FEARLESS
Living

FEARLESS
Living

Live Without Excuses
and
Love Without Regret

Rhonda Britten

DUTTON

To protect privacy, pseudonyms have been used and certain characteristics have been disguised in the case histories recounted.

DUTTON
Published by the Penguin Group
Penguin Putnam Inc., 375 Hudson Street, New York, New York 10014, U.S.A.
Penguin Books Ltd, 27 Wrights Lane, London W8 5TZ, England
Penguin Books Australia Ltd, Ringwood, Victoria, Australia
Penguin Books Canada Ltd, 10 Alcorn Avenue, Toronto, Ontario, Canada M4V 3B2
Penguin Books (N.Z.) Ltd, 182–190 Wairau Road, Auckland 10, New Zealand

Penguin Books Ltd, Registered Offices: Harmondsworth, Middlesex, England

Published by Dutton, a member of Penguin Putnam Inc.

Fearless Living™ is the trademark of Rhonda Britten.

First Printing, April, 2001

3   5   7   9   10   8   6   4   2

REGISTERED TRADEMARK—MARCA REGISTRADA

LIBRARY OF CONGRESS CATALOGING-IN-PUBLICATION DATA
Britten, Rhonda.
Fearless living : live without excuses and love
without regret / by Rhonda Britten.
p.   cm.
ISBN 0-525-94579-2 (alk. paper)
1. Fear. 2. Change (Psychology) I. Title.

BF575.F2 B75   2001
158.1—dc21   00-050832

Printed in the United States of America
Designed by Eve L. Kirch
Set in New Baskerville

This book is printed on acid-free paper. ∞

My mother wasn't able to live her newfound freedom for long.
Yet by her example, I was able to pick up where she left off.
This work is my gift to her.

Thank you for giving me the courage to live fearlessly.
I love you, Mom.

CONTENTS

PREFACE

If you have ever been too threatened by failure to go for something you want . . . too apprehensive to share your feelings . . . too comfortable with your success to take a chance on making your life better . . . too intimidated to stand up for yourself when someone is putting you down . . . too afraid that you're unlovable to end a bad relationship . . . too nervous about getting hurt to risk trusting another . . . too sensitive to criticism to speak out and be counted . . . too worried about losing your children's devotion to put your foot down . . . too fainthearted to strike out in a new direction because you think you might not be up to the challenge . . . then what you are about to read has the power to change your life.

And you are far from alone. In the course of my career as a speaker and life- and career-coach, I have discovered that the vast majority of people, no matter how confident they appear to be, harbor paralyzing fears that lurk beneath the surface of their psyches. These inner demons are always at the ready to whisper skeptical objections and plant doubts about anything that might shake up the status quo: Do you really think you should do that? Are you ready for a big step like this? Why don't you get somebody else's opinion? Are you sure you're not getting in over your head? What will people say?

These menacing messages, whether we are conscious of them or not, allow us to rationalize that we are better off not taking those chances. This does not apply to clinical emotional disorders such as depression and anxiety that require professional help. I am not advocating recklessness. I mean the virtually universal human tendency to make excuses and deny the type of fears that hold us back. Those subtle, gnawing fears that make up what I call the Wheel of Fear control our lives in myriad unseen ways.

Even little incidents along the way can contribute to your fears. The time you were accidentally separated from your mother in the grocery store when you were five years old may have been the beginning of a fear of being abandoned. The cruel words of a childhood bully might have added to your fear that you are stupid. The criticism of a Little League coach when you were doing the best you could may have made you fear that you're worthless. Fearless Living is a program that will teach you to recognize and master those fears. Mastering fear does not imply you will never experience fear again. But rather, you will know what actions to take to move beyond your fear at will and the frequency of occurrence will diminish.

As for more extreme traumas, I'm living proof that the most unspeakable of experiences can be harnessed as a force for hope. Before I went on the *Oprah* show to reveal at last the terrible secret you'll read about in the Introduction, I had already established my personal program of self-growth to overcome a troubled past. Alcoholism, nervous breakdowns, and suicide attempts were the misguided efforts I had previously used to deal with my fears. Yet as a result of my program, my self-destructive behavior has become a mere memory. I am astounded as I look upon my own life now. I see loving friendships, healthy family relations, a handsome income, a beautiful home, and creative fulfillment through my speaking engagements, books, videos, and audiotapes. Most important, my sense of self is always intact, breeding self-confidence, personal power, and clarity of purpose. In short, my life is governed by freedom.

I designed Fearless Living to help you triumph over the fear that prevents you from living a fulfilling life. As of this writing, thousands of people have attested to the life-changing payoffs acquired by following the Fearless Living program. Instead of theories and concepts, Fearless Living entails practical applications for real-life situations that will work for you. In Part One, you will learn how your individualized fears operate, perpetuate, and manifest. In Part Two, you will discover the power behind your day-to-day actions and uncover how they sustain your fears or help you move beyond them.

There is no "right" time to begin living fearlessly. Wherever you are is the perfect place to start. So get ready to take a journey that will transform your life.

Welcome to the world of Fearless Living.

Rhonda Britten
June 2000

FEARLESS
Living

Fear is a killer.
It kills hopes.
It kills dreams.
It kills careers.
It kills relationships.
In a flash, it killed my parents.
It almost killed me.

How is it killing you?

INTRODUCTION

My Story

A steady downpour pummeled the windowpanes of my childhood bedroom in northern Michigan on a chilly June morning. I snuggled deeper under the warmth and comfort of my blankets, wishing I didn't have to face what lay ahead. The year was 1975 and I was fourteen. Father's Day back then in my little hometown meant families trooping to have brunch at local restaurants where buffets were considered the height of elegance. Part of me was looking forward to the salad bar and the slices of roast beef, but I dreaded the get-together. My parents had been separated for almost a year. This obligatory reunion with my father was sure to be strained.

I wondered whether my two sisters, and for that matter my mother, felt as uneasy as I did. Still, I told myself, nothing really upsetting was going to happen. We'd be in public, after all. Everyone would be on their best behavior. In spite of all that had gone on between my parents behind closed doors, they had always been very good at putting up a front. They cared too much about what the neighbors might think.

Reassured, I threw the covers off, got up, and picked out the white cotton dress my mother had finished making for me only days before. An accomplished seamstress, she took pride in out-fitting her girls. I treasured everything she created, but this dress was one of my favorites. She had sewn me a long white scarf with black polka dots, an accessory that made me feel very sophisticated. I wrapped it around my neck as a kind of testimony of her love. In return, I loved her so much that it almost hurt. I have a photograph of just the two of us taken before my younger sister, Linda, was born. My mother was holding me on her hip. My little head was leaning on her shoulder. On the back she had written, "When you were the baby of the house, Rhonda." The image and the message gave me strength and a sense of being very special. I looked at the picture and read her words whenever the trials of teenage life started to get to me.

On that Sunday morning, I had gotten dressed, and while my sisters were still fighting over the bathroom, I walked by my mother's room. She spotted me through the open door.

"Oh, you look so pretty!" she said with a lilt in her voice. "Come in. I want to show you something."

My heart skipped a beat. As the middle child, I cherished every moment when I was alone with my mother. She put down her omnipresent coffee mug after taking one more sip, and did the rest of her makeup. I perched on the bed, careful not to rumple the spread, and watched her smooth the rouge into her cheeks after gliding the blue shadow over her lids. Even without the help of cosmetics, she was a true beauty. I wanted to grow up to be exactly like her.

"How's the new boyfriend?" she asked after she had put on her lipstick and spritzed herself with perfume.

Girl talk. I was thrilled by this private, intimate moment. "Okay," I giggled. "So far, anyway. How's Bill?"

Her eyes lit up. Bill was my mother's first attempt at finding love again, and my sisters and I approved. He was a big man with a heart to match. Since meeting him, my mother smiled a whole lot more.

"That's what I wanted to show you," she said, dusting off her hands and reaching for something in the basket beside her. She held up a blue-and-red-striped polo shirt.

"I made it for Bill's birthday," she said. "Do you think he'll like it?"

"Oh, yes! It's perfect!" I said, feeling like my mother's friend and daughter all at the same time.

That's when the doorbell rang, shattering the coveted one-on-one connection with my mother. "Your father is here," she said, quickly folding the polo shirt and hiding it under the bed. Neither of us wanted any evidence of Bill in the room. My father, unable to let my mother go, was wildly jealous of her relationship with Bill.

"Go let your father in. I'll be right there," she continued. Her expression said the rest: *Be nice, put on a smile, give your father a hug, and keep our little secret.*

I stood up. After a reluctant pause, I began moving toward the front door as my mother had asked. My father had called me a week before Father's Day, even though I hadn't spoken with him in months, asking me to come and live with him. I had begged off. Why me? He loved Linda, my little sister, the best. Once, when I had somehow irritated him, he had chased me and pinned me down, putting his hands around my throat. My screams had brought Linda to the scene. Because of her, he had released me. Yet now he wanted me, not Linda. He said I would thank him someday. For the suffering? Did he think that would make me a better person?

I opened the front door. The rain had slowed to a drizzle. My father stood on the stoop, a little damp but looking absolutely wonderful and normal—exactly the way I remembered him from when I was a little girl. There was no sign of the angry, troubled man I had come to expect. Pleased and relieved, I felt compelled to hug him after I ushered him inside.

As he entered, my mother came toward us, shrugging into her raincoat and saying something about wanting to warm up her car. The yellow 1973 Buick Apollo was a gleaming symbol of my mother's newfound freedom. Leaving my father after almost two decades of verbal abuse had proved to be an incredibly liberating experience for her. Mom was a farm girl who had never learned to drive anything other than a tractor. Getting her driver's license and buying that Apollo had been a crucial step toward her independence. I watched, smiling, as she dashed through the raindrops with her car keys in hand.

Then I glanced at my father. His eyes were following my mother, who was dodging puddles on the way to her car. Abruptly he said, "I'll be right back. I need to get my coat from my trunk."

He loped across the lawn to his car. It was parked a couple of feet from my mother's. I opened my mouth to call to my sisters that we were just about ready to leave. Before I could utter a syllable, I saw my father pull not a coat but a rifle from the trunk of his car.

Every second that passed as I made my way from the door frame onto the edge of the porch is burned into my mind forever. My breath stopped. My heart stopped. My father was yelling at my mother, "You made me do this." His hand wrapped around the rifle stock, the barrel aimed straight at her.

"Daddy, don't!" I screamed. "Dad, I'll live with you. . . . Dad, I'll take care of you!" Oh, my God, I had to stop him. Maybe the rain was drowning out my words. Maybe he couldn't hear me. Maybe he didn't care.

My desperate cries did nothing to dissuade him. His hand tightened around the trigger as he trapped my mother between the two cars. Still, I kept pleading, hoping to stop him. But my voice was powerless. Why didn't he hear me? Why didn't Linda hear me? He would listen to her. Where was she? And where was my older sister, Cindy?

My mother said hoarsely, "Ron, don't you do this. Don't you do this."

"You made me do this," he countered. "It's all your fault. You gave me no choice. If I can't have you, no one can. No one will."

While he raged, she looked him squarely in the eye, showing her courage in the face of the man who had controlled her for so long. Instinctively, she wrapped her arms around her body in the vain hope of deflecting what was to come. As I watched, I kept running scenario after scenario through my mind. I had to save her. I could jump between her and the gun. I could do something to distract him, maybe throw a chair or bang on the metal garbage pail, and she could run. But my body was frozen.

Crack! The sound of the rifle firing tore a hole in my life. Everything moved so slowly that I felt as though I could reach out and stop the bullet in flight. The way my mother looked right before and after the bullet entered her abdomen is my most vivid memory. She was so beautiful and scared and alone. When the bullet penetrated, she fell forward ever so slightly, her body wrenched in pain. She grabbed her stomach the way you would if you were going to throw up. I remember her face, twisted in agony, still eye to eye with her killer. She was silently begging him to stop. I think for one part of one second my father didn't believe what he had done. I know I must have been screaming, but all I remember is the surreal silence.

The click of the gun recocking broke the stillness. My father's gaze and the barrel of the gun turned my way. I was sure it was my time to die. But the gun swung back and found my mother again. As the second bullet hit, she fell through the open door of her prized car. The bullet went straight through her and lodged in the steering wheel. The blaring of the car horn ripped into the quiet of a small-town Sunday morning. To this day, the sound of a horn has the power to unnerve me unless I call forth all the inner resources I have stockpiled to free myself from fear.

The horn was still keening as my father ran toward me. Rain soaked, he fell to his knees at my feet, the gun upright at his side. He rested his right temple directly against the end of the barrel and pulled the trigger. His every motion was seamless, as if he had planned and rehearsed diligently for this final act. The sound of the gunshot at close range was deafening. My father's blood splattered on the white dress that was my mother's last gift to me. His body collapsed beside me.

The only sound was my own harsh breathing, waking me up to the realization that what had happened was not a dream. It was real. I began to shudder. In that moment, I was gripped by a potent fear that I didn't deserve to be alive. Why was I still standing? After all, my father had proved that I wasn't worth living for. In fact, I wasn't even worth killing. And I—the only person on the scene—had failed as my mother's savior. What earthly use was I anyway?

I turned and retreated into the house, heading for the sanctuary of my mother's bedroom where just a few minutes earlier I had felt safe and singled out for her confidences. I got down on my knees, and folded my hands against the bedspread. The scent of her perfume was still in the air. I prayed with all the faith I had ever had. "Please, God," I begged, "don't let her be dead." Yet I knew even then that she was already gone.

The news traveled fast through our little town. Arrangements were made and within hours we were at my aunt's house. I am told that I was hysterical, then silent. I suppose I changed out of the bloodstained dress. I remember very little from the time I knelt to pray until hours later. I vaguely recall phoning my boyfriend and blurting out what had happened, but after that everything is just blank. My aunt had convinced Cindy to put me on medication. I took the pill, more for their sake than for mine. But I refused to eat. These people, my relatives, were convinced that if I would just eat, things would be better.

They had no idea. I had failed to save my mother. I didn't deserve sustenance. Each mental replay admonished me more. In a haze of medication and self-loathing, I kept thinking I could have done something to stop my father from killing my mother. I could have stepped in front of the gun. I could have figured out something better to say. At the very least, I could have run over to the car where she lay slumped against the steering wheel. Maybe she had been waiting for me to come to her. If I had gotten to her, maybe she would have pulled through. But I had left her there. Looking back, I know that part of the fear that was etching itself into the very essence of my being was the idea that everyone else blamed me as well. Perhaps they were even pointing the finger at me for what my father had done. After all, he had once told me that it was all my fault that my mother had left him. I had no idea what he meant, but that didn't stop me from being afraid that he was right.

And yet that evening, as I did every Sunday, I went to the local indoor ice rink. Continuing with the routine I had always known seemed like the only thing to do. I didn't get much skating in, though. Once I got to the rink, I had to take care of my friends. They had shown up not knowing what to do or say. At first, they shifted from one foot to the other and avoided my eyes. This was a pattern with which I would become all too familiar in the months and years ahead. In a world where almost nothing was unmentionable any longer, a murder-suicide— especially one involving your parents and certainly if you were the only witness—turned out to be the last taboo.

Finally, my friend Julie let herself react. She hugged me, sobbing into my shoulder. I was glad she was crying. My fear was already hard at work, keeping me from sharing my real feelings. I held her, letting her vent her grief and fury, all the while keeping mine in. I was afraid that if I let them loose, the world would not be able to withstand my heartache. I was afraid of myself. Afraid to be human. The consequences were too terrible to imagine.

The next day, Cindy—who at eighteen had become the one in charge—left Linda and me with our aunt while she and my mother's friend Sharon went back to the house to get some of our things. Cindy told me later that when they were in the bedroom, Sharon started to cry at the sight of my mother's favorite mug on the vanity, half full of coffee long since gone cold. I never got to see the mug. I wish I had. But no one would let me go back to the scene of the crime. They all thought they had to protect me. They meant well, but they didn't understand. After what I had seen, the damage was already done. The fear had become part of me, feeding on the ordinary fears I already had until it was a force that dictated my every thought and every action. One minute, I had been a young girl in the cocoon of her mother's love with my dreams stretching into a future full of possibilities. The next, I was not only an orphan but also the person who hadn't prevented my parents' tragic deaths. I wanted to scream, "You can't keep me safe! It's too late for that!" But the fear choked me and kept the words inside. After a while, the fear was so completely in control that I didn't even know what the words were anymore. I only knew that I must never, ever unleash them.

Monday went by in a blur. My sisters say we picked out the caskets. I'll have to take their word for it. Visitation and viewing at the funeral home were on Tuesday. That I remember in exquisite detail. All afternoon, with my pen in hand and a smile on my face, I politely guided each person to the guest books, one for my father and one for my mother, and pointed out the next available space. While my sisters milled around among the mourners, I played "hostess with the mostest." I remember crying very little during that time, feeling a deep obligation to tend to all these people who had so loved my mother, or my father, or both. I had to make sure they were okay. If I couldn't save my parents, at least I could do that much.

After the majority of people had arrived, my sisters and I sat in the family section of the funeral home and received condolences together. When it was time for us to say our final farewells before the caskets were closed, the funeral director pulled a red velvet curtain around us for privacy. I said good-bye to my father and I remember looking at him with amazement. There was no indication that he had shot off part of his head. I had never imagined that I would be having a conversation with myself regarding funeral directors' artistic abilities, but they should get an award, I thought.

Yet if I was detached as I looked at my father's body, I was profoundly moved by the vision of my mother. It is seared into my brain. I scanned every part of her, afraid I might miss something. She wore her favorite long evergreen dress with white polka dots, the one she had bought for the first Christmas party she gave on her own after the separation. Mom had spent more money than she usually allowed. The gown had been a gift to herself, one of her small acts of freedom during her brief reprieve from a life of fear.

Her hair and makeup were perfect. My mind flashed back to the Sunday morning only a few days earlier when I had sat on the bed, watching her "put on her face," as she called it. How could it be that this simple pleasure, and all the rest of life's miracles, would never be hers again?

The funeral director reappeared, rousing me from my reverie. He took my mother's engagement and wedding rings off her hands and gave them to Cindy. Then I saw that Cindy had put her class ring on my mother's finger. And Linda had placed one of her most beloved bracelets on my mother's wrist. Both pieces of jewelry were gifts to take to the Great Beyond. I couldn't believe my eyes. Nobody had told me about this! I felt so betrayed, as though I had been slapped in the face, yet so ashamed that I hadn't thought of this gesture myself. Was this my sisters' way of punishing me for not saving Mom? Then I stopped myself. This moment was about my mother, not me. My pain had to wait. The urgency of the situation called for immediate action. I knew that if my mother were buried without a symbol of my love, I could never forgive myself. What did I have to give her?

The answer came to me quickly. My boyfriend had given me a promise ring just two weeks earlier, a pearl set in silver. I had been secretly longing for that ring. It was the most valuable thing I owned. I twisted the ring off and placed it on Mom's little finger. I had righted a wrong the best way I knew how. I was so angry that my sisters hadn't included me, but I also knew I could never express my shame to anyone, ever. I buried it along with my feeling of worthlessness.

The funerals were on Wednesday, the day that would have been my parents' twentieth wedding anniversary. I insisted on singing at their funerals. My mother had always called my voice a gift from God. She had swelled with pride when I was invited to join the senior-high chorus the year I was still in seventh grade. She made sure I had lessons, and she was as thrilled as I was when my voice teacher recommended that I attend the 1975 summer session at the world-renowned Interlochen Arts Center near Traverse City. That was to have been my first time away from home, a big step toward the career that my mother was sure was my destiny. The least I could do now was to sing a memorial tribute.

I picked a song called "Thank You" intending to sing it at both funerals. The irony of that title for my father's funeral was lost in my denial. I truly believed I had instantly forgiven him. Even so, I did not shed a tear during his 1:00 P.M. service. After we laid him in the ground, we had a scant half an hour before my mother's funeral began at 3:00 P.M. During that brief interval, I realized which song I had to sing for her. My mom's favorite was Olivia Newton-John's hit "I Honestly Love You." I had been chosen to sing it with my friend Tammy as a duet for a choir concert earlier that year. Afterward, my mom had asked me to sing it whenever anyone stopped over.

Everyone tried to talk me out of going ahead with my plan, but I was determined. I grabbed Tammy and convinced her we had to do it. She agreed. I don't know whether someone went to her house to get the music or if someone went to mine. As I said, it was a small town. We both lived within minutes of the church. In any case, we got the music and rehearsed it once in the church meeting hall. Then I took my place with my sisters outside the sanctuary, greeting family and friends.

From the minute my mother's funeral began, tears streamed down every cheek and great wails of grief punctuated the proceedings. When it was my time to sing, I had to make my way from the front pew all the way back down the aisle and then up the steps to the choir loft in the rear of the church. So that I wouldn't break down, I deliberately avoided any eye contact. My aunt had begged me to take a pill before the funerals, but I had refused. I wanted to be completely myself and totally awake to my feelings. I wanted to remember everything. I didn't want to sing on drugs. I didn't want to cry on drugs. I didn't want to see my mother for the last time on drugs.

In a strong and clear soprano, while Tammy's voice harmonized with mine, I sang the song for my mother, to my mother. I sang it with every ounce of my being. There is a place near the end of the lyrics where I spoke the words "I love you," followed by a long pause. In my silence, the congregation could not contain the sobs that told of their grief and their compassion. The sounds of sadness swelled into a lamentation I can hear to this day.

As I returned to my seat, all eyes were on me. Everyone was surprised I had pulled it off, but I wasn't. I'd had to do it. The song was the last gift I would give to my mother. It had to be perfect, and it was.

Nothing after that moment was perfect for many years to come. At the cemetery, the emotional dam that had been holding back my tears finally broke. The brilliant sunlight and the fresh breeze off of Lake Superior seemed to mock the unbearable ache in my heart. I threw myself on my mother's coffin, crying, "Don't leave me! Please don't leave me!" My grandmother, a formidable woman with a no-nonsense philosophy of life, wrenched me off the casket and said, "That will be enough of that. It's over." As she led me away, her hand in a vicelike grip on my wrist, the fear that it was not right to be me took a firm hold over my life.

The more that people tried to shield me from my pain, the more frightened I became of my own feelings and the harder I worked at keeping them in check. Many relatives became remote. Friends disappeared. I felt totally left out. People hushed when I entered a room. I remember overhearing adults prep visitors. "Be careful not to bring up the subject of parents," they would say. I developed a sense of shame about sharing my story with anyone. I was terrified that I would be accused of not having stopped my parents' deaths. I was afraid of who I was.

Much later, while attending college on scholarship, I was seen as normal, a high achiever with much to be proud of. No one would have guessed the fears that were running my life. I kept others at arm's length to avoid the fear of being discovered and to dodge the inevitable questions. Fear was my constant companion, giving me permission to lie. "How are your parents?" someone would ask. "Just fine," I'd respond. For a long time, my parents were "just fine." Eventually, in the briefest of terms, I began telling people what had happened, followed by ". . . but I'm over that now. I've handled it. I'm fine."

At the time, I had talked myself into believing that I was fine. But I wasn't. Fear was taking its toll. I was worried that I would never have enough money. I doubted my ability to succeed. I dreaded the responsibility of growing up. I was uncomfortable being alone. Yet I was anxious about falling in love because I was sure any man would discover what my father must have already known: I was worthless. My expectations regarding friendships could never be fulfilled. Intimacy and trust were elusive. Love was never part of the picture. I was easily angered and at times, suicidal. Although my intellect and body had survived, my heart and soul were deeply wounded. Happiness was beyond my reach.

Nothing I tried—not the therapy I sought, not the books I read, not the courses I took, not the grief groups I joined—showed me how to get beyond my fears to experience the wholeness I yearned for. More than that, I noticed that people from all walks of life had the same challenges I had. I began to wonder if maybe this is all there was. I took to rationalizing my fear away. "This must be the way life is. Everyone else complains, whines, and moans. We each have our lot in life. This must be mine." I figured the best I could hope for was camaraderie through my pain. Maybe you've felt the same way. Maybe you have come to the conclusion that the best you can do is learn to deal with it and try to control it the best you can.

I believed that for a long time. Then I began to notice that there were individuals who did not make choices based in fear. They took risks and lived fully. When I asked them how they did it, they couldn't articulate it. They had no formula or pattern. Sometimes they were afraid while other times they were able to move past it. With that knowledge, I became determined to help myself. I wanted to know the answer to the questions "What is fear?" and "How does it run my life?" And I wanted more than haphazard freedom. I wanted more than understanding. I wanted actual things to do that would help me get through my doubts, worries, paralysis, and defensiveness at will. I wanted to know that my fear hadn't eclipsed any good left within me. It all started with a calendar and some gold stars. Each day I would write down exactly what I had done that was kind and loving to others as well as myself. I was vigilant. At that point, it was all I had. At the end of the month my calendar was covered in gold stars. I knew I had a fighting chance. From the seeds of that first exercise, I have come to realize there is a way to get beyond the fear. And it isn't always necessary to understand how your fear developed. What matters is that it did.

We all have our stories, our scars, our wounds, the things that give us the excuses for why life isn't exactly as we had hoped. My story may be more dramatic than others', but the basic fear I experienced as a result of my parents' deaths is the same basic fear we all have to confront: We are afraid that—in some if not all areas of our lives—*we're not good enough.*

I've learned this, not only because I have overcome the fear that kept my story in place, but because I have worked with countless clients who have mastered their fears as well. Of course, people don't walk into my office with the insight to say, "I'm afraid they'll find out I'm not good enough." But that's what they mean when they say, "I'm afraid my husband is going to leave me." . . . "I'm afraid I'm going to lose my job." . . . "I'm afraid I'm going to end up homeless." . . . "I'm afraid my kids aren't going to turn out well." . . . "I'm afraid I'm never going to do anything that makes a difference." . . . "I'm afraid I'm not going to live up to my parents' expectations." . . . "I'm afraid to open up my own business." . . . "I'm afraid to get involved with anybody." . . . "I'm afraid people will make fun of me." . . . "I'm afraid to speak up." . . . "I'm afraid I will never fulfill my potential."

Even people who become highly successful by societal standards are not immune. Why, after all, do celebrities suffer from stage fright other than because they fear that a performance won't be good enough? As for the rest of us, just about any situation can call up that basic fear that we're not good enough. What keeps a man from asking a woman out on a date? What makes someone put off sending out résumés in order to get a better job? What makes a mother find reasons to blame herself when a child is sickly or gets a failing grade or doesn't have any friends? Why does a person who has put on a little weight come up with excuses not to go for a checkup that would mean stepping on a scale in front of a nurse or doctor?

There are a lot of words we could use to define specific aspects of the fear of not being good enough. "Unlovable," "inadequate," "stupid," "untalented," "worthless," "weak willed," and "loser" come to mind. The label doesn't matter. Any definition that rings true for you is fine. What does matter, as I have seen over and over again with my clients, is that once people recognize the basic fear, all of the offshoot fears are rendered manageable at last.

Better yet, the fear becomes not an enemy but an ally. Instead of causing you to shy away from situations that could result in the sting of failure, the fear gives you the impetus to take on new challenges. You no longer spend your time and energy trying to avoid showing the world you're not good enough. You move to a level where you respect and love who you are. When that happens, you experience an exhilarating sense of freedom. You are no longer trapped in the false security of boredom and routine. You are released to experience life's limitless prospects fearlessly, in spite of the fact that failure is always a possibility. In the words of legendary sportswriter Grantland Rice, "When the

One Great Scorer comes to write against your name/He marks not that you won or lost, but how you played the game."

Fear has been instrumental in setting your course whether your parents are alive or dead. Whether you grew up happy or sad, wealthy or poor. Whether you know it or not. Fear has developed your likes and dislikes, picked your friends, and raised your children. Fear has limited your potential, excluded possibilities, and controlled your choices.

We can change that. What took me years to learn will take you months. I know this because so many of my clients have done it. A life worth living is attainable. I know, too, because I am living it. Now is the time to begin the work that can set you free. Let's get started. . . .

Part One

WHAT ARE YOU AFRAID OF?

Courage faces fear and thereby masters it.

Martin Luther King, Jr.

What Is Fear?

Imagine that you are enjoying a walk in a woodsy area of a state park on a perfect summer day. The sun plays in patches on the leafy canopy overhead and you breathe in the earthy scents carried by a gentle breeze. Birdsong fills the air. You are at peace, relaxed, thinking of nothing in particular. Out of the corner of your eye, you spot something in the underbrush next to the path. It is brown, large, and coiled. Your brain registers, *Danger! A snake in the grass!* Your bodily state changes instantly. Your heart races, your palms sweat, your stomach and throat clench, your scalp tingles, your skin prickles with goose bumps.

What does this have to do with the basic human fear of not being good enough? Your body's reaction to fear is the same whether you are faced with a physical threat or an emotional one. What happens is that the hypothalamic-pituitary-adrenal (HPA) system in your brain releases chemical messengers, mainly dopamine and adrenaline. The HPA also triggers an out-pouring of the hormone cortisol that in turn activates a small, almond-shaped area of the brain called the amygdala. Your blood sugar and blood pressure rise steeply to give you a burst of energy. Your digestive system shuts down so you can use that energy either to meet the threat head-on or run away from it.

This is the well-known "fight or flight" phenomenon, first described as such in 1932 by eminent Harvard physiologist Walter B. Cannon. It is the most primal of survival mechanisms, not only in humans but in virtually all species ever studied for the fear response, including fruit flies and snails. The problem is that a real or perceived threat signals the hippocampus—an area near the amygdala—to store the experience in long-term memory. That's good in the sense that when you get visual clues that make you think you see a snake, your body goes into overdrive and you get out of there fast.

But maybe it wasn't a snake after all. Maybe it was a fallen tree branch. You didn't stop to find out whether the danger was real or not. You beat a hasty retreat without even contemplating what you were doing. As famed fear researcher Joseph LeDoux put it in his book *The Emotional Brain,* there is a "quick and dirty processing pathway" that "allows us to begin to respond to potentially dangerous stimuli before we fully know what the stimulus is. . . . The brain is programmed to detect dangers, both those that were routinely experienced by our ancestors and those learned about by each of us as individuals."

Throughout life, we add to our ancestral fears with a long list of perceived threats born of experience. We aren't simply afraid of physical danger, such as snakes or sticks that might be snakes. We are afraid of any imagined situation that might evoke a painful emotion. We run away from the danger of being failures, of being ridiculed, of being rejected, of being belittled, of being embarrassed, of being played for a fool. In the same way that a child who accidentally touches a hot iron will never do so again, we don't want to risk being twice burned psychologically and emotionally. Every negative experience, however fleeting, can be a lesson in fear that is well learned by our subconscious minds. The result is the all-too-familiar heart-racing and palm-sweating, as well as suppression of the immune system and of activity in areas of the brain concerned with short-term memory, concentration, inhibition, and rational thought. When this happens on a daily basis over many years, mental, emotional, and physical health are clearly in jeopardy. So are the ability to function at peak capacity and the simple ability to enjoy life.

That's where Fearless Living comes in. LeDoux's research—mainly with rats conditioned to fear a sound previously associated with an electrical shock—has shown that erasing the memories of fear is in all likelihood not feasible. But the difference between rats and humans is that we have something called "consciousness," which is our ability to be aware. When we become aware of how fear is running our lives and what our fears are, we have the power to break free of our conditioning and make choices about how we behave. Otherwise, our unconscious minds and our conditioning decide for us, just as they do for the rats. Fearless Living will show you how to outsmart fear rather than allowing the memory of fear or fear itself to determine your life. As LeDoux says, "It is thus completely possible that one might have poor conscious memory of a traumatic experience, but at the same time form a very powerful implicit, unconscious memory of a traumatic experience. . . . We may not be able to get rid of the implicit memories."

I agree. Whether we have a clear recollection of a traumatic experience—as I do of my parents' deaths—or whether the trauma is not something we remember vividly, the memory is in the unconscious mind ready to invoke fear. You can't delete your amygdala's personal cache of fear-laden triggers. Yet I know that you can go beyond the fear. My clients have done it. I have done it. You can too.

Fearless Living Means Moving Beyond the Fear

Let's start with my definition of "fear": Fear is both the cause and effect of the feelings, thoughts, or actions that prohibit you from accepting yourself and realizing your full potential. Fear stands between you and your ability to go anywhere you like, do anything you want, and meet anyone you please. To help you stay safe, fear motivates you to hide your essential nature by thwarting your ability to express yourself truthfully.

Renowned psychologist Abraham Maslow, in his classic work *Toward a Psychology of Being*, described the process in this way: "This kind of fear is defensive, in the sense that it is a protection of our self-esteem. . . . We tend to be afraid of any knowledge that could cause us to despise ourselves, or to make us feel inferior, weak, worthless, evil, shameful. . . . We also tend to avoid personal growth because this, too, can bring another kind of fear. . . . This is the struggle against our own greatness. . . . Thus to discover in oneself a great talent can certainly bring exhilaration but it can also bring a fear of the dangers and responsibilities. . . . The moment of fright is understandable, but it must be overcome."

Fearless Living is about helping you do precisely that, not just once but as a way of life. Fear's function is to keep you from getting hurt, but in so doing fear also keeps you from becoming your best and truest self. Fear has been with you all along, filing away all the hurt and heartbreak—the time you didn't make the cheerleading squad or the way you were teased about your accent or the fact that you were ignored by the people who were supposed to love you the most.

Fear heard you cry, "I don't ever want to feel like that again." It took you seriously. It became determined to keep you safe. It assumed the role of guardian of your feelings. Now, when a situation presents itself in which you think you may not be accepted for who you are, fear flashes warnings, telling you, "Don't go there. Don't do that. And definitely, don't say that." You could potentially experience rejection, disappointment, or the feeling that you're foolish. Dangerous!

Fear's number-one job is to guard you against any negative feelings that would confirm your worst fear—that you are not good enough. This perpetuates your inability to accept yourself.

Yet deep down, we want to own our power and strength and courage. In order to do that, we must embrace the fullness of who we are, and that includes our limitations. Again, fear sees that as a little on the risky side.

Think of it this way: Fear is the gatekeeper of your comfort zone. Your comfort zone is whatever is familiar to you. As a little child, your comfort zone was your mother's lap. You ventured away out of curiosity but scurried back to safety when you felt threatened. Now your comfort zone is the people you already know, the routines you're used to, the places where you feel at home. Whether these are bad, good, happy, or sad is immaterial. As the old saying goes, "Better the devil you know than the devil you don't know." People stay for years in bad marriages, boring jobs, and other belittling situations because breaking the bond to the familiar and trying something new feels too scary. Your comfort zone is what you are comfortable with, where you feel safe.

But how satisfying is safe? Fear keeps us from feeling alive when there's a danger of not being accepted, approved, or understood. Therefore we deny our essential nature. Fear doesn't know you are an adult who craves adventure and love and fulfillment. It doesn't know that you could handle it from here. That is why a crisis is sometimes what's necessary to shake up your world and give you the courage you need to show your fear who's boss.

The crisis in your life that gets you started on the journey from fear to freedom need not be as obvious or life shattering as mine. But there is almost certainly some level of crisis manifesting itself in your life right now. Maybe you are simply sick of letting yourself down or listening to your own excuses. Perhaps you've had enough of never finding the courage to stand up for yourself. It could be that you are through with neglecting yourself, or you are fed up with being walked on, or you can't face putting up a front to keep the peace with your boss, coworkers, family, spouse, or kids one more time. Maybe you are tired of not earning what you're worth just because you can't bring yourself to put a real value on your contribution and ask for that raise or promotion. Perhaps you are tired of being dependent on others or doing everything alone. Maybe you've had it with letting other people take public credit for work that you've done behind the scenes. You may not even be able to pinpoint what's going on, but you know something isn't quite working. Your soul yearns for more. That's all we need to get you started.

Meredith's Story

Meredith's crisis started years ago, but she ignored the warning signs until she was forced to face it the night her husband walked out on her after eighteen years of marriage. "There's got to be more to life than this," he said. "All we ever talk about is the kids' homework and how we're going to pay the bills and what kind of fertilizer to use. Apparently this is enough for you. Well, it's not enough for me."

Meredith opened her mouth but no words came out. Fear strangled her. How would she manage on her own? What would people think of her when they found out she hadn't made a go of her marriage? What was it about her that had driven Phil away? If he didn't love her after all they had shared, who could?

"Look, there's no point in dragging this on any longer," Phil continued. "I'm going to stay with my brother for a while. We'll work everything out down the line about the money and the custody and stuff."

"Is there someone else?" Meredith finally managed to whisper.

"No, no, that's not it," Phil said. "The thing is, I just can't stay here and let life pass me by."

He opened the door and she caught a whiff of the crisp evening air. She heard the crunch of the car wheels on the blacktop as he backed out of the driveway. And then he was gone.

The children, twelve-year-old Lucy and ten-year-old Sam,

were asleep upstairs. Meredith sat immobile at the kitchen table, grappling first with the terror of being a single mother and then with anger at Phil for leaving her like this. Meredith had always been a loyal wife and a devoted mother. Her mind reeled with the realization that this was actually happening to her after eighteen years of putting her husband and children first. When she had wanted to take a painting class at the local community college, her husband had pointed out that canvas and paint were expensive. She never mentioned the idea again. Fear, disguised as reason, told her that Phil knew best when it came to family finances. Anyway, she shouldn't spend money on something selfish. And when she went on a trip with her sister, Phil had fussed about how hard it was when she was gone. Fear, disguised as understanding, convinced her that this was the way he showed his love. And now, after eighteen years, he had as much as said she was insignificant!

After the divorce was final, Meredith sought me out. She said she wanted to "start living." I knew that she meant she wanted to live fearlessly. She had come to the right place. Over the course of our sessions together, we discussed the elements of Fearless Living, including claiming your essential nature, building self-confidence and self-caring, the power of accountability and choice. As we talked, it was clear that she had a sense of what she didn't want more than of what she wanted. No longer did she want to break promises to herself, let others have the final word, or put herself last. She wasn't even sure what she liked. She had gotten so used to going along with what Phil liked that she had assumed her desires and Phil's were one and the same. It became evident that Meredith had lived most of her married life as a people pleaser and, more specifically, as a Phil pleaser. Meredith hadn't shared any feelings or thoughts that were different from his in years. She never confronted him about the way the money was spent. She never told him she didn't agree with one or another of his decisions. She rarely picked the restaurant they were going to go to. Sure, she complained to her friends about him, but she never shared her frustrations with him or stood up to him. Then as she began to work the Fearless Living program, she realized she had been bowing to Phil's wishes in order to avoid appearing selfish, which was the way she thought she could keep from experiencing her most dreaded feeling, that of being insignificant.

That realization began to unravel her world as she started to see how most of the decisions in her life had been made to avoid feeling insignificant. Somewhere fear had rationalized that if she made everyone else happy, she would be important to them rather than insignificant. Therefore, she had thought it was better to accept the love she had than question whether Phil's love fulfilled her needs. "That would be too much to ask," she had always felt, "and ungrateful." Yet ironically, as I helped her to understand, the very reason she had behaved the way she had for eighteen years was now the very reason Phil was leaving her.

Scared to Seize the Day

The crisis of the divorce was the impetus Meredith needed to open her eyes to the fact that she had always expected to be happy in the future. This is a heartbreakingly common fallacy. Far too many people wish their lives away, letting fear keep them from making the most of every moment. They are always waiting for "someday" to come. As Meredith reasoned, hadn't she always been a good person and done the "right" thing? "Someday," she constantly promised herself, "it will be my turn."

Like most of us, Meredith had been waiting for something magical to happen so she could finally be happy. Maybe it would be when the kids left home or when Phil retired. She wasn't sure. But her turn never came until she began doing the Fearbuster Exercises in the Fearless Living program. Before that, she had never given herself the internal permission she needed to make her own happiness. People wait for a multitude of things:

for the weather to change, the perfect mate to come along, the winning lottery numbers. Some are waiting finally to be heard by their spouses. Others are waiting to be appreciated by their bosses. Still others are waiting to be loved for the first time. We are waiting. Waiting for something to change outside of ourselves that sweeps away the fear of taking a chance or trying something new, something that would grant us the courage and the permission we need to live with passion.

We are waiting for a guarantee that if we risk, nothing bad will happen. You reason that if only your boss would see that you're a great asset to the company, then his confidence in you would translate into increased self-confidence. And that is exactly what you would need to have the guts to open the catering business you've always dreamed about. Or you figure that if only you had the winning lottery ticket, then you could chuck the life you have for a whole new persona with no fear of making a mess of things and ending up homeless. And of course if you would only meet Mr. or Ms. Right, then you'd finally have the motivation to lose weight and make a lot of interesting friends and take your career off hold. If only . . .

But there is never a guarantee. While we wait for circumstances or people to change that are outside of our control, we can end up feeling sorry for ourselves, resentful, or helpless. Waiting validates our negative self-image. When we wait, we feel powerless. When we passively wait, we are living in fear.

Meredith realized how she had been waiting and wishing for someone to give her the answers that would "fix" her life. But no one is in charge of "saving" Meredith. When Meredith began mastering her fear, she no longer was waiting for life to happen to her. Instead, she began to make life happen.

I began to make my life happen on the twentieth anniversary of my parents' death. I was thirty-four years old. I had spent two decades searching for something or someone to take the pain away. I had blamed my parents' deaths for just about everything. How could I be happy when they were dead? How could I flourish after my sisters and I had been left as teenagers to bring ourselves up with barely any help? How could I make anything of myself when my father's point-blank killings had permeated my psyche with the fear that I wasn't worth the air I breathed? Yet at last, on that twentieth anniversary of their deaths, I looked in the mirror and said to myself, "Your life is up to you." I knew that after all the work I had done on my fear by embodying the principles of living fearlessly, I was ready to own my life. Only then would I accept myself fully and be the person I was born to be.

For Meredith, the crisis of her divorce from Phil gave her the courage and focus she needed to take back her power and become accountable for her life. As the Roman poet Horace put it: "Adversity has the effect of eliciting talents that would otherwise have lain dormant." The woman who walked into my office blind to the fact that she had been petrified of living was now shining from the inside out. As she fearlessly stepped out into the world, she began to ask herself the simple question, "What does Meredith like?" Sometimes, fear came up as she tasted freedom and tried new ventures. But after our work together, she knew how to face her fear and move beyond it.

Being Willing Makes You Able

The first thing I shared with Meredith was that in order to make any permanent changes, she had to be willing. Willing to see things differently. Willing to experience new ideas. Willing to listen to the people who cheered her on rather than ones who echoed her fears. Willing to admit that her fear had been in charge during her marriage. When we are willing to shift, move, or change—whether in one or all areas of life—we open ourselves up to true transformation. Not just temporarily, but permanently.

Our resistance to change is a symptom of how strong a hold fear has on us. Have you heard this definition of "insanity"? Insanity is when you do the same thing over and over again expecting different results. Well, that is how fear tricks us. It wants us to believe that if we only tried harder, then we could get it right. Before I developed my program, I used to say to myself, "I should know this. Why can't I figure this out? What is wrong with me? I'm afraid they'll find out I can't cut it." I was beating myself up with negative self-talk, and that lowered my self-confidence by making me afraid I was a loser. To get rid of that fear, I would make an even greater effort to succeed by doing more of whatever I had been doing—taking on more work, promising to meet deadlines I couldn't meet, saying I got the point when I really didn't. The thought of trying anything unfamiliar by taking a risk felt impossible. I couldn't ask for help, I couldn't plan a reasonable work load, I couldn't admit I needed advice. Each time that happened, fear won again.

Like me, Meredith had listened to fear one too many times. Yet when she found herself alone with no one to blame for her life but herself, she became ready and willing. I am happy to report that Meredith invested most of her nest egg in a small antique store that has become quite profitable. She loves running the store. She travels around the country hunting for antiques, and for over a year she has been dating a wonderful man who finds her fascinating and shares her newfound passion for life. Not bad, especially considering the fact that Meredith had only held a part-time job during her marriage. At forty-three, Meredith finally took some risks. And she learned to her great joy that risk is one of the keys that move you from fear to freedom. Taking risks built Meredith's courage, confidence, and consistency, giving her the ability to see herself differently. It propelled her to make more choices aligned with what was now true for her. With the insight that risk is inherent in any change, Meredith moved beyond her fear to live fearlessly.

The Origins of Fear

Our fear, and more precisely what I call our Wheel of Fear (which will be explained in detail in Chapter 2), begins to develop before our first memories. For example, just about every firstborn experiences a certain fear of abandonment and betrayal when the second baby is born. And plenty of only children acquire very early on an exaggerated fear of not fulfilling their parents' expectations of their ideal offspring. Also, since no one is good at everything, we have each had our share of failures and frustrations that instill the fear that we just don't measure up. Maybe you struggled to understand algebra, or you didn't get a part in the school play, or you were hopeless when it came to spelling, or you were the only one in your crowd without a date for the prom, or you couldn't kick a soccer ball to save your life. Never mind that you were a shining success in other arenas. Somehow, humiliation trumps approval every time and proves to you once again that your fear of not being good enough is true. In fact, success starts to make you nervous because you're sure you'll be found out sooner or later. Even child prodigies who seem to lead charmed lives can have this reaction. It's hard to follow your own act and keep topping yourself. There's always the nagging fear that you've peaked and won't be able to keep this up.

In my case, the reason that I was propelled onto my Wheel of Fear may seem obvious. But no single episode, not even one as traumatic as witnessing the crime of passion that took my parents' lives, puts a person on a Wheel of Fear. Like virtually everybody else, I had already accumulated a series of large and small insults to my ego that would have put me on the Wheel even without the murder-suicide as a catapult.

More important, we are all affected not only by what happens in our lives but by the way key people do or don't help us cope with the events. Our parents and the other people who love us want what is best for us, and therefore they try to protect us.

Unfortunately, meaning well and doing a good job are often poles apart. The way the adults in a child's life handle fear-provoking situations often exacerbates the fear. My relatives had no idea how to handle the murder-suicide, so we did not talk about it for over twenty years. After my grandmother lifted me off of my mother's coffin where I was sobbing inconsolably, and shushed me, my aunts and uncles tacitly agreed with her that I needed to stop wailing and get ahold of myself. At fourteen, I had no permission to cry or talk about what had happened ever again. Period. The message I received from this rule laid down by the adults in my life was "It is not okay to express who I am." Or put another way, "The people I value won't be proud of me if I am who I am."

That is one of the chief messages that formed my Wheel of Fear. Somewhere along the line, messages you received from adults in your life went into forming your Wheel of Fear as well. Maybe you were a tomboy who was dragged to ballet lessons because your mother didn't want you to play baseball even though you loved it and were good at it. Maybe you were a gifted visual artist who was pushed into sports by your father the jock. Maybe you showed your English teacher the beginnings of a science fiction novel and were told you should set your sights on a more practical career. Whatever the particulars, you no doubt haven't thought about any of the incidents for years and years.

False Perceptions Based on Fear

And that's just fine. You don't need to know what the cumulative events were that added up to your fear that it's not acceptable to be you and that you're not good enough. As we move along, you'll learn how to overcome the fear whether you are aware of its roots or not or, as LeDoux put it, "have a poor conscious memory" of the event. What I am interested in is how your fear does what I call "filtering." If you're afraid you're unlovable and someone says, "I love you," you'll pass the words through your filter and all that will be left in the sieve, so to speak, is your reaction: "But you don't know I'm not worthy of your love."

Here's another example. I have one client, Anna, who is an administrative assistant. She told me that when her boss asks her to do anything new, she invariably feels as though she is too stupid and too slow so she will surely fail. Anna grew up with a mother who was old-school strict, constantly berating her and seldom giving compliments. Consequently, Anna passes compliments through her filter and all she gets is her reaction: "He doesn't know what he is talking about. I hope I don't get caught. Any success I have had has been pure luck with very little chance of a repeat performance." Anna is smart and very able to handle any task brilliantly, but her fear-based filtering system makes her believe her feeling that she's not very capable or accomplished after all. Put another way, based on her fear-driven filtering system, Anna's perception is that her boss is mistaken when he says she's good. She fears that she'll never live up to what's expected of her. She feels incompetent, even phony. She minimizes anything positive in her life. Secretly, she wonders when she will be fired. Yet the truth is that she's good.

Each of us has a unique filtering system, but the mechanics of the system are always the same. Your filtering system may leave you with the perception that you are being taken advantage of when in fact you have been afraid to say no. You may have the perception that you have no choice but to accept your lot in life when in fact you are afraid to risk change and possible rejection. And to keep those perceptions in place, you need to build evidence to support them.

Proof That Your Perceptions Are Correct

Anna had amassed plenty of evidence to support her perception that the boss was wrong when he said she was good. She reminded herself often that she does not have A+ typing skills.

She always took longer to finish a task than anyone else in the office. And anytime she started to think about asking for a raise, she would remember that humiliating moment when she had forgotten to make her boss's plane reservations for their yearly corporate meeting. He wasn't able to attend the opening keynote. He was not happy. How much more proof did she need that it was silly to believe any compliments from her boss? He was just being kind in keeping her.

Human beings are experts at building evidence to uphold their fear-based beliefs. Let's say you are afraid that computers are too hard for you to understand. In turn, you believe you could never learn to use computers. Now whenever you see an article in the paper about how difficult technology is, you read it and nod your head. Suspicion confirmed! But if you see a headline that promises an article about the way elderly people at senior day care centers are mastering computers with ease, you skip right past that—not on purpose necessarily, but unconsciously. You don't want your fear to be challenged or disproved. You're nice and safe believing what you believe, thank you very much. In fact, you'll even go out of your way to find evidence to support that belief. If you have a friend who is a computer geek, you'll ask questions that will get that person to elaborate on the perils and pitfalls of his profession. You'll listen eagerly to his stories about system crashes and lost data, all the while filtering out his evident satisfaction at solving those problems. Then you'll say to yourself, "Aha! I was right."

Admit Your Perceptions Aren't Working

And that is what fear likes to hear, because fear has a secret weapon: it knows you like to be proven right. It filters all the information you receive so that you invariably accept only what aligns with what you already know. Fear uses your desire to be in control, your high standards of perfectionism, and your effort to look as though you've got it together to keep you just the way you are. It tells you what you want to hear, giving you a false sense of being protected from the outside world. Being right has become the way you prove to yourself that your life is all right, that your decisions are okay, and any mediocrity in your life is not your fault. It is the basis for your ability to justify your excuses and complaints, push away responsibility, and blame others for any problems in your life.

Think about this. What if your desire to manage, avoid, and deny fear were actually keeping it in place? What if your idea of perfection were keeping you from who you desired to be? What if your need to look like a winner were the reason you didn't feel as successful as you could? Attempting to manage fear only perpetuates it. Even if you do set a goal and reach it, fear minimizes it by bringing up those nagging doubts and worries. You're always running scared. The truth is, you're afraid of breaking out of your self-imposed limitations because you are unsure of what lies ahead. You might fail. You might get chastised. Your hesitation came from the voice of fear asking, "Are you sure this is what you want? Do you think you can handle this?" Fear has won again. You become convinced that this success was an accident. The bottom line is fear can motivate you to try really hard, and you can get what you tried for, but inherent in fear is the inability to enjoy what you've got. The Wheel keeps spinning.

Frank's Story

That's what happened to Frank. He was a hard worker and ambitious. Those are two traits that are admirable and sought after, but he had exhibited those qualities for one reason and one reason only: Frank was afraid of failure. He was driven to avoid being seen as a failure. That goal consumed him. To say the least, his life was out of balance.

Frank is not alone. Fear keeps many people motivated by reminding them they could be criticized or be shown to be a fake if they don't work harder. Frank would ask himself daily, "What if I don't accomplish such and such. What will 'they' think?" "They" could be his spouse, parents, the next-door neighbor with the bigger house, his classmates from college, the boy who teased him when he was nine, his boss, his kids, or a thousand other people he probably doesn't even remember. To keep his fear at bay, Frank ate, drank, and slept real-estate home sales. He was consistently "Salesperson of the Month," but his marriage was in shambles and he didn't even know if his kids preferred McDonald's or Taco Bell. Intimacy was not his forte. Fear was.

Fear creates deceptive results. On the outside, Frank appeared successful. He made six figures a year, his children went to a top private school, and his picture was plastered on billboards all over town. Everyone knew Frank. But Frank didn't know himself. He just kept thinking that if he could make the next sale, then he would have time to spend with his family. But the next sale always had another sale right behind it. Life was slipping by.

Frank's fear-driven behavior stemmed largely from the fear he inherited from his father. Remember what LeDoux said about fear and our heritage? Parents can have a huge influence on the way we process fear. Frank's father had lost everything in the Depression, and Frank could still remember how hard his father worked to put food on the table. Frank was tutored daily on what it takes to succeed, and the number-one ingredient was hard work. The shame his father experienced when he went broke was not lost on Frank. The fear of experiencing that same shame kept Frank going.

The good news is that Frank's ability to be focused, persistent, and go the extra mile could eventually be used to move him from the Wheel of Fear to what I call your Wheel of Freedom (which will be explained in detail in Chapter 3). When he started the Fearless Living program, I prescribed homework that was designed to instill in him a willingness to give up the perceptions that were keeping his fear in place and to rebuild his filtering system so that it empowered him rather than diminished him. That may sound difficult. But if you, like Frank, have been struggling with fear every day of your life, learning how to master fear will be easy by comparison.

Did Frank have to give up his career success to master his fear? No. But what he did have to do was face the fact that he wasn't happy, his wife wasn't happy, his children weren't happy, and his life was not what he thought, or portrayed, it to be. I worked with Frank to quiet the voice of fear that constantly whispered in his ear, "You are going to lose everything. The next sale might be your last and then what will you do? Everyone knows that your numbers are just a matter of luck. One day your luck will run out and then what? Everyone will know the truth about you." We also had to change his answer: "I'll show them!" That internal dialogue was fear talking to fear. The minute you let others decide how you are going to act, fear is on patrol.

When was the last time you accomplished a goal that "should" have made you happy, yet instead left you empty and cold? Frank wanted success more than anything. He believed it would make his life worthwhile and vindicate his heritage of poverty. But fear was the only thing pushing him to succeed. Fear can be a great motivator, but at the end of the day, it doesn't necessarily make us feel satisfied or give us peace of mind.

Love Thyself

Of course, Frank's fear of being criticized and of being seen as a failure is understandable. Caring what others think about us is normal. The desire to belong is basic to human nature. But in order to feel like you truly belong, you must accept yourself for who you are. That is critical to Fearless Living. Accepting yourself can be tough when you aren't at peace with your present state. But self-acceptance is necessary in order to have a true sense of belonging.

Like so many of us, when Frank attempted to connect with people—both those who were already important to him and those he was hoping to get to know—he let fear keep him from revealing his essential nature. "Put up a false front," fear says, "They won't accept you for you." We all want approval. Letting the key players in our lives see that we are scared or lonely or not sure we're worth loving is almost unbearable. Yet unless we allow others to know our truth, fears and limitations included, there can be no trust and no genuine intimacy. How can we hope to cultivate friendship, love, and support if we can't risk being vulnerable enough to let people experience who we really are? Acceptance of yourself and others is crucial if fear is going to loosen its grip on you.

Thriving, Not Just Surviving

And fear uses evidence to keep our filtering systems and perceptions in place. After my parents died, I used the filtering system called "It's me against the world." Meredith's was "What can I do for you today?" Frank's was "I must not fail." All of those systems denied us the chance to accept our true selves. That is called surviving. Not living. The title of this book is Fearless Living, not Fearless Surviving.

Think of the last twenty-four hours. What percentage of those hours was spent just surviving? Surviving means you are settling . . . waiting for the other shoe to drop . . . hiding yourself from other people . . . doubting yourself . . . never allowing anyone really to get to know you . . . having friends that are more like enemies . . . doing things because you think you have to, need to, or should . . . waking up and dreading the next twenty-four hours . . . hoping someone will take you away from all of this . . . complaining . . . saying yes when you really want to say no . . . worrying for no reason at all . . . giving up on yourself before you ever try . . . putting your needs last . . . protecting yourself from being hurt . . . never questioning authority . . . holding yourself back when you want to whistle, giggle, or sing . . . having a ton of good excuses why your life is the way it is and having the evidence to prove it . . . not asking for support when you need it . . . holding a grudge . . . spending money you don't have on things you don't need . . . comparing yourself to anyone and everyone . . . being unwilling to love first . . . blaming your parents for the way you turned out . . . being unwilling to rock the boat . . . figuring everyone knows more than you do . . . drinking too much . . . not speaking up when you feel ignored, unimportant, or undervalued . . . waiting for something—anything—to change . . . manipulating others to get your way . . . eating foods that you know aren't good for you . . . being so ashamed of your body that you wear clothes two sizes too big . . . holding it all together even though you feel as though you're falling apart . . . priding yourself on not having cried since your pet mouse died when you were four . . . listening to fear when it tells you this is all you're allowed to have and believing it . . . saying things you will regret just because you feel other people deserve it . . . not admitting there could be two sides to the story when your relationship doesn't work out . . . giving your opinion to people who haven't asked for it . . . hesitating to speak up . . . defending your position no matter what . . . seeing losing as bad . . . wishing things could be different but doing nothing to change the status quo . . . calling yourself stupid . . . denying your creativity.

Living, on the other hand, means saying no when you mean no . . . being grateful for the good in your life . . . smiling out of the blue . . . having someone in your life whom you are blessed to call your friend . . . never holding a grudge . . . giving yourself a break . . . doing your best and praising yourself for all of your efforts . . . dancing down the hallway . . . being willing to fall in love without a guarantee that you won't get hurt . . . wearing your favorite shirt for no reason at all . . . singing in the car even though you are tone deaf . . . anticipating that everything will work out . . . being someone's confidante . . . giving up your worry list . . . telling yourself you can do it when fear makes you think you can't . . . asking the people in your life to help you through a difficult time and telling them how to do that . . . crying because you need to . . . standing up for what you want in life without walking over anyone . . . living with an attitude that there is enough to go around . . . waking up just happy to be alive . . . being willing to be wrong . . . learning something that you've always wanted to learn . . . giving your time to a service organization because you care rather than because it would be good for business . . . trusting yourself . . . saving up your money for that frivolous item that you've been yearning for . . . acting as if people like you . . . taking steps toward your vision . . . saying yes to you.

Living is what we're working toward. Fearless Living.

Pick a Place to Start

Maybe there is already an area of your life that is not governed by fear. Perhaps you are passionate about your work or you have a wonderful marriage or you are good at helping others who are less fortunate than you are. That's terrific. But is there also an area of your life that is marred by dissatisfaction, frustration, or disappointment? Are you happy in your relationship but miserable at work? Are you financially successful and well respected in your field but unable to lose weight and stick to an exercise regimen? Are you a creative dynamo but you come home to an apartment empty except for your cat? If the answer is yes, you're not alone. And what you may also learn as we work through this book is that even in the areas where you are ostensibly in control, fear may play a much bigger part than you had ever realized.

The simplest way to learn how fear may be driving you, consciously or unconsciously, in any area of your life is to focus on the one area that is most obviously not satisfying. As you do the Fearbuster Exercises throughout the book, be sure to concentrate on that area. When you master one area of your life, you are gaining the skill to master any area—your career, your relationships, your physical health, your creativity. Think of an area you would like to work on. Whatever comes to mind first is perfect.

However, before we do any more work, I want to lay down some ground rules:

- For now, keep this work to yourself.

  Until you've mastered the basic principles of Fearless Living and experienced some results, sharing this work with other people—especially the wrong people—can undermine your efforts by activating the very fear we're out to vanquish. I'll guide you through the process of choosing the best Fearbuster Team in later chapters.

- Set aside at least ten minutes a day to do the Fearbuster Exercises.

  I know you're busy. That's why I want you to build this work into your agenda and stick to it. Get yourself a notebook, or if you're a computer maven, set up a folder and some documents for this purpose. Then have a look at your schedule. Can you set the alarm a few minutes earlier so you'll be up before the demands of your family take over your morning? Can you do the written exercises on the commuter train? Is there some quiet time after dinner when everybody else is watching TV? Could you carve a little time out of your lunch hour? At the very least, can you do the work when you're in the privacy of the bathroom? Somewhere in your routine, designate a slot for the purpose of taking care of yourself through doing the Fearbuster Exercises.

Understanding the aspects of fear is vital to your ability to loosen its hold on you. Now we're ready to break down fear through identifying the four key aspects that form your personal version of the Wheel of Fear. . . .

2

The Wheel of Fear

When you are trying to control fear, you are keeping it in check, just beneath the surface where it is ready to erupt at the slightest provocation. When you manage fear, it keeps you off track by telling you to focus on the circumstantial issues of life rather than the actual fear itself. Therefore, the fear is making your decisions for you passively, unconsciously, reactively. On the other hand, mastering your fear means facing it down, allowing you to feel it move through without getting stuck in it.

The minute Connie got the e-mail message saying that her in-laws were coming for a two-week visit, her throat closed up. Not that she hadn't invited them to make the trip up from Florida. The baby was their first grandchild and she knew they were eager to see him. Still, the idea of having Bob's parents as houseguests sent Connie into a tizzy. Maybe she should buy new sheets for the guest room. At the very least, she'd have to clean that room top to bottom, including the slats on the Levolors. And she really should plan to have her parents and her brother and his family over for dinner the night her in-laws got there.

But what could she serve that would stand up to her mother-in-law's cooking? Anyway, everything was complicated by the fact that Connie, who had been the press secretary for the CEO of a major corporation before her pregnancy, was now running her own thriving public relations business from a home office. Whenever the baby was finally napping, Connie felt she had to be at her desk fielding calls and meeting deadlines.

By the time Connie's in-laws were scheduled to arrive, she was exhausted and looked it. Besides that, she hadn't lost the "baby fat." Connie smudged concealer over the circles under her eyes and picked out a blousy outfit she hoped didn't look too much like her maternity clothes. Then she put the baby in a strap-on carrier to keep him quiet, and rushed around making her from-scratch menu of stuffed Cornish game hens, vegetable soufflé, seven-grain bread, and key lime pie.

Let's cut to the chase. The evening was a disaster. The baby was cranky, wouldn't take his bottle, and subsequently spit up on Grandma's silk blouse. The bread burned. The soufflé fell. The pie was watery. An irate client called while Connie was clearing the dishes and chewed her out for letting a typo slip by in a press release she had prepared for him. And Connie's mother-in-law—never one to be big on tact—said, "My goodness, dear, are you getting enough sleep? You don't want to lose your looks. Right, Bob?"

Connie had failed miserably in her attempt to avoid being judged as—and this is the word she used when we worked together—"incompetent." What happened then? She tried even harder to avoid having anybody think she was incompetent. She got up early to make pancakes for breakfast, forgetting that her father-in-law was on a low-cholesterol diet and couldn't eat them. She laundered the towels every day as though she had to compete with the Hilton hotel chain. She stayed up until all hours to write her press releases so that she'd be free to spend time with her in-laws during the day. She leapt out of bed every time the baby whimpered so he wouldn't be a bother and disturb anybody else. But no matter what she did, she couldn't achieve the standard of perfection she was sure was expected of her.

One evening toward the end of the week, she found herself standing in the kitchen sobbing uncontrollably. She had started to slice a tomato for the salad and suddenly the thought of all the chopping and dicing ahead of her—the peppers, the celery, the mushrooms, the carrots—overwhelmed her. Bob came in just then and she blubbered something about how she just couldn't face cooking one more meal.

"Get a grip!" Bob said. "You used to handle high-pressure situations at the office every day. Now you can't even cut up a tomato without losing it. And you used to leave here every morning looking like a million bucks. These days you never even fix yourself up before dinner. Okay, okay, the baby takes up a lot of time. I help when you let me and I am trying to be understanding, but you're not the first person in the world who ever had a baby. It's been six months already. When are you going to get it together?"

Bob's uncharacteristic outburst hit Connie right in the solar plexus. She gasped for air, the tears still streaming down her face. Later, Connie would tell me that at that agonizing moment, when Bob turned on his heel and left the kitchen, she had gone from thinking she was incompetent to feeling utterly unlovable. It was then that Connie reached for the pack of cigarettes she kept hidden in a top cupboard just for times like this. She had quit smoking when she found out she was pregnant, but she had found nothing to match the power of the first deep drag on a Benson & Hedges when it came to numbing her emotional pain.

When Connie flushed the butt down the toilet, the relief the cigarette had brought her turned to unbearable shame. She had locked herself in the bathroom with a can of air freshener to get rid of the smell of her transgression. She looked in the mirror and saw the puffy, tearstained face of an incompetent, unlovable human being. She called herself some choice, unprintable names and vowed to try even harder to live up to the standards she had set for herself. Resolutely, she marched back into the kitchen, opened her cookbook, and set about making beef Bourguignon instead of simply grilling the steaks she had on hand. That ought to impress everybody. "I'll show them!" she muttered to herself as she pulled the meat out of the refrigerator and got to work.

Connie was on the Wheel of Fear. It is a classic vicious cycle, a looping of events in which the apparent solution to a problem causes a new problem that brings us right back to the original problem. My Wheel of Fear is a perfect example. I'm afraid of being seen or thought of as a loser. To me—and this is my definition—that means I should be able to do everything for everyone, and perfectly. Therefore, before I developed my program, I was in the habit of saying "yes" when I should have said "no." I would give myself unrealistic deadlines. I would take on too many projects. Superwoman was my role model. I was always trying to prove I wasn't a loser, but of course I unconsciously set things up so that I couldn't possibly fulfill all my obligations or get everything done the way it should have been done. I was always trying to beat the clock and I was impatient with myself and everybody else. In the end, I would believe that I was—you guessed it—a loser. The next step? I would indulge in any one of my favorite emotional painkillers—alcohol, wild spending sprees, isolation. Then I would beat myself up. The result was that my excruciatingly painful feeling of worthlessness would kick in. That would send me to the beginning of the cycle, taking on too much in order to avoid what I fear and making my Wheel of Fear go around and around endlessly.

Each of us has an individual Wheel of Fear that has been formed by our family heritage, belief system, and life experience. Each of us keeps the Wheel of Fear in perfect operating order, greasing it with the evidence we continually find to prove that our fears about ourselves are correct. Only when you identify your Wheel of Fear will you be in a position to stop it from spinning. However, even though your Wheel is yours and yours alone, the mechanism that keeps the Wheel of Fear spinning is identical for everyone. Over the years, with client after client, I have seen the same cyclical process at work.

- First, something happens that *triggers your fear* of being thought of by yourself or anybody else as having what you believe to be a serious character flaw. You urgently want to avoid that outcome, so your body prepares to handle the emergency. To at least some degree, you experience the physical symptoms of fear, including a racing heart and sweaty palms.

- Second, your *fear response* makes you do something, usually unconsciously, that is meant to ensure that you avoid the dreaded outcome. Just as you would run away from an object you perceive to be a snake, you try to run away in the figurative sense from the thought that terrifies you. Ironically, your response—for example, trying harder to succeed or making promises you can't possibly keep—almost certainly guarantees that the outcome will in fact happen. In a cruel trick of nature, we unerringly choose behavior that only serves to confirm our worst fear about ourselves.

- Third, as you realize you haven't avoided what you fear, the consequence is that you experience the gut-wrenching *negative feeling* of not being good enough—whatever your particular version of that is. This is what you are truly afraid of. The thought you are trying to avoid is a cover for the feeling that you can't bear to face. That feeling is always underneath your thoughts and responses, both of which keep you distracted, helping you avoid the very thing you must confront: your version of not being good enough.

Self-loathing is next. You globalize from this one instance, and you fear that you can't do anything right.

- Fourth, you find some way to numb the emotional pain, almost invariably *self-destructive behavior* such as drinking, gambling, eating unhealthy food, or shutting yourself off from the very people who could support you. Remember, the degree to which you indulge in this behavior isn't the issue. The motivation is.

If you toast with a glass or two of champagne at someone's wedding and also eat a piece of the wedding cake, you're probably not using the alcohol and the sugar as emotional painkillers but as ways of celebrating. Yet if you go home after a bad day and pour yourself a drink because you "need" it, your behavior is fear driven even if you don't get drunk and even if you don't do this all that often. In other words, don't tell yourself, "I'm not an alcoholic, so this section doesn't apply to me."

Similarly, if you stop off at your neighborhood 7-Eleven to buy a quart of ice cream because you messed up at the office, and then you thaw the ice cream slightly in the microwave so you can eat it right out of the carton, you're almost certainly on your Wheel of Fear. Don't try to let yourself off the hook by pointing out that you're not overweight and that you don't make a habit of overeating. Finally, if you go off to a writer's colony where you can be alone with your thoughts, that's a positive motivation for solitude. But if you stop answering the phone and your e-mails because you're feeling like an idiot and you don't want to relate to anyone, that's unhealthy isolation whether it's for one evening or chronically.

In any case, since self-destructive behavior doesn't give you any lasting relief and usually in fact makes you feel even worse, you end up exactly where you started: trying in vain to keep the fear at bay. The fear becomes a self-fulfilling prophecy. And the Wheel goes on and on.

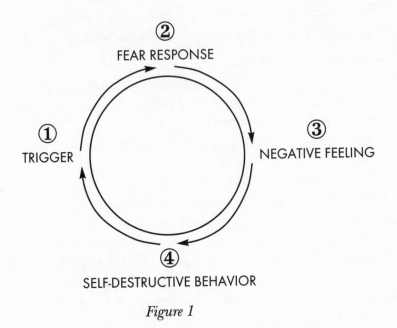

Figure 1

Find Out What's Keeping You on the Wheel of Fear

In order to get off the Wheel of Fear, you have to understand what triggers your cycle. To that end, I'm going to use the technique that is effective time and again with clients who are working through my Fearless Living program. I'm going to ask you to complete four statements. Let's begin with the one that starts the Wheel spinning.

First, study the following list:

1) selfish
2) stupid
3) weak
4) incompetent
5) ordinary
6) a loser
7) a fake
8) lazy

9) invisible
10) rejected

Next, pick the one word from the list that gives you the most intense reaction when you put it in the following sentence:

If someone I love, respect, or admire thought I were _____, I would be devastated.

When I did this exercise with Meredith, the loyal wife whose husband left her after eighteen years of marriage, she said she couldn't pick just one. She said all of them would devastate her. You may feel the same way. However, experience has shown me that if people identify the main trigger that sets the Wheel of Fear in motion, they are in a much better position to defuse all the fears that can accompany it. Awareness is the key. When you know what you are most afraid of, you are better able to realize when your actions are knee-jerk responses to fear instead of proactive, conscious choices.

In order to figure out which word to write, narrow the list down to the top five items that would really bother you if your best friends said them about you. After that, I want your top three, the ones that would horrify you if the person you most respect in your life told you them about yourself. All right, let's get it down to one—the top one that would be by far the worst, the one you would do just about anything to avoid having people think about you. That's the trigger for your Wheel of Fear.

Meredith, a quintessential people pleaser who had spent her entire adult life putting her husband and children first, picked the following for her top five: "selfish," "lazy," "incompetent," "rejected," "a loser." Then she narrowed her list down to the following three: "selfish," "rejected," "a loser." Finally, she found her main trigger: Meredith would do anything to keep people from thinking she was selfish. Yet ironically, her eighteen years of denying her own needs in order to be her idea of a perfect wife and mother had backfired. That's what happens when someone is driven by the Wheel of Fear instead of unfolding naturally through his or her Wheel of Freedom.

Connie, the working mother whose trigger was the fear of being thought of as incompetent, overcompensated and got just what she was trying to avoid. Frank, the real-estate salesman who didn't want to be thought of as lazy, worked relentlessly but never felt sure of himself and he never had time to enjoy his loved ones. I behaved much the same way in my attempt to avoid being thought of as a loser. My workaholism and perfectionism guaranteed that my worst fear would be confirmed.

Core Negative Feelings

The next statement I want you to complete is designed to elicit your core negative feeling—your version of fearing you're not good enough.

Study the following list:

1) a failure
2) unlovable
3) a disappointment
4) worthless
5) helpless
6) foolish
7) inadequate
8) insignificant
9) an outcast
10) damaged goods

Now, fill in the following blanks:

If the people I care about really thought I was (the trigger you identified goes here) _____, I would feel as though I were _____.

Again, narrow the list down to five, then three, then one. At the end of a bad day, when nothing has gone right, how do you feel about yourself? The sixteenth-century Spanish poet and mystic St. John of the Cross called it "the Dark Night of the Soul," and later F. Scott Fitzgerald wrote, "in the real dark night of the soul, it is always three o'clock in the morning." Others call it their shadow side. What feeling lurks in your psyche that you want desperately to override? In our most fear-driven moments, we suspect that our core feelings could very well be the truth about us. And each time we go through the cycle, the Wheel of Fear takes a stronger hold upon our conscious and unconscious decisions. Eventually, we typically believe that the negative feelings we have about ourselves are facts.

I assure you, they are not. As we work through the program, you will learn to take positive actions that will put you on the path to positive feelings. You will own them. Simply put, you will be you—and you are not those negative feelings you fear. You'll love who you really are. You'll greet each new day with enthusiasm and anticipation instead of dread. Naturally, you'll still encounter unpleasant and maybe even cruel people and events along the way that trigger your Wheel of Fear. However, you'll be able to deactivate it because you will be equipped with the emotional stamina to handle even the most upsetting situations. Remember, the past does not equal the future. You can change ingrained patterns and keep history from repeating itself. You're not a laboratory rat. You're a human being. You can master your fears. But first you have to know them.

Meredith, who had resisted picking one trigger, found that picking one core feeling was easy. That is often the case. You can deliberate about what thoughts you're afraid of, but feelings are visceral. Also, once you have identified your trigger, examples of incidents from your life may pop into your head that might make you experience the very feeling we're trying to identify. For Meredith, pinpointing that she was always striving to avoid being thought of as selfish made her realize that every time she made herself a human sacrifice, she was in effect crying out, 'Look at me! Notice me! Appreciate me! I matter! You can't do without me!' As she said to me when she had gained insight into her behavior, "When they seemed to ignore me or take advantage of me anyway, I had this horrible feeling that I was completely insignificant. I felt like I didn't matter after all. So I'd go into hyperdrive to try to get rid of that feeling and prove I did matter. Over and over again, day after day, year after year."

The trigger Connie identified was "incompetent" and the feeling was "unlovable." The trigger Frank identified was "lazy" and the feeling was "failure." The trigger I identified was "loser" and the feeling was "worthless." Interestingly, my sister Linda, who picked "ordinary" as her trigger, also picked "worthless" as her feeling. We started at different places and ended up with the same awful, empty, gut feeling that we are worthless. Linda, the baby of the family—doted on and adored, coddled and cherished—had envisioned herself doing something extraordinary with her life. She has a head for math, and she dreamt of working for NASA. Instead, she is a high-school math teacher. That just didn't seem big enough to her. She felt, most days until she found her Wheel of Freedom, worthless.

Responses

The third statement I want you to complete elicits your responses to your trigger as well as your responses to your core feeling.

1) Go down the following list and put a check mark (✔) next to everything you do to avoid your trigger—that thought that you couldn't bear to have others think about you. Meredith for example checked "being a peo-

ple pleaser," "perfectionism," "workaholism," and "comparing yourself to others" as her fear responses to avoid being thought of as selfish.

2) Go down the list again and place an X next to anything you do to stop the emotional pain when your core feeling kicks in. This is usually our more self-destructive behavior. Some of the items may get both a check mark and an X. Others may get one or the other. Meredith put an X next to "comparing yourself to others" along with "isolating," "apologizing for everything," "taking everything personally," "overeating," "insomnia," and "hating yourself." Then she paused for a long time and finally put an X next to "shoplifting."

"I've never told a soul about this," she said, flushing and blinking back tears. "My whole life I would just give, give, give. Phil was so tight I never spent any money on myself. So sometimes I'd snap and go to the mall and slip something into my bag. It was never anything big. Maybe a tube of lipstick or a scarf. Thank goodness I never got caught. But of course I always felt worse than ever afterward."

And that is how the Wheel of Fear spins. We have a thought that perhaps we are lazy or weak or stupid, which triggers our fear responses. They are the reactions that tell us if we just do that behavior, it will prove that the thought isn't true. But inherent in the reaction is the feeling you have been avoiding all along. If you play out the reaction, it is only confirming your worst fear that you really are worthless, helpless, or whatever your personal version of not being good enough is. And when you experience that feeling, it pushes you into self-destructive behaviors.

What you will come to discover is your judgment of your thoughts is what pushes you off center, keeping your Wheel of Fear revolving. When you can't be thought of a certain way, it triggers reactions and self-destructive behavior that become a way of life. They give you a temporary, false sense of security, just as a child who clings to a tattered baby blanket has the illusion of safety even when his parents aren't there to protect him. But sooner or later the fear takes hold again and you start all over. Ultimately, the thought you are avoiding is the same thought that must be embraced in order for the fear to lose its power.

Here's the list of fear-driven responses:

being a people pleaser
isolating
blaming
compromising
shopaholism
negative attitude
sleeping too much
procrastination
apologizing for everything
moving to get away
    from problems
taking everything
    personally
being manipulative
staying in an Internet
    chat room until 3:00 A.M.
surfing channels on the
    TV until all hours
giving up
doing drugs
bulimia or anorexia
kicking the cat/dog
making jokes about
    yourself
workaholism
shutting down

emotional drama junkie
self-pity
drinking too much
whining
exercise addict
being promiscuous
arguing with anyone about
    anything
escapism
name calling
gambling
lying and pretending
cheating
shoplifting
smoking
putting other people down
insomnia
suicidal thoughts or attempts
crying uncontrollably
physical abuse to yourself
negative self-talk
comparing yourself to others
constipation/diarrhea
headaches/migranes
stomachaches
high blood pressure

verbal abuse to yourself
or others
making a preemptive
strike on others
being irresponsible
overeating
perfectionism

making excuses or
complaining
endless daydreaming
hating yourself
intentional sleep
deprivation
heartburn

Now fill in the following:

1) When I want to avoid the thought that I am _____
(your Wheel of Fear trigger goes here), I do the following:
(items check-marked ✔ only)

_____

_____

_____

_____

2) When I want to get rid of my core negative feeling that
I am _____, I do the following: (items with
an X only)

_____

_____

_____

_____

The important thing about all of these responses is that they
masquerade as your problems when they are simply your attempt to avoid confirming your worst fear about yourself and
to ease the pain of believing it is true. Connie, for example,
had always imagined that nicotine addiction was her problem,
and had tried all sorts of techniques to solve it. She used

over-the-counter patches and gum, she put No Smoking signs all over the house and on her desk, she had her teeth professionally whitened, she had her clothes cleaned, she threw out her ashtrays, she read every scary article she could find about lung cancer and emphysema, she kept lollipops and gum in her desk drawer. And at last she proved to herself that she could quit when she gave up smoking during her pregnancy. But even though she had kicked her physical addiction to cigarettes, she would still find herself using nicotine to short-circuit her feeling of being unlovable. Only when she worked through the exercises in the Fearless Living program was she able to give up smoking once and for all. Similarly Frank, whose workaholism was destroying his marriage, finally got some balance in his life once he got with the Fearless Living program.

Your Wheel of Fear

Now you're ready to put your Wheel of Fear down on paper. Fill in the blanks:

When I want to avoid having people think I'm (your trigger goes here) _____, I react by (your checked responses ✔ go here): _____

_____

_____

When that doesn't work and I end up feeling (your core negative feeling goes here) _____, then I (your responses marked with an X go here):_____

_____

_____

_____

Good Work! And remember, you can add to your list of responses as we go along. The more thorough you are when you list your responses, the more you will start recognizing your Wheel of Fear even in the minutiae of your everyday life. In fact, you can add specific responses that are not on the general list I gave you. For example, let's say you go to the grocery store and the box of cereal you want is on a top shelf. You can't reach it. You feel impatient and mutter to yourself that the store is "stupid" because the shelves are too high. Instead of asking someone to get it for you, you leave without the cereal. You don't want to bother anybody. You don't want to risk having the stock boy roll his eyes and act put upon on your account. In that seemingly unimportant moment, your inability to ask for help kept the Wheel of Fear spinning. So add "Can't ask for help even from people paid to help me" to your list.

Other examples of situation-specific responses to fear: You grab the restaurant bill to prove you're not a failure, even though your credit card is maxed out and sure to get declined. . . . You stay late at your East Coast office so you can make sales calls during West Coast business hours even though you have more than met your quota. . . . You say yes just to keep the peace and then you hate yourself afterward. . . . You go out for drinks and stay up too late the night before an important meeting. . . . You let a once-in-a-lifetime opportunity slip away because you can't make up your mind. . . . You spend money you don't have on stuff you don't need. . . . You shut everybody out and devote all your free time to playing computer games. . . . You crack jokes about how hopeless you are when it comes to relationships, or making money, or cooking, or losing weight, or driving. . . . You laugh when somebody else makes fun of you. . . . You call in sick the day of a meeting because you're afraid you'll make a fool of yourself. . . . You put off making crucial decisions, unable to make up your mind. . . . You fail to delegate even though you're the boss now and you have a whole staff to help.

Those responses may seem justifiable to you in certain situations. Yet it is never appropriate to put yourself (or others) down or abuse yourself (or others) in any way. Every time you put off calling the insurance company about a mistake you think was made in a claim . . . every time you turn down an invitation to a party with the excuse that you're too busy . . . every time you compare yourself to someone else and conclude that you don't measure up . . . every time you hesitate to order what you really want in a restaurant because you're sure the waiter thinks you could lose a few pounds . . . every time you tell yourself you might as well eat the whole box of Girl Scout cookies because you can never stick to a diet anyway . . . every time you go to bed disappointed in yourself because you didn't check off enough items from your To Do list . . . every time you wake up in the morning with the sense that this day is just one more day in a long list of days . . . every time those things or things like them happen, you are on your Wheel of Fear.

Symptoms That Mean You're on Your Wheel of Fear

However, recognizing when you're on your Wheel of Fear may be tough in the beginning. You may not be able to catch yourself thinking that thought or taking those actions. A good way to become more aware of your behavior is to pay attention to the symptoms that mean you are on your Wheel of Fear. In the same way that a scratchy throat and a runny nose signal the start of a common cold, certain emotional symptoms are a sign that you're not in optimum emotional health. The symptoms are legion, varying from person to person, but the most common ones are when you feel:

Impatient You want instant results and instant relief from suspense. What did the boss think about the report you turned in? You can't stand it. You can't wait. You have to know now. You feel irritated and edgy, like somebody stuck in traffic. Why can't they all hurry up? What's taking them so long? Why don't they get back to you?

Exhausted You're dragging through your days. Everything takes so much effort, but nothing seems worth the effort. You're racing around, doing a million things, but nothing ever seems to get done, let alone done well, and you're just worn out with it all.

Self-Righteous They're all jerks! Everybody in the whole industry is impossible to work with! They don't appreciate anything you do. You practically give blood at the office every day and everybody else takes all the credit. People take advantage of you right and left. Even at home, somebody always wants something.

Misunderstood People take everything the wrong way. They get their feelings hurt when you mean to be nice. They give you blank stares as though you're speaking Greek. Nobody gets it. You just don't feel heard.

Paranoid You suspect others are out to get you or don't support you or that what you are doing needs to be protected. You feel you need to keep your defenses up. Somebody might steal your ideas, sabotage your plan, get there first.

Paralyzed You are so numb to your feelings and thoughts that you deny that anything is wrong. Yet you draw a blank when you try to figure out what the next step should be. Nothing motivates you or appeals to you. You can't get anything accomplished and you may tell people that you're just "spinning your wheels." Actually, you are spinning on your Wheel of Fear.

Shame You feel guilty about anything and everything. When somebody casually mentions there was a slip-up at the office, you immediately wonder if it was your fault. Your five-year-old is diagnosed with dyslexia and you assume you did something to damage him during your pregnancy. You come down with the flu and you find a way to blame yourself.

Defeated You sent out a batch of résumés and didn't get one response. You went to a singles event and no one approached you. You went shopping and came home empty handed after suffering from three-way-mirror trauma. Whatever the situation, you have magnified one small setback into a great big suspicion that you just can't win no matter what.

Out of control Maybe you're spending the afternoon at the office jumping from Web site to Web site, none of which have anything to do with what you're supposed to be working on. Or you're standing up in the kitchen at two in the morning, polishing off the cold pork chops and downing a quart of ice cream. Or you're on a shopping spree, buying the latest gadgets that you don't need and can't afford. Whatever you're doing, you can't stop yourself. You don't feel in charge.

Confused Life isn't turning out the way you thought it would, but you're at a loss to say exactly why. You feel scattered and spent. You're going nowhere fast. You can't make up your mind about anything. Should you look for a new job? You don't really know. Would things be better if you moved? You have no idea. Is your current relationship as good as it gets? You have no reference point. You don't have clear criteria for making decisions, so you don't make any. You just keep muddling through, constantly bewildered while you are buffeted by life's inevitable challenges. The best you can do is to keep up the status quo.

Overwhelmed You are about to begin a huge and exciting new undertaking. Yet whether you're on the verge of planning your wedding or buying your first home or launching a Web site for your business, the project suddenly seems like more than you can handle. The enormity of what you've set out to do hits you, killing all the joy you felt when you decided to go for it. You feel incapable of taking even one small step toward your goal. Days go by while you're frozen with fear. The deadline looms and that makes the situation even worse. What were you thinking when you agreed to this? You marvel at other people who have pulled off something similar. What do they know that you don't? Why can't you deal with this?

Victimized You've sacrificed some of your own dreams in order to give your kids every advantage and every opportunity, but all you get from them is attitude. Your boss is trying to please *her* boss, and you end up with the piles of paperwork that will make her look good. Your wife keeps nagging you to make as much money as your brother does. You feel like the helpless victim of some grand scheme to keep you from living your life the way you were meant to live it. You're not helpless. You're just scared. Scared of believing in yourself. Scared of alienating people. Scared of being you.

❋ FEARBUSTER EXERCISE ❋

- Define the words you chose for your trigger thought and your core feeling.

    Since they are yours and yours alone, you will define them in your own way. The more thorough you are at defining your words, the better you will be able to recognize when you are in your Wheel of Fear. No dictionaries, please. There is no wrong way to define your words. List anything that will help you identify them. This is for your eyes only. However, to get you started, I'll share with you my definition of "loser": "They are all laughing at me. So-and-so was right. I don't deserve success. I'll never win. Who am I kidding?" My definition of "worthless" is: "What's the point? I want to hide or die. No one cares."

- Keep track of the symptoms you experience on a daily basis. The sooner you can identify the symptoms, the sooner you can get off the Wheel of Fear. However, when you first become aware of the symptoms you may feel worse than you ever did. This will pass. The symptoms were there all along, you just didn't know it. They were draining your energy and taking up your time. Only, now that you recognize them for what they are, you'll be able to get past them. This will take practice. Be patient and kind to yourself. Hold firm to the belief that you must know your symptoms before you can change them.

- Write down the title "My Wheel of Fear" and write your own version as you did on page 50. Put the slip of paper someplace where you can see it every day. This will help remind you that when your fear comes up, it is something you can change rather than something that is wrong with you. Remember, you are not your Wheel of Fear.

- Pay attention to how and when you find yourself spinning on the Wheel of Fear.

- Fill in the blanks:
    If I mastered my Wheel of Fear, the following would be possible for me regarding:

    my career

    my intimate relationships

my finances

my health and well-being

social life and friendships

my family

my spirituality

my intellect and knowledge

my emotional development

my home/living space

my creativity

Nobody can make you an emotional victim without your permission. The good news—and it is very good news indeed—is that now that you have identified your Wheel of Fear, you can begin to move beyond your fear. When you move from fear to freedom, you are altering your filtering system by shifting your focus and thereby your choices. You are going from fear-based thoughts to freedom-based qualities that will access your essential nature. In the same way that little things have triggered your Wheel of Fear for so long, little things will begin to show you that you don't have to be afraid. Each small act of courage will go a long way toward giving you the confidence to handle the big events. Every time you call a friend to ask for help . . . every time you call a friend to *offer* help . . . every time you find a gentle way to get your mother off the phone when you're trying to meet a deadline . . . every time you listen to someone's angry words without shouting back . . . every time you have a good cry . . . every time you let someone know you need a little time to yourself . . . every time you laugh out loud when you see the absurdity of your fears . . . every time you do things such as those, you are leaving your Wheel of Fear behind. Every day of your life, you are creating an environment of fear or fearlessness with each choice you make.

Fear Is an Affirmation of Growth

I am going to tell you the secret that became the foundation of Fearless Living: Fear is just an affirmation of your growth. It's just a way of letting you know you are alive and walking out into the unknown. The Wheel of Fear may be triggered during the big risks in your life but it will no longer be a daily occurrence. And when your Wheel of Fear does start spinning, you'll know that is a sign for you to be sure that you have prepared, that you have done the best you can, that everything is in order. After a moment, a day, or a week, your Wheel of Fear subsides because what you're doing is no longer a new experience for you. Think about this: Who would be afraid to take a chance if fear were a positive force, not a negative one?

All along, fear has not been the enemy. It has been your friend, letting you know that this is unfamiliar territory as well as giving you a heads-up when it is time to acknowledge yourself. Whenever the fear of being a loser or the feeling of worthlessness comes up for me, I acknowledge myself for taking a risk. I acknowledge myself for being true to myself. I acknowledge myself for being alive.

As we live with the intention to move through our fear, not only do we learn to feel without attaching ourselves to the feeling but we also learn how to move through the fear with ease, grace, and love. In that process, we discover who we are. There springs up from within us a life force that I call the Wheel of Freedom. And we come to see that in embracing our humanity, the things that we saw as weaknesses or character defects are but the path back to ourselves. Not something to deny, but something to welcome and celebrate.

Turn the page, and continue the process of learning how to choose fearlessness. . . .

The Wheel of Freedom

The Wheel of Freedom is not the opposite of the Wheel of Fear. However, virtually all of the people I've worked with have assumed at first that the Wheel of Freedom is simply a positive version of the Wheel of Fear. Remember Connie, the harried working mother who was afraid of being thought of as incompetent and who ended up feeling unlovable? Since she was afraid of being thought of as incompetent, she believed she would be free of fear if she managed to prove she was competent, and that she would feel lovable as a result. Before I developed my program, I was laboring under that same misconception. I didn't want to be perceived as a loser, so I reasoned that the solution was to act like a winner, and that I would therefore feel worthwhile instead of worthless.

Unfortunately, as we have seen, that kind of thinking is exactly what brings about the behavior that keeps the Wheel of Fear revolving on the downward spiral that makes you more afraid and more disgusted with yourself than ever. So if the Wheel of Freedom is not the opposite of the Wheel of Fear, what is it? Listen to Connie as she talks about the day during the second week of her in-laws' visit when she experienced the life-affirming upward spiral of the Wheel of Freedom for the first time:

"Bobby had fallen asleep in my arms. Dawn was breaking and he looked so beautiful in the half-light. We were breathing in exactly the same rhythm. I made a move to get up and go put him in his crib so I could start breakfast. But Bobby let out a shivery sigh the way babies do, and I was afraid I'd wake him up. Suddenly, looking at his sweet face, I was so filled with love for him that tears ran down my cheeks. In a very real way, I had waited all my life for him. My little miracle!

"At that moment, in spite of the work and worry of the week I'd just gotten though with my in-laws, I felt exhilarated. A surge of energy shot through me. The craziness about washing the venetian blinds and making gourmet meals and beating myself up for missing that typo in a client's press release seemed plain silly. What did any of that have to do with the love I felt for Bobby? Or for that matter, the love I felt for my husband, my parents, and even my in-laws? Or for how much I love my work? I remembered what Rhonda had said about trying to live up to unrealistic expectations and I realized that all of my behaviors had been caused by my Wheel of Fear. They weren't making me a good wife and mother, or a good daughter, or a good daughter-in-law, or a good businesswoman. The only thing they were doing was making me feel incompetent and unlovable. And they certainly weren't letting anybody know that the real Connie is all about being compassionate to myself and everybody else—not about trying to earn the Good Housekeeping seal of approval for everything from polishing the silver to catching typos, and then freaking out on myself if I blow it."

Inspired by that insight, Connie decided to give herself a break. Instead of pushing past her exhaustion and going to the kitchen to start breakfast, she took Bobby into bed with her and curled up under the covers next to the man she loved. With her precious baby cradled in her arms, she fell into a deep and peaceful sleep. When she woke up, refreshed and relaxed, it was . almost noon. Bobby was still asleep. Six hours was a record for him! Connie tucked him in his crib. Looking at him, she was reminded once more that compassion was her real state of being. Going back to sleep had been a conscious, positive action that came out of being true to herself. She was ready to do even more. Connie pulled on her robe and slippers and padded into the living room where her mother-in-law was happily absorbed in "her" soap opera.

"Hi, dear," Connie's mother-in-law said, glancing away from the screen as a commercial came on. "The men have gone to play tennis. I hope you don't mind that I made breakfast. We just couldn't wait any longer."

That comment brought up Connie's fear of being incompetent. She was on the verge of getting defensive when she recalled how that behavior was just a response to her fear. She made a conscious choice not to say something she might regret. Instead, she said, "That's great. Thanks so much. I guess I really needed some sleep."

"Well, my goodness, yes!" her mother-in-law said. "You look like a new woman. I remember what it was like after Bob was born. I've never been so worn out in my life. You have to take care of yourself."

Connie nodded, feeling not only lovable but loved. She sat down next to her mother-in-law on the couch. The soap opera was almost over when Bobby started to cry. Connie turned to her mother-in-law and decided to take a risk. "Would you mind giving Bobby his bottle? I would love to catch up on some work at my desk."

At first Connie's mother-in-law seemed startled and Connie was sure she had overstepped her bounds. Connie was just about to apologize when her mother-in-law broke into a grin.

"Mind? I can't wait! You know, dear, it's okay to ask for help. Let me go get him right now." And with that, she stood up, headed toward the nursery with a spring in her step, and sang out, "Grandma's coming, Bobby. Grandma's coming."

Connie practically fell over. She had been a very attentive hostess, not wanting to put anyone else out, yet she had just learned that her mother-in-law had felt as though she didn't have permission to do anything. Connie never would have guessed, and if she hadn't taken a risk, she would never have known.

By the time Bob and his father got back from the tennis court, Connie and her mother-in-law had spent a delightful afternoon chatting, playing cards, and enjoying Bobby. Connie had decided to forgo her daily ritual of laundering the towels, and she didn't protest when her mother-in-law ran the vacuum. But watching her mother-in-law vacuum did bring up all of Connie's insecurities. The Wheel of Fear, disguised as concern, whispered in Connie's ear, "I guess you didn't clean your house very well, since your mother-in-law feels compelled to vacuum." Connie quickly identified her Wheel of Fear's new attempt to trick her into feeling ashamed. Not this time. When her mother-in-law finished vacuuming, Connie asked her to watch the baby while she freshened up. She took a bath, did her makeup, and slipped into a fresh dress—guilt free.

"Hey, gorgeous!" Bob said when he came in the door behind his father, who headed for the living room to turn on the TV. Alone in the foyer, Connie instinctively reached out to Bob and gave him a hug. He seemed surprised at first, since she had been cool to him after his outburst in the kitchen the night before. But then he relaxed and hugged her back. Connie experienced peace of mind and with it the sense of being whole. He pulled her even closer and gave her a sweet, urgent kiss. She didn't resist. "Maybe tonight?" he whispered in her ear. "If you're not too tired."

"Mmmmm," she said. "Not too tired at all."

"Have I told you lately that I love you?" he said.

"I love you too," she said.

Just then, Connie's father-in-law appeared with Bobby in his arms.

"The little fella was fussing and I could tell nobody else heard him, so I went and got him," he said. "Hope that's okay."

"Oh, thanks!" Connie said as her father-in-law swooped the baby into the air, eliciting coos and giggles.

"Do I smell dinner cooking?" Bob asked.

"Yes," his mother said, emerging all smiles from the kitchen and wiping her hands on her apron. "My pot roast. Connie had some business calls to make, so she asked me to be the chef tonight. Wash up. The roast is almost ready."

Connie stood for a moment, taking in everything around her—the people she loved and who loved her, the air redolent with spices, the sound of the baby's laughter, the taste of her husband's kiss. She was in the present, and glad to be alive.

Connie had deliberately put herself on the Wheel of Freedom. She knew that in order to get off her Wheel of Fear, she had to decide how to behave instead of simply reacting. In the instance of the visiting in-laws, Connie had realized she was on the Wheel of Fear because of certain symptoms she was experiencing—feeling overwhelmed, exhausted, and defeated. She also noticed how she was reacting—cleaning, cooking gourmet meals, answering her business line after hours—all in a frantic attempt to avoid being thought of as incompetent. Her attempt only resulted in the feeling that she was unlovable and pushed her to crave a cigarette.

Based on our coaching sessions, she understood the process of consciously moving onto the Wheel of Freedom. After building her awareness and consistent practice, she was able to do just that. With time and patience, you can do it as well. Here's how it's done:

- First, you identify your *essential nature,* the state of being that fuels your passion and gives you an abiding sense of purpose. This is your true self, although it is most often masked by fear. This is who you really are, who you were born to be, the pure self that existed before environmental influences began to shape you, making you afraid that this self is not good enough.

- Second, you consciously engage in *proactive behavior* by doing things that allow you to get in touch with your essential nature.

- Third, as you take the actions that help you get in touch with your essential nature, you dispel your fear of not being good enough and experience a sense of *wholeness*. This is your essential nature brought to its highest and most expansive level. Think of your essential nature as your unblemished, newborn self. Then think of your wholeness as that evolving self brought to maturity in a positive and fearless way. Your wholeness gives you a sense of fullness and power. Life for you is now full of limitless possibilities and you are eager to embrace them. Taking risks ignites you instead of frightening you.

- Fourth, your sense of wholeness frees you from the fear of not being good enough and you instinctively engage in *self-*

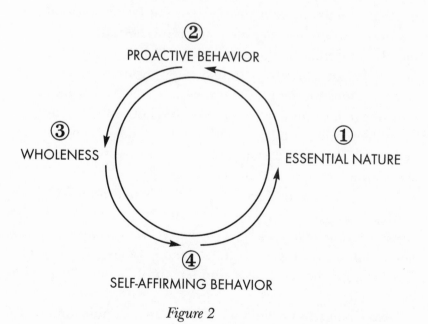

Figure 2

affirming behavior. You are able to make a contribution to yourself and to the world without judging yourself or fearing the judgment of others. In so doing, you go back to the beginning of the cycle where your essential nature inspires a new round of proactive behavior. As a result you feel even more true to yourself, and more fearless than ever about making your contribution.

In Connie's case, her essential nature was to be compassionate to herself and others. She realized that she certainly wasn't being compassionate while she was furiously scrubbing and baking and typing in an attempt to ward off her fear of being incompetent. When Connie had that awareness, she knew that the next step was to do something proactive. Her first choice was to get some much-needed sleep. After that she asked for help at the risk of being judged by her mother-in-law, and in so doing gained compassion for her mother-in-law's disappointment at not having been allowed to help with the chores and the baby. Connie went a step farther and asked her mother-in-law to cook dinner so Connie could finish her office work. Connie also took the time to soothe herself with a bath and make herself feel attractive by putting on a pretty dress.

As a result, she sent a silent message to her husband. When they hugged, Connie moved to new level of wholeness and she was able to initiate intimacy with her husband—a self-affirming behavior. His positive response gave her precisely the feeling she yearned for. She felt loved.

On her Wheel of Freedom, Connie's definition of "good enough" changed from "someone who keeps a spotless house, cooks from scratch, has a perfect baby who never cries, and never makes a typing error" to "someone who is good to herself and to those she loves, and who lets those people be good to her as well."

That change was profound. It meant that Connie didn't have to live up to unrealistic expectations in order to prove she wasn't incompetent. In fact, her fear of being seen as incompetent was transformed into a conviction that she was uniquely capable of loving her family and of receiving their love, and her confidence in her ability to make a success of her business soared. She no longer felt unlovable or incompetent. She felt necessary, both in her relationships and in her work. That gave her joy. Her senses were heightened, and she appreciated the people and situations around her. She was able to make a contribution far greater than a pile of clean laundry or a flawless press release or a key lime pie. She became a person who acted out of compassion, not fear. And everyone—from the baby to Connie's husband to Connie's in-laws to Connie's clients to Connie herself—was richer because of that. Within a year, Connie had not only established firm bonds with her family, but her income had doubled and she was so swamped with clients that she had hired an assistant.

My own Wheel of Freedom is another good example. My essential nature is authenticity. My definition of that word—and this is mine alone, but it works for me—is to be true to myself. When I am not being who I truly am, I react to my limited perception of myself from the paradigm of fear that brings up frustration and victimization. Not attractive. Yet, when any of those thoughts or feelings occur, I immediately know the Wheel of Fear is deciding my fate, and it is never for my highest good. I choose new actions. That might mean no longer monitoring myself to see whether I'm fulfilling other people's expectations, not saying yes when I mean no, not taking on too much work just to prove how capable I am, not rushing to meet self-imposed deadlines and ending up missing the simple pleasures in every moment of every day. The sum of those actions always leads me to self-acceptance. That gives me my sense of wholeness. From there, I naturally engage in self-affirming behaviors—thanking people for compliments, giving compliments freely, smiling at a stranger, admitting what I don't know, asking for help, giving help. I am free to contribute to the world.

Self-acceptance keeps me on track, on purpose, and in my passion. When I accept myself fully, I am filled with an inner joy and contentment and I become more productive as a result. That moves me back to my original state of being, which is authenticity, and an even stronger intent to live fearlessly.

Get on the Wheel of Freedom

Just as we discovered your personal Wheel of Fear, we're going to discover your Wheel of Freedom.

First make a "hero list" by answering the following question:

Who are the five people—dead or alive, real or fictional—whom you most admire, respect, or secretly envy?

1)_____

2)_____

3)_____

4)_____

5)_____

Now, put your hero list aside. We'll refer back to the hero list after you complete the next step.

Essential Nature

Study the following list:

1) authentic
2) creative
3) compassionate
4) accountable
5) loving
6) beautiful
7) courageous

8) focused
9) generous
10) trusting

You know the drill by now: Narrow the list down to five, then down to three, and finally pick the one that is your essential nature. Now fill in the following:

My essential nature is that I am _____.

Meredith, just as she did with fear triggers, insisted she couldn't choose. In this case she felt that everything on the list was part of her. She was absolutely correct. But claiming one quality as your own automatically frees you to claim the others as well. The access point is your essential nature. Remember that Connie claimed being compassionate and her nature radiated out into being more courageous (risking her mother-in-law's judgment; hugging her husband first), more trusting (letting her mother-in-law take care of the baby), and all the rest.

In any case, Meredith finally picked "generous." That's when I asked her to get out her hero list and choose one essential nature for each hero, using the same list we used to pick her own essential nature. I want you to do the same:

1) Hero_____ Essential Nature_____
2) Hero_____ Essential Nature_____
3) Hero_____ Essential Nature_____
4) Hero_____ Essential Nature_____
5) Hero_____ Essential Nature_____

Meredith had listed her grandma Rose, her best friend Sue, Joan of Arc, Martin Luther King, Jr., and Elizabeth Dole. She stared at her list for a long time. Finally she assigned "courageous" to all of them except Sue, for whom she wrote "creative."

"My grandmother was the most courageous woman I've ever

known," Meredith said. "She was a first-generation immigrant who came to this country alone with her two young sons—my dad and my uncle—after she was widowed when my grandfather died in a mining accident. She started her own millinery business on the Lower East Side of Manhattan and she was a huge success. Nobody walked all over her, for sure.

"And Joan of Arc, well, that's obvious. As for Martin Luther King, Jr., he stood for his beliefs even though they weren't popular at the time. That took guts. Elizabeth Dole, well, being the first woman to announce a candidacy for the presidency was certainly a courageous act. I really admire all of those people. And my friend Sue, the creative one, writes and illustrates children's books. I'm in awe of her, and I'll admit that I envy her too."

When Meredith had finished her explanations, I asked her to think about the essential nature she had picked to describe herself: "generous."

"Is that really who you are, Meredith?" I asked.

"Of course," she said. "We've already established that what triggers my Wheel of Fear is the idea of being thought of as selfish. So I'm generous instead."

"The Wheel of Freedom is not the opposite of the Wheel of Fear," I gently reminded her. "The Wheel of Freedom is who you are. And you, Meredith, have just shown me that you are courageous."

"Me?" Meredith said, absolutely taken aback. "Oh, no. I'm not courageous. Sure, maybe I want to be courageous. But I've never done anything courageous in my life."

"I bet you have, but you may not have identified it as such or given yourself credit. Besides, there's no time like the present to start claiming it as true for you," I said. "Because being courageous is who you really are. Being generous is just who you think you ought to be. And the beauty of claiming your essential nature is that in so doing you will be freed to claim a genuine generosity that springs from truth, not from fear."

Her eyes welled up. Then I asked her to claim her essential

nature by writing it down and then saying it out loud. After she wrote, she cleared her throat and waited until she had composed herself. Then she said in a barely audible whisper, "I am courageous." Finally she said it again, in a clear and committed voice. "I am courageous!"

Think about what you originally picked as your essential nature. Is it the same as the essential nature of at least three out of five of your heroes? If so, you identified your essential nature correctly. If not, then your Wheel of Fear tricked you into picking the essential nature you thought you should pick. The essential nature of the majority of your heroes is your true essential nature. We can only see in others what lies within ourselves. Fill in the following blank:

My TRUE essential nature that has just been revealed is that I am _____.

Wholeness

Now, study the following list:

1) integrity
2) personal power
3) self-acceptance
4) peace of mind
5) passion
6) intimacy
7) inspiration
8) confidence
9) inner joy
10) faith

If you could give one gift to the world as your contribution, which quality of wholeness would you choose? _____

In other words, if you claim your essential nature by taking actions that are consistent with it, which of the expressions of wholeness on this list will you feel? Or you can think of it this way: If you have children, what one quality would you like to pass on to them as their parent? What about your spouse or best friend? The quality you yearn to give to others is inherent within you and indeed is your gift to yourself and the world. As always, narrow the list down to five, then three, then one. Here again, the miracle is that when you feel the one that is most central for you, the others will follow. Now fill in the blanks:

When I claim (your essential nature goes here)_____,
I will feel (your wholeness goes here) _____.

Meredith, whose essential nature turned out to be "courageous," picked "personal power." And indeed, she went on to have the courage to invest most of her nest egg in her antique store and gain an immensely gratifying sense of personal power that led to all the other feelings as well, including "creative" (inspiring her to take those painting classes after all) and "intimacy" (allowing her to attract a man who loves and respects her for her essential nature).

My essential nature is "authentic" and if I consistently take actions that are true to that nature, I attain my wholeness, which is "self-acceptance." From there, I have all the rest, including "passion" and "inspiration." Consequently, I can make a contribution working with my clients and through my speaking engagements as well as teaching seminars and writing books. When I own my wholeness, I am free of my fear of being a loser, and instead have "personal power" and "faith" propelling me forward. I am free to live fearlessly. Because of that, my contribution goes beyond measurable accomplishments. Yours will too. It will include the joy you bring to others when you smile, the comfort you give when you are a good listener unencumbered by your own fears, the release of tension you inspire in everyone around you, the spirit of cooperation you promote in a place where competitiveness had prevailed, the infectious enthusiasm you exude. When you are on your Wheel of Freedom, you're not trying to prove anything, not trying to hide, not trying to save face, not trying to put up a facade, not trying not to get caught, not trying to cover up. You are simply being you. When you are on your Wheel of Freedom, the whole world is better for it.

One Hundred Proactive and Self-Affirming Behaviors

To get on your Wheel of Freedom, particularly if something threatens to trigger your Wheel of Fear, you need to take conscious actions that work for you. In fact, to help myself fend off fear in any given situation, I have written down a list of actions that I know from experience are effective. When I am in a crowd, I draw deep breaths or take a mental vacation to an open space such as a deserted beach or a grassy field. When I am alone, I cry or do jumping jacks or clean out the cupboards or file papers. When I am in an intimate gathering, I focus on someone I love and let my love show or I turn a negative remark around with a positive comment. The reason I have my lists at the ready is that thinking up the actions while threatened by the Wheel of Fear is extremely difficult. I recommend that you, too, find the actions that will move you toward your Wheel of Freedom, then write them down on a wallet-size card, laminate it, and carry it with you.

To get you started on your list of actions, I have given you one hundred possibilities. Put a check mark (✔) next to all the ones that instinctively appeal to you—the ones you would really do and that you feel would work:

Say, "I don't know," when you don't

Give a compliment

Ask for help

Take a cooking class
Learn a new sport
Be honest
Stand out in a crowd
Confess your blunders
    to a friend
Say no when you mean no
Accept a compliment
Take a break
Give a gift for no
    reason at all
Stargaze
Smile at a stranger
Cultivate good friends
Make a daily checklist
Keep a journal
Ask for something
    you want
Share your interests
    with others
Risk embarrassment
Hire a coach
Attend a craft fair
Be considerate in traffic
Forgive yourself
    (or another)
Speak the truth
Brainstorm
Listen
Initiate a conversation
Complete the task in
    front of you
Let someone else go first
Paint a wall
Wear something daring
Pamper yourself

Meditate
Put emotional boundaries
    in place
Create something
Take the class you have
    been putting off
Breathe
Eat right
Get enough sleep
Speak so others can hear you
Call someone who loves you
Pet the cat
Give yourself a
    positive treat
Do something kind for
    someone else
Appreciate the weather,
    rain or shine
Listen to music
Take a mental vacation
Clean the bathroom
Go to the grocery store
    with a list
Watch a comedy
Throw a dinner party
Say you're sorry
Stand for your convictions
Exercise
Get professional help
Plant some flowers
Sing out loud
Dance
Design a new business card
Walk the dog
Cry
Listen to the birds

Send a love note
Hug—a lot!
Take a nature walk
Hit a pillow
Spend time alone
Ask questions
Lie on the grass
Focus on a hobby
Knit
Do research on the Web
Join a dating service
Express gratitude daily
Adjust your standards
Renegotiate your
  agreements
Visit a museum
Practice the art
  of conversation
Read a book
Be interested

Smell a flower
Pray
Flirt
Attend a recital
Write five affirmations
Change your mind
Be willing to be wrong
Get (or give) a massage
Eliminate silent contracts
Take a bath
Obtain knowledge
Run through the sprinklers
Focus on one thing at a time
See another's point of view
Check in with a friend
Get out of your own way
Break your own rules
Say hello to everyone you
  encounter
Follow your intuition

Next, go back over the list and put an X beside the ones that you realize would begin to come naturally if you attained your wholeness. Meredith, for example, checked such items as "Eliminate silent contracts" and "Obtain knowledge" for her list of proactive behaviors in order to claim her essential nature of being courageous. Then she put an X next to such items as "Smile at a stranger" and "Share your interests with others" for her list of life-affirming behaviors that would evolve as she attained her wholeness of personal power. I checked "Ask for help," "Speak the truth," "Dance," and "Paint a wall." I put an X next to "Put emotional boundaries in place," "Take a nature walk," and "Create something."

Your Wheel of Freedom

Now you're ready to create your personal Wheel of Freedom. Fill in the following blanks:

In order to claim my essential nature, _____,
I engage in the following proactive behaviors: (items with check marks ✔)

_____

_____

_____

_____

_____

When I claim my essential nature, I feel my wholeness, _____. This allows me to engage in the following life-affirming behaviors: (items marked with an X)

_____

_____

_____

_____

_____

Congratulations! You now have the power to free yourself from the Wheel of Fear. Remember, it doesn't matter where on the Wheel of Fear you realize that you are spinning. Like many people, you may recognize your fear when the core feeling you so desperately are trying to hide from surfaces. Or perhaps you may recognize your fear when you are already engaging in self-destructive behavior. That's fine. Remind yourself of your essential nature by saying it out loud if the situation allows, or at least thinking it. Then sneak a look at your laminated wallet card of behaviors and start doing something immediately to transform fear into freedom.

When you get better at recognizing your fear, you'll be able to identify the thought that is your trigger that starts the Wheel of Fear spinning. This takes practice. Our thoughts go through our minds so fast that many times they are almost impossible to catch. Yet as you gain awareness, you will be able to release fear at every juncture and get right on your Wheel of Freedom.

Signs That You are on the Wheel of Freedom

You'll know you're there when you experience one or more of the following states of mind. They will become more intense and last longer as you become more and more adept at getting on your Wheel of Freedom with every choice you make. At first you may experience these states of mind only briefly. You may even feel uncomfortable and attempt to push them away. That's normal. This is unfamiliar territory. The thing to remember is that you have made a great beginning. Keep going until you begin to trust the process. This is not about perfection and not about having freedom all the time, but rather about noticing when you do have the signs of freedom and giving yourself credit for your expansion.

Being present You start thinking about the problem you have to deal with at work tomorrow when you're in the middle of a pleasant dinner with your wife. You stop yourself. You look into her eyes and share the love you feel for her. Or maybe you are about to call all of your friends to get the gossip about your blind date for this weekend. Instead, you decide to go on the date without getting anyone else's opinion. You give yourself and your date an opportunity to discover each other without outside influence. Or you are walking down the street and see an estranged friend. Instead of spending five minutes debating

whether to say hello, you say hello immediately. All life is decided in the moment. No other place are choices made. The
more you are able to be present to your negative thoughts, feelings, and behaviors, the more you will be able to override them
the moment they occur. Investing in the moment-by-moment
process of living gives you the awareness to bypass your conditioned responses to life. Focus on what is happening right in
front of you as well as what is transpiring within you. When living in the present becomes instinctive, life will be richer.

Acceptance You want to go to the latest romantic comedy
but your husband wants to see an action movie. You flip a coin.
Action it is. You make a conscious choice not to complain about
the result and instead find ways to enjoy your time with your
husband. Rather than spend all of your time frustrated and
whining, you accept the situation as is, becoming open and
flexible to any new opportunity that comes your way. I am
not talking about putting up with the status quo or settling. I
am talking about distinguishing between your reactions based
in fear and your conscious decisions based in freedom. When
we go with the flow rather than fighting upstream, acceptance is
an effortless outcome and finding the goodness inside each new
opportunity is an adventure.

Inner strength Your friend Sally said something cruel to you.
Instead of brushing it off one more time, you speak up. The inner strength you are accumulating will propel you to speak and
act according to what is true for you. Standing for yourself will
no longer be a dream but a reality. You are cultivating the inner
strength through your commitment to your Wheel of Freedom.

Centered As you live more and more in your true nature,
you will be more centered in yourself. No more looking outside
of yourself for the answers. You begin to experience the truth
that you have all the answers within you. All you have to do is

keep eliminating your conditioned responses by following the path to freedom and claiming your essential nature and your wholeness. Clarity is no longer elusive. Calm is available no matter how chaotic the situation may appear. There is deep sense that all is well.

Empowered The conversation turns negative. You turn it around. Work isn't going well. You write positive affirmations to help focus you back on your Wheel of Freedom. You are capable, strong, and know your boundaries. When you feel empowered, you have internal permission to do what must be done in order to live by your essential nature. You are internally focused and experience a surge of personal power. You begin to trust the process and, more important, to trust yourself.

Detached You asked for a raise. Rather than judge how well you did by whether you get the raise or not, you know it is in the asking that character is built and freedom is released to work miracles in your life. Of course, you prepared and acted as if you would receive the raise, yet your day wasn't destroyed if you were turned down. This became another opportunity to learn more about the process of being you. When you are able to be objective with no attachment to what is right and what is wrong, there is space for life to work itself out for your benefit. No stress, strain, or pressure. Being detached from your feeling of not being good enough will put you on the Wheel of Freedom faster than you can say, "Yes to you!" Not taking things personally frees you up from blame, shame, and guilt. Remember, other people's fears have nothing to do with you. Expecting a certain outcome is a thing of the past when you know that life is anything but static.

Abundance Rather than grabbing all you can out of fear that there won't be any left, you affirm that there is enough to go around. Your heart has expanded and generosity of spirit is your calling card. You give compliments freely, share your ideas and resources with others, and believe that there is plenty of love and support in the world. When abundance is your state of mind, your conversations and actions reflect that and you attract as well as give more love, knowing that it is a boundless resource.

Energized Each day is an opportunity to be yourself. Energy moves through you, so you can complete your daily tasks. Excitement pulsates all around you and others gravitate toward your enthusiastic view of life. No more feeling tired and run-down. Instead, you feel relaxed and ready to rest after a job well done.

Satisfaction A strong sense of accomplishment is pervasive. Feeling satisfied that you can indeed do the task in front of you gives you the courage to take the next step, and the next, and the next. Satisfaction builds your self-confidence so you can do more and be more, all aligned with your passion and purpose.

Synchronicity This is the place where you accomplish what's before you without stress, strain, or sacrifice. Opportunity and timing converge. Life is sweet. As you begin to spend more and more time on your Wheel of Freedom, those instances will increase. And they show up in big ways as well as small. Let me share something that happened to me recently to illustrate the power of daily synchronicity.

I was flying from Los Angeles to a speaking engagement in the Midwest. During a layover, my head began to pound, and my eyes blurred. I knew this was the beginning stage of a migraine and I had a two-hour flight ahead of me.

Pre–Fearless Living days, I would have "toughened up" and suffered in silence in my attempt to hide my pain from the people around me for fear of being thought of as weak or vulnerable. But now, on my Wheel of Freedom, authenticity is my state of being, and to help me achieve that state, my actions must be authentic. In this case, that meant asking for help and not denying my health challenge. Risking rejection, I went up to the flight attendant in charge of boarding and explained my situation, asking to preboard. Whew! I was sweating. What if she looked at me and scoffed? Or said, "Sorry, against company policy." Or worse, thought I was lying. That notion almost stopped me, but I reminded myself that was only fear talking. During those few minutes, fear told me I was acting like a baby, when in truth, I was taking care of myself. Speaking up was a risk for the old, fear-filled Rhonda. But the flight attendant smiled and said, "No problem. I get migraines myself. I know what you're going through."

As the plane was about to board, the flight attendant graciously ushered me down the walkway. Again, my fear of being seen as dramatic and selfish surfaced. I persevered and kept walking. As I was just about to get on the plane, a man came up from behind me and asked, "Are you feeling ill?"

Now, in my fear-filled days I, superwoman Rhonda, would have turned to him and said, "No, I am fine," and made my grandmother proud. Back then, I was so afraid of being viewed as worthless that there was no way I would ever need anyone. No way, not me. I couldn't risk having them reject me or think of me as a loser and, ultimately, not worth their time. Keep it to myself, I would think. This time, though, authenticity won out. I was willing to be vulnerable. I cautiously admitted, "Yes. I am not feeling very well."

The next words out of the other passenger's mouth bowled me over. "Please take my seat."

"Excuse me?" I exclaimed.

"Please take my seat," he repeated. "You'll be more comfortable." And with that William Belgard handed me his seat assignment marked 2D, first class.

I was flabbergasted. First class? I couldn't, I thought to myself. That would surely be selfish. That just wouldn't be fair, I reasoned, I'm not that sick. Yet anyone who gets migraines knows I was indeed that sick. My denying how sick I felt stemmed from my fear of feeling less than worthy.

Again, Mr. Belgard repeated his simple phrase: "Please take my seat." And he went on to say this was his way of helping. With that honest admission of concern, my Wheel of Freedom was set in motion and I accepted his seat with gratitude. A few minutes later, I was sound asleep in a leather recliner in first class.

Why did he give me his ticket? Yes, to be helpful. Yes, because he was kind. But he never would have had the opportunity to share his generous spirit and I never would have received such kindness, if I hadn't been willing to be authentic. First, I had to be willing to be rejected by asking for help from the flight attendant. Next, I had to admit I wasn't feeling well, which to my Wheel of Fear is a sure sign of weakness. Finally, I had to say yes to the kindness of a stranger. My Wheel of Fear tried to trip me up at each juncture, yet I stayed focused on my true state of being, authenticity. This experience was synchronicity on the Wheel of Freedom.

Everyone you meet is helping you either on or off your Wheel of Fear. William Belgard was helping me off of mine by giving me an opportunity to embrace more of my authentic nature. I was sick. I needed help, and his offer was a gift from a stranger. It's up to us to pay attention and be alert to the many magical moments that cross our paths. Remember, we are responsible for our state of being, what actions we take, and how we contribute to ourselves and to those around us.

Those are just a few of the sensations you will experience as you begin to release fear from your life by embracing the attributes of freedom. This isn't about comparing one day to the next. Rather, it is about sustaining the process. Always, it is about doing the best you can and knowing that's good enough. No one is perfect all the time, no matter how tough that is for us to admit. When you accept that this is a process, results are more aligned with your truth and happen effortlessly. Remember, each time you let go of your fears by taking actions consistent with your essential nature, the power of fear is diminished.

You may be stronger in one area of your life than another. That is normal. You could be living on your Wheel of Freedom seventy-five percent of the time when you are at work and plummet to twenty percent when you are with your significant other. Everyone will have one or more areas that are fairly easy to master and others that are more of a challenge. But the challenging ones will eventually get easier as you work the program. I have seen countless people go from living a very frustrating existence to owning their power and loving their lives. And it didn't take long. But what it did take was a commitment to their Wheels of Freedom over all other commitments they had ever made to themselves.

FEARBUSTER EXERCISE ✹

- Define the words you choose for "essential nature" and "wholeness." As I said about the Wheel of Fear, this is yours and yours alone, so no two people will define the words in exactly the same way. The more thoroughly you define your words, the more quickly you will recognize your Wheel of Freedom. Again, no dictionaries, please. This is for your eyes only if you so choose. Remember, my definition of my essential nature, "authenticity," is "true to myself." My definition of my wholeness, "self-acceptance," is "I like myself. I enjoy my own company. I see my beauty. I don't compare myself to others but see the value of my uniqueness. I don't expect others to understand me all the time. I am fully responsible for myself and my behavior."

- Keep track of the signs of freedom you experience on a daily basis. The sooner you can identify the signs, the sooner the Wheel of Freedom will be a constant.

- Write down the words "I am my Wheel of Freedom." Then write your essential nature and your wholeness just as you did on page 78. Put the slip of paper with your "Wheel of Fear"—perhaps both as a sign over your desk and as a laminated wallet card. Remind yourself daily that you are either on the Wheel of Fear or the Wheel of Freedom based on each decision you make.

- Pay attention to when you find yourself on your Wheel of Freedom.

- Fill in the blanks:

If I carry my laminated list of proactive behaviors with me, I will feel _____.

If I don't carry the list of behaviors with me, I will feel

_____.

If I claimed my essential nature, I could

_____.

If I claimed my wholeness, I could _____.

If I were on my Wheel of Freedom, I could

_____.

By now you have learned what fear is and you have identified your Wheels of Fear and Freedom. As we go on, you will learn concrete aspects of the Fearless Living program that will make your Wheel of Freedom ever more present and powerful for you and allow you to consciously move beyond your Wheel of Fear.

I hope you have heeded my advice about keeping this work to yourself during the initial stages. Now here's some very good news: The time has come to reach out for the comfort, companionship, and counsel of friends and family members whom you can count on to support you as you continue to learn to move off your Wheel of Fear and onto your Wheel of Freedom.

But be careful! You need to tune out the advice of anyone—well meaning or not and related or not—who is likely to keep you down or nudge you onto your Wheel of Fear. Read on to find out who those people are. . . .

Fear Junkies

Olivia wanted to quit her high-powered job as an advertising-agency executive and turn her backyard greenhouse into a business. She was making great money at the agency and had a corner office with a window, but she didn't enjoy her work. Not a day went by that she didn't think about how much fun it would be to do what she really loved. Everybody raved about her plants, especially her orchids. She knew she had the proverbial green thumb and she felt frustrated that her greenhouse was nothing but a hobby.

The trouble was that at fifty-two, Olivia was worried not only about giving up her salary but also about losing her benefits package. She'd have to roll over her 401(k) and get individual health insurance. Besides, she was concerned about whether she had enough of a financial cushion to float her if the business went under. Still, she didn't want to end up seventy years old, looking back and regretting not having gone for it. So Olivia had the courage to make a decision to resign. The night before she was planning to let the boss know she'd be leaving, she happened to run into her neighbor, Larry, in the produce aisle at the supermarket.

"It's a good thing the store is open twenty-four hours," Larry said. "I would never get my shopping done otherwise. Man, I'm beat. I was at the office until seven P.M. You, too, I'll bet. It's tough."

"Well, yes," Olivia said. "I was at my desk pretty late as usual. But that's about to change. Tomorrow I'm going to give my notice. I'm quitting. You're looking at the future owner of Olivia's Orchids. Good-bye day job, hello the real me!"

"Whoa!" Larry said. "Are you for real? Don't you know that most new businesses fail within two years? Anyway, if it's shorter hours you're after, forget that. You'll work harder for yourself than you would for anybody else. Look, just about everybody has dreamt of being an entrepreneur. I know I have. Jennie and I have always talked about opening a bed-and-breakfast. But unless you've got a trust fund, you're making a huge gamble starting your own business. Are you sure you're doing the right thing?"

Olivia winced. Larry had just brought up every argument against opening Olivia's Orchids that she had thought about herself before she came to her decision. Hearing him voice the risk factors she had already dismissed made her doubt herself. The sense of exhilaration she had felt moments earlier gave way to a surge of fear.

Larry was what I call a Fear Junkie. Like the Wheel of Fear itself, Larry wanted Olivia to choose safety over risk to prevent a variety of unfavorable outcomes such as getting taken, being disappointed, losing money. Of course Larry did not mean to hurt Olivia's chance for a life she loved by squelching her dream. In fact, like almost all Fear Junkies, he believed he was doing Olivia a favor. And, of course, in some ways he was. His cautionary tales were all true. But because Larry lived on his own Wheel of Fear, terrified of taking a chance on opening that bed-and-breakfast, he was unable to move from caution to precaution. Fearless Living isn't reckless living, after all. Olivia had in fact done the arithmetic that assured her that quitting her job was not going to spell immediate financial disaster. She had prepared for her fearless move. Yet Larry's recital of the risks put her back on her own Wheel of Fear.

The denouement of this story, fortunately, is a fearless one for both Olivia and Larry. She came to me for coaching. Along with teaching her the principles of Fearless Living, I sent her to the Small Business Administration. After a couple of meetings, the fact that Olivia was ready to make her venture a reality became clear to her again.

Three years later, Olivia's Orchids is a huge success. And inspired by Olivia's triumph, Larry and Jennie have opened Stop Inn, a B & B with a decidedly contemporary decor and cuisine that has attracted a younger and more affluent clientele than had frequented the area's more traditional Victorian-style establishments. Olivia, Larry, and Jennie are all making a good deal more money than they had before beginning to live fearlessly. That, to my delight, is a very common occurrence.

As Larry demonstrated during his supermarket encounter with Olivia, everyone has a Wheel of Fear. Think of the people you love. No matter how together they seem, they, too, have fears. And they, like Larry, may project those fears onto you. Most of them don't mean to. They just can't help it. They are unaware of how their own fears are coloring their conversations with you. They don't know that their hesitations or doubts or worries are their own fears projected onto your latest project or new love. Your job is to become vigilant about what you share and with whom. This is not about withholding your love. It is about understanding the fact that just because you love certain people and they love you as well does not automatically guarantee they will be supportive of you.

However, you may need to leave certain people behind by severing a toxic friendship or even ending a destructive marriage. Some people in your life may be suffering from debilitating or dangerous emotional disorders or addictions. If so, guiding them toward professional help or twelve-step programs is ideal. Saving those people is not your job. If they resist help, get yourself safely away from them. This is one instance in which fear is making you aware of a genuine threat to your well-being. There truly is a reason to be alarmed and to beat a retreat.

Most of the time, though, you can maintain cordial and even loving relationships with key people in your life who turn out to be Fear Junkies, unwitting or not. You can learn, for example, not to take your mother-in-law's dire warnings about life personally and simply maintain polite interaction with her at family functions. Similarly, you may be annoyed with a friend because she is always complaining about how she feels stuck at her current job, yet never gets up the nerve to do anything about the situation. Yet you might welcome her guidance when it comes to child rearing, since you admire the job she is doing with her own kids. The trick is to figure out what you value in any given relationship and learn how to focus on the positive aspects. If you want to stay connected, then soak up whatever advice and affirmation you can, and remind yourself that the things that bother you have nothing to do with you. Your friend gripes about her job because she is on her Wheel of Fear. When you understand that, you are able to relish what you love about her and filter out the rest. In other words, the next time she starts in about her dead-end job and won't let you get a fearless word in edgewise, realize that she may be one of those people who doesn't want to change. Take care of yourself by tactfully changing the subject to child rearing, the topic that is not derived from fear.

The friend in that hypothetical example shows that people who are basically dear to you may temporarily prove to be Fear Junkies in certain areas. Also, some people may temporarily act as Fear Junkies when specific situations present themselves. I'm thinking about the period when I was the culprit in a situation involving my best friend, Marta. Most of the time, we are completely supportive of each other. But when it came to the question of whether her teenage son should have a job, we were at loggerheads. Alder had turned sixteen, and I believed he should get a job. After all, I had worked from the age of fourteen. Well, Alder didn't get a job. I was beside myself. But in

Marta's opinion, school was top priority and if Alder didn't work, she understood. I was furious. "What do you mean it's okay?" I'd say. How is he supposed to become responsible and develop a good work ethic (like me)? How is he going to learn the value of a dollar (like me)? How is he going to prepare for a life of sacrifice (like me) if he doesn't work and pay for his own way (like me)? Each argument I had—and of course I just knew I was right—would end up in our disagreeing on the basic idea of working during high school. I thought it was a must and she saw it as an option. From the time Alder hit sixteen until he was nineteen, I couldn't talk to Marta about her son. Each time she brought his name up, I would start giving "the speech."

Of course my Wheel of Fear fueled all of the anger. I was jealous that Alder didn't have to work during high school, while I did. I was angry he was allowed to be a kid when I hadn't been. I was beside myself because I couldn't get Marta to understand the "right" thing to do—the "Rhonda Truth."

I now realize that each family needs to look at the issue of working during high school in the context of each child's needs and abilities, and then decide accordingly. But during that time, there was no talking to me. I unconsciously wanted to make sure my unfortunate adolescence was vindicated. During the stretch when Marta and I didn't agree about Alder and work, we continued to empower one another in other areas. If you expect your best friend or your spouse to be able to talk about anything and, more important, to be everything and support everything, you are setting yourself up to be disappointed. The key people in your life do not have to agree with every decision you make in order to have an ongoing supportive relationship.

However, certain people are more likely than others to hold you back rather than cheer you on. Let's look at profiles of the five most common types of Fear Junkies. As we move through the following list, be sure to jot down the people in your life who fit into each category. Some may belong in more than one category, depending on the circumstances, and some may be negative influences in some areas and positive influences in others. The idea is to clarify in your mind whether there are people in your life who are hindering your pursuit of Fearless Living. Like Larry, Olivia's neighbor, they may eventually be inspired by your example and stop living in fear themselves. But whether they do that or not, don't let them keep *you* from finding freedom.

Dream Drainers

The members of this group are the most dangerous of all because they mirror your Wheel of Fear. That is, they believe that you need to be protected from the possible results of risk taking such as rejection, disappointment, and the feeling of incompetence or worthlessness. As a result, they mimic and reinforce your own inner voice of fear.

Dream Drainers say such things as:

- Are you sure you want to try it?

- What makes you think you're capable of accomplishing that?

- What if you make a fool of yourself?

- What if you lose your shirt?

- Why rock the boat?

The Dream Drainers don't want you to get hurt, so they do everything they can to make you see how impossible your dreams are. They love you and they think they know you better than you know yourself. Usually they're trying to keep you in your rut because they are comfortable in theirs. If you listen to the Dream Drainers, your essential nature will be suffocated even more quickly than if you had only been listening to your own voice of fear reiterating the reasons why what you want to do won't work. Their hesitations become your hesitations. They can't distinguish your dreams from their fears.

Of course, the Dream Drainers honestly feel they have your best interests at heart and they are absolutely correct that if you try to achieve your dreams, you might fail and get hurt. So if you do go for your dream in spite of the Dream Drainers and don't succeed immediately, the Dream Drainers in your life will be right there to tell you, "See, I told you so." But if you don't try, you will never know what you are capable of. You may not accomplish all you set out to on the first attempt, yet you may on the second or the fifth. And you will never know if you don't go for it. Each precious moment of your life in which you are frozen with fear is a moment when you are not being all you can be. In the end, that hurts more than anything. Succeeding or failing does not determine if we are surviving or living. Rather it is in our ability to reach beyond our present self-imposed definition of who we are, and to risk becoming more, that we are able to feel fully alive.

Example of a Dream Drainer in Action: Valerie's Mother

On hearing that her daughter planned to move to New York to pursue a modeling career, Valerie's mother said: "You want to be a model? Get the stars out of your eyes. You'll probably end up thirty-five years old and still waitressing at Denny's, for Pete's sake. What you need to do is go to college and get a teaching certificate. That way you could land a job anywhere. Plus you'd get health insurance and a pension. Also, the hours are perfect for when you have kids. Trust me! I know about dreams that lead nowhere. Anyway, those show people are always getting into trouble. I'm afraid that even if you did get your career going, you would end up miserable. I love you too much to wish that on you."

She's afraid. Dream Drainers are always afraid for you. But you've got plenty of fear of your own to master. You don't need any more than you already have. Like Valerie you may not want to resist or hurt your Dream Drainer. Valerie's fear made her think that her mother might be right, but her intuition kept telling her to go ahead with following her dream. Valerie worked with me on how to step back from the situation to be sure she was on her Wheel of Freedom and then consciously decide whether modeling was for her. When she did, she was able to see the situation for what it was: her mother's fear of failure projected on Valerie. She decided that she was not going to accept her mother's fear as her own. To get herself centered, Valerie picked an action from her list of proactive behaviors. She took some deep breaths and took the action. Afterward, she was able to thank her mother for sharing her concerns as well as how grateful she was that she loved her enough to care. Then she courageously told her mother that she was going to go ahead with her plan anyway. She asked her mother to support her in spite of her reservations.

Valerie's mother wasn't used to having Valerie stand up for herself. She took a minute or two to digest this new behavior. This frequently happens when anyone starts facing up to the people who drag them down. Valerie braced herself for another speech. But her mother finally said, "I understand. Okay. I am still scared for you. But I will try to be supportive."

The changes that happen in the dynamics of your relationships when you begin to stand for your dreams are amazing. Instead of letting the Dream Drainers take control, you take control. Not accepting their fear as your own frees you and also gives them a chance to see things differently. Remember, Dream Drainers are just scared. If you quit buying into their fears, they have a better chance of finding freedom themselves.

Who are the people in your life who put doubt in your mind, use love as their excuse to take your dreams away, or, even worse, give you the feeling that it is not okay to be you? List the individuals whom you thought of as Dream Drainers. Separate the people you must associate with due to work or family relationships from the ones who are optional. Pick one individual who isn't obligatory and think about how you interact with that person. Do you feed their worries? Do you talk about your problems without actively discussing solutions? Are your doubts the only thing you share? If so, you may be contributing to the Dream Drainer's fears. Perhaps instead you could choose to share only powerful positive aspects of any event. Silence is also very powerful when you don't know what else to do. Practice with someone who is not a "must" in your life and then move on from there.

Complaining Buddies

These are the guys who confirm your worst fears about life being hard, tough, or a dead end. When you're on the verge of turning around and looking for a way out of the maze, they remind you that you're wasting your time. Relationships with Complaining Buddies are definitely not good for you. But they feel good in a perverse sort of way. As the old saying goes, misery loves company. The trouble is that Complaining Buddies are the friendliest and easiest of fear-based relationships to maintain because they appear to be harmless.

The sob stories of the Complaining Buddies can be very seductive as well. Like all fear-inspired behavior, their tales of woe do a convincing imitation of the truth. You can easily get sucked into believing them. Hearing that other people are dealing with pretty much the same seemingly hopeless struggles that you are facing gives you the perfect excuse to decide there are no solutions. Sometimes your Complaining Buddies may attempt to help you solve a problem, but in the end their advice always turns into some version of "You can't," "You shouldn't," or "What makes you so special that you think you can change things around here?" The result is that you're feeding on each other's fears and perpetuating the myth that you're powerless to change the status quo.

Complaining Buddies say things such as:

- The rich get richer, but guys like us don't stand a chance. I guess if we were meant to be rich, we would have been born that way.

- He dumped you? Men are all alike. Why bother?

- Some people have all the luck. Too bad we're not some people!

- You can't save any money? Me neither. It's the tax bite. The more you make, the more they take.

- I told you so. You just can't win around here.

Example of a Complaining Buddy in Action: Craig, a Coworker of Steve's

Steve worked in an advertising agency. Craig was the guy in the next cubicle. When Steve brought up the idea of asking for a promotion, Craig went into his litany of complaints.

"Man, there is absolutely no chance for advancement in this place," Craig said. "You and I deserved to get promotions and raises after we busted our butts bringing in that new account last month. But let's face it. The boss didn't even say thank-you. And here we are, still pushing papers and barely making ends meet. You know what I mean? It's not fair! Sure, we could try to get new jobs, but if we moved to another company we would probably have to start at the bottom. I've worked too hard to start over. At least I have my three weeks of vacation, and my profit sharing kicks in next month. I have too much to lose if I leave. Well, gotta get back to the grind. I guess that's life. Listen, it's been great talking to somebody who understands what it's like around here."

No, it hasn't been great—not for Steve and not for Craig. All that has happened is Craig's attempt to convince Steve that there's no way off the Wheel of Fear.

Who are your Complaining Buddies? Be honest with yourself. Admitting that your best friend could be the very one keeping you down in certain areas of your life isn't easy. Yet this often happens when you are growing at a faster rate than the other person is. And your Complaining Buddies probably don't even know they are squelching you. The ideal, of course, would be for them to learn eventually from your fearless example. In the meantime, stay friends but consciously filter out the complaining.

Be aware of whether you are the one initiating the complaining behavior. We all like to feel connected, and lamenting about life's injustices can become a habitual way of feeling part of the pack. Listen to yourself for a day or two, and if you find that you always start a conversation with a gripe, even one couched in humor, begin to make a conscious effort to reframe your remarks in the positive or to look for something to celebrate, however small.

Puppeteers

These are the people who want to manipulate you—all for your own good, of course. And in truth, most of them do think they're doing the right thing by "guiding" you. Stage mothers are a classic example and so are Little League dads. As noted psychiatrist Carl Jung explained, "Nothing has a stronger influence psychologically on their environment and especially on their children than the unlived life of the parent." Parents (or grandparents or favorite aunts and uncles) who need to live vicariously through the children in order to fulfill failed dreams of their own share a powerful fear that the younger generation will lose out just as they did. Teachers and coaches can be Puppeteers as well. What all Puppeteers have in common is that they make you afraid that the life path being foisted on you is the only one that could satisfy you. And if you don't live their dream, you will surely live to regret it and be labeled a loser for the rest of your life. The Puppeteers have spent a lifetime building evidence to prove their position and they are convinced what they are suggesting is the only way. But whether or not you have the talent, the smarts, or the looks to go through the motions while they pull the strings, everyone concerned will be disappointed and miserable if you don't also have the desire. And you must be successful or their efforts will be in vain. If not, blame and shame are sure to follow.

Puppeteers say things such as:

- When I was your age, I would have killed for a chance like this.

- I know you'll do me proud.

- We're all counting on you. Do this for the family.

- You're too young to know what you want. You'll be sorry later if you don't listen to me now.

Example of a Puppeteer in Action: Tyler's Grandfather

Tyler had been accepted to Harvard Law School. Very impressive indeed. But after working through the Fearless Living program, Tyler suspected that fear, not desire, was what had made him apply in the first place. He told me about something his grandfather had said: "When I was your age, I would have given anything to go to law school. We lived in a tenement on the Lower East Side of Manhattan. My dad did odd jobs and my mother took in laundry. There were six of us kids, so there was no way I was going to Harvard, which is what I always dreamt of doing. So now, my boy, it's your turn. I've made good money running the deli all these years. I can afford to give you the opportunity I never had. We'll finally have a Harvard lawyer in the family!"

The trouble is, Grandpa never stopped to ask whether Tyler had even the slightest interest in passing the bar, let alone litigating for a living. And until he identified his Wheel of Fear, Tyler had no idea he was basing his entire future on a reactive response to fear. What sounded like the chance of a lifetime for Tyler was nothing but a guarantee that he would be controlled by a fear of not measuring up to his grandfather's expectations. Tyler would end up being afraid to be true to his essential nature.

What did Tyler do? He began preparing his family by dropping hints here and there. Many people do drop hints but stop there. However, dropping hints is just the preparation stage for the honest dialogue that must eventually occur between the people involved. After hearing a few well-placed hints, the Puppeteers are better prepared emotionally to handle the conversation.

Tyler and I rehearsed before the big showdown. In reality, it wasn't that at all, but that is what it felt like to Tyler. His fear of being an outcast and rejected by his family was foremost in his mind.

In the end, he did very well. Instead of talking about how he didn't want to go to law school, Tyler began the conversation with the concept of loving your work, being happy, and living with purpose. He and his grandfather had a great discussion, and then Tyler told him what he intended to do: write poetry and make a reasonable living as a college professor. His grandfather balked. But then he saw the determination in the set of Tyler's jaw. "Tell me more about this dream of yours," Grandpa finally said.

Tyler experienced immense relief that the conversation did not become the huge confrontation he had imagined. He was ecstatic. Grandpa had ended up not only understanding, but agreeing to put the money that he had earmarked for law school toward Tyler's Ph.D.

Who are the Puppeteers attempting to control your life? Ask yourself whether their dreams for you are the same as your own. If not, I challenge you to stand for your own dreams and desires by putting healthy emotional boundaries in place with the Puppeteers in your life.

Rivals in Disguise

These people aren't easy to recognize because they often seem so genuinely helpful. They'll tell you how to handle a job, what to wear, who to butter up, where to be seen, what to say, and offer plenty of other hints that sound as though they are meant to help you get ahead. The trouble is that the advice is deliberately misleading. Rivals in Disguise, in fact, are the only people on this list who are tripping you up on purpose. Everybody else we've been discussing means well but gives you a bum steer because each person's Wheel of Fear is in control. Rivals in Disguise are also coming at you from their Wheel of Fear—fear of failure or of not being good enough or of being worthless—but they are aware that they are hoping to bring you down.

They are usually highly competent or talented, but they feel threatened by your competence and talent anyway. They have a need to get you out of the way in order to make progress of their own, as though life were a race with only one possible winner. They are so trapped in their own Wheels of Fear that they are stunted morally and emotionally, and they believe there is not enough to go around. Scarcity, lack, and limitation are concepts that keep their Wheel of Fear spinning. They don't understand that we can all be winners in our own way. After all, life is not about win, place, and show. It's about personal best—and the peaceful acceptance that our personal best is continually expanding and refining as we change and grow.

How can you tell a Rival in Disguise from a genuine mentor? When you make a specific request for information or advice, they brush you aside, change the subject—or worse yet, give you a misleading answer. Intuitively, you know you shouldn't trust them. And you're right. They are smiling while they plan your demise. They want to know everything about what you are doing yet share none of their plans. Also, the green-eyed competitors can't resist slipping in a catty remark or a put-down when they make "helpful" remarks.

Rivals in Disguise say things such as:

- I'm glad you let me have a look at the notes for your presentation. You can use all the help you can get. Anyway, I see that you've hit on a lot of the points the boss always goes for. But you're better off surprising him with a couple of ideas that are really off the wall. I'd totally rework this if I were you. Trust me.

- Let me tell you something, just as a friend. That dress isn't you. Certain people can pull off a look that's really dramatic, but your style should be a lot more low key. Why draw attention to yourself?

- Come on, one more drink won't hurt. The night is young! You'll be more relaxed for that interview in the morning if you chill out now. I'll bet you were a nerd in high school. Ha ha! Like, you actually "just said no" and you never stayed out past your curfew, right? Loosen up, man!

- It doesn't matter how I got my last promotion, what matters is helping you move up and out. So quit asking questions about me, what have you been doing lately?

Example of a Rival in Disguise at Work: Georgia's Writing Teacher for Her Adult Education Course

The teacher called Georgia up to her desk after class one evening and said, "I'm glad you told me that you got a letter published in the newspaper. But please don't take that as a sign that you could become a professional writer. Your work is nice, but this is a tough business. I ought to know. I've had my share of rejections like everybody else. Take it from me. There's no sense getting your hopes up. I mean, *this could be a nice hobby for you, but don't quit your day job.*"

Georgia was crushed and she let her teacher's remarks hold her back for a while. Then she enrolled in one of my seminars and began facing her fear. She realized that whenever she wanted to submit something in order to try to begin a professional writing career, she literally saw her teacher's face and heard his words. Because he was more experienced and a teacher, Georgia thought he knew best. But the instructor was just downright jealous of Georgia's talent. And that jealousy was twisted into a piece of advice that was not helpful at all but harmful.

Rivals in Disguise are masters at dispensing that kind of advice. And if you confront them in any way, perhaps asking them for more information or questioning how they formed their opinion, Rivals will brush you aside or question why you don't trust them, implying that you must be insecure.

The best way to deal with the Rivals in Disguise in your life is to avoid them. If you can't do that, then just don't listen to them. These sinister people are not worth having in your life. They will change only if they finally wake up one day and wonder why they don't have any true friends. You can't force them to change. They have to do it on their own.

Who are your Rivals? They are threatened by you. Get out of their way because if you don't, they will attempt to mow you down.

Rearview Mirrors

These are the people who bring up a subject when you are past it, supposedly to show how far you've come. The last thing you need is a reminder of the Wheel of Fear's self-destructive behaviors you've worked so hard to transform. Yet when you have a Rearview Mirror in your life, the incidents you've processed, released, and moved beyond will be brought up again and again.

I am not talking about you and your best friend or therapist processing the past or using it to congratulate yourself for all the changes you have made. Many times we must look back in order to acknowledge how far we have come. But Rearview

Mirrors, in contrast, are sabotaging your growth by not letting you forget any of your blunders. Instead, they keep building evidence that your worst fear about yourself is true by constantly bringing the past into the present. Rearview Mirrors evoke memories that leave you disempowered, making you wonder if you can hold on to your transformation. What makes them do this? They sense that you are evolving emotionally and they are afraid—often rightly so—of being left behind. If possible, help them to move forward with you. But whatever you do, don't let them pull you back.

Rearview Mirrors say things such as:

- Do you ever hear from John? How long has it been since you broke up? I still can't believe you were involved with somebody like that!

- I'll never forget the day you didn't make the cheerleading squad and I did. You were this little geek with the pointy glasses and you couldn't do a split to save your life. Of course you were on the debate team and I wasn't. But the jocks don't exactly go out of their way to hit on geeks. High school sucks, right?

- Remember your college nickname? Shorty! I think you're the first guy under six feet who ever got into Sigma Chi.

- Congratulations on making partner! Wow, if they ever knew you failed the bar three times, they'd probably revoke your license to practice law! Ha!

- Are you going to Julie's Labor Day barbecue this year? Remember how drunk you got last year? Didn't you throw up in her geraniums? Julie sure can throw a party.

Example of a Rearview Mirror in Action: My Friend Ken
After I had begun working earnestly on my personal development, I faced the fact that I had relied on alcohol to get me through much of my pain. It was time to let it go. This was a dif-

ficult period for me, particularly when I began to remember the embarrassing situations I had gotten myself into. After I quit, looking at myself in the mirror some mornings and dealing with my remorse was hard enough, but my friend Ken made things even worse. He would repeatedly bring up—in front of other people—stories about my past that I wasn't too proud of. He wouldn't put those memories to rest. I know that for him the stories were entertaining, yet I was trying to change, and being reminded of those episodes made me feel as though he didn't approve of the new me. They also kept bringing up feelings of shame about how I used to be, which made me doubt my ability to succeed in maintaining my sobriety and my new way of thinking. I'm sure Ken, by sharing the intimate details only good friends would know, was trying to prove how important he was in my life—not realizing that the very thing that he was doing to stay close was actually pushing me away. His constant references to the past brought up my Wheel of Fear, causing me to relive events that made me feel worthless just when I was in the process of learning how to master my fear and accept myself.

Eventually, I realized this and I quit hanging out with Ken. That was hard. He had been one of my best friends, yet he was no longer behaving like a friend. He was pulling me back into the past. I see now that he was doing it in an attempt to keep me in his life because he was afraid I was drifting away as I changed. But at the time, neither he nor I had the skills to discuss what was going on. We just avoided the subject and eventually quit talking to each other. I'm sure he thought I was ungrateful and stuck up. At the same time, I thought he was immature and thoughtless. Neither was correct. Ken's fear of losing me was dictating his behavior, and that brought up my fear of being a loser. Fear had won again, ending our friendship.

Do you have anyone in your life who is having a hard time accepting and supporting your essential nature? Someone who keeps repeating stories of the past that you would like to put behind you? Name the people who keep talking to you as if you were the same person you were five, ten, twenty years ago—or maybe just a year ago.

You do not have to have the same outcome I had with Ken. Maybe your Rearview Mirror is someone you would like to keep around. If so, the next time this person tells a story about your past, politely say, "Gosh, that was forever ago. Let me tell you something that happened to me just yesterday." And then take charge of the conversation.

✳ FEARBUSTER EXERCISE ✳

- List the people you know who belong in each of the following categories: Dream Drainers; Complaining Buddies; Puppeteers; Rivals in Disguise; Rearview Mirrors.

- Do you have to be in a relationship with any of these people due to work or family? If you do, use the techniques in this chapter to deal with them. If not, ask yourself if you are willing to let the present state of the relationship go. This doesn't mean confronting or giving an explanation, it simply means no longer participating with them. If you want to keep your relationship going, name one way you can handle the next encounter with them differently. (A good place to look is your Wheel of Freedom proactive list). Remember, don't spend your time trying to change their behavior. That would be frustrating and ultimately fruitless. You can only change your response to their behavior with any certainty.

- Pick one proactive behavior that you can rely on whenever you encounter someone who belongs to one of those groups. It might be walking away or smiling or saying, "That's interesting," and then changing the subject or breathing through the conversation while silently reminding yourself that they do not support you.

- How and with whom do you exhibit the qualities of a Fear Junkie?

- Choose one relationship you would like to alter and pay attention to your behavior each time you encounter that person. Consciously choose to take actions consistent with your Wheel of Freedom.

Now you know who your Fear Junkies are. Let's move on to the people you cherish, the beloved and loving ones who help you even as you help them in the lifelong challenge of outsmarting fear and living free.

5

Your Fearbuster Team

A
sking for support from the right people at the right time helps you summon the courage to show more of who you are to the world. Yet when most of us attempt to connect with people—both those who are already important to us and those we're hoping to get to know—we avoid truly revealing ourselves. Of course, hesitating to trust is not always bad, as we have just shown in Chapter 4 when we listed the Fear Junkies who unwittingly or purposely thwart your essential nature persuading you to be afraid to follow your passion. But as the poet Maya Angelou said, "Nobody, but nobody, can make it out here alone."

She is absolutely correct. Central to Fearless Living is identifying the people in your life who not only have your best interests at heart but also have the generosity of spirit and the compassion to give you unqualified love and support. Of course, that works both ways. Never forget that relationships are two-way streets. The beauty of Fearless Living is that as you master your own fear, you'll be in a better position to look after the people you care about when they're the ones who need help.

And you won't lose your own sense of self as you reach out to them.

I'm going to refer to all of the key people in your life as friends, although some may be related to you by blood or marriage. In other words, certain family members are friends and others are not. Remember the Puppeteer parents we met in Chapter 4? That's a perfect example of relatives who aren't behaving as friends. Similarly, you might have one brother who is a friend and one who is not. On the other hand, you might have a friend who is dearer to you than any family member.

All of the people you identify as friends are vital members of what I call your Fearbuster Team. Unlike the Fear Junkies we talked about in Chapter 4, the members of your Fearbuster Team don't fall into neat categories. They play different roles for you at different times. Yet what they share is enthusiasm for who you are and who you are becoming, along with an abiding delight in your emotional prosperity. And you, of course, reciprocate their enthusiasm and delight.

Identifying at least three and preferably five to seven people who are members of your Fearbuster Team is valuable. They don't need to know one another. The point is that they all qualify because they are eager and able to support you in various ways, and vice versa. That is extremely important because as Meredith found out on the night when Phil walked out on her, being dependent on one relationship only is not healthy. No one can fill all your needs all the time—not even a spouse who actually is a genuine lifetime soul mate. For example, there will surely be certain challenges and changes in your life that call for input from someone who has the wisdom of experience in that area. Your mother, if you have a good rapport with her, can be in a better position to help you through the physical effects of your first pregnancy than your husband is. Your sister the CEO may be in a better position to help you gain business acumen than your brother who is fresh out of college. All of this perhaps appears to go without saying, but I have seen far too many clients who have either relied on one other person for support in all areas or who have solicited counsel and solace from the wrong people given the situation at hand.

That's why you need a Fearbuster Team, not just one significant other. The team is essential to your growth and success. Incidentally, if you are already successful in the sense that you are prominent or even famous, you need to reach out for Fearbuster Team members just as much as everyone else. It truly can be lonely at the top. People can see you as a kind of icon, not as a human being with frailties and needs. They can't believe—indeed, don't want to believe—that you have fear just like everybody else. You might have lots of groupies, but nobody you can really turn to. They all want you to be the strong one. They are afraid to see your vulnerability. Don't let that happen to you. Find people who know that in spite of your accomplishments and status, you have a Wheel of Fear just like everybody else.

FEARBUSTER EXERCISE

To help you begin to identify the members of your Fearbuster Team, do the following exercises:

- List your friends and immediate family members.

- What is your present relationship to them? Are you estranged? Close? Is yours an I-have-to-see-them obligatory relationship?

- In which area of life are they supportive? Career? Relationships? Leisure? Child rearing? Write the area next to their name. Some people may be supportive in all areas, but that's not often the case. Most will support you in one or two areas. Your best friend, or even your spouse, is not in charge of guessing everything you need.

- Define friendship. What does it mean to you?

- What qualities of friendship do your family members and friends embody? Are they loving? Compassionate? Jokesters? Nonjudgmental?

- Do you embody those same qualities?

- What kind of friend are you? What qualities of friendship do you embody?

- How do you contribute to the people you call friends?

- In what areas of life can you be counted on for support?

- What are the challenging areas of friendship for you?

- What would you like to change about your relationships?

Fearbuster Teams in Action

As we begin to identify our Fearbuster Team members it is crucial to remember that there will be central members who are the core of the group while other members come and go depending on what is happening in your life. I have nine people I count on regularly to help me break through my fear, yet I have numerous other people whom I go to for specific situations. For instance, my writers' support group consists of Carol, Chellie, Linda, and Victoria. They are there for me twice a month, yet Victoria is on my team above and beyond the writing group.

Here are the members of my main team:

1) Marta, my best friend
2) Cindy, my older sister
3) Linda, my younger sister
4) Greg, a friend and colleague
5) Kimberly, a friend
6) Victoria, a friend and member of my writing support group
7) David, a friend and colleague

8) Bonnie, a friend and colleague
9) Ras, a friend

Meredith, the onetime husband pleaser we met in Chapter 1, now lists:

1) Lucy, her teenage daughter
2) Nigel, her new beau
3) Barbara, a friend
4) Judy, a friend and fellow antique lover
5) Ralph, her brother
6) Cathy, her ex-husband's sister
7) Tracy, a friend

Nigel, Judy, and Tracy are friends Meredith acquired after she began the process of living fearlessly. She met Nigel at a neighborhood garage sale, where she spotted him fingering a vase that she suspected was worth far less than the price tag. With her newfound courageous essential nature, she approached him and offered her expert opinion. He was charmed by her forthrightness and her obvious passion for her work as an antique dealer. The rest is history. As for Judy, she is a valued customer at Meredith's store who has become a dear friend. And Tracy is a member of an online support group for suddenly single women that Meredith joined. Tracy and Meredith e-mail one another regularly and have made plans to meet in person when Meredith is in Tracy's area antique hunting.

Lucy, Ralph, Cathy, and Barbara had all been a part of Meredith's life when she was still stuck on her Wheel of Fear, but she had never effectively included them in her decision-making or her dreams. Before her divorce, when Meredith wasn't clinging to Phil, the only people whom she frequently connected with were her Complaining Buddies. All they did, of course, was reinforce her fear. Barbara, a dental hygienist at the office where Meredith had worked part time as a receptionist, was one of them in those days. Over lunch at a diner near the office, the two women used to whine endlessly about how the dentist they worked for was a tyrant and how the patients were all difficult. Barbara and Meredith also loved to moan about how their husbands and children took them for granted. Barbara, a natural comedian, made Meredith laugh in a bitter sort of way with her tales of being the classic doormat. Needless to say, neither Barbara nor Meredith felt better after their exchanges. Then, after Meredith quit her job and opened her antique store, she kept Barbara in her life by meeting her for lunch occasionally. But she stopped being a good audience for Barbara's "stories of the day." Every time Barbara complained, Meredith shifted the subject to something positive—either a genuine compliment for Barbara ("Your hair looks great. Where'd you get it done?") or an acknowledgment of herself ("I contacted a couple of Web designers today to get quotes on what it would cost for me to launch a site for my store"). Meredith tried the same tactic with all of her Complaining Buddies, but only Barbara responded positively. I reminded Meredith that changing other people is not possible because they will only change if they want to, not because we push them. And in reality, the only one we can truly change is ourself. As we become more aligned with the proactive and self-affirming behaviors on our Wheel of Freedom, the people around us will respond either positively or negatively to our transformation. We cannot choose their response or force it. And those who respond negatively consistently will usually no longer be interested in being our friend. In their eyes we will have changed, and more than likely not for the better. As we grow, we must be willing to allow the friendships that need to move on to do just that and accept new ones in our life. I acknowledged Meredith for being open to Barbara, and advised her to focus on enjoying their revitalized relationship. Barbara had begun making fearless changes in her own life, including looking for a job with a more reasonable boss.

Lucy, Ralph, and Cathy had not been Meredith's Complaining Buddies. They had simply been on the emotional fringe of Meredith's life. After she began living fearlessly, she became much closer to all of them as she allowed them to cheer her on. This often happens. Be open to inviting people into your process. You'll probably be surprised at how pleased many of them are to share your fearless journey.

To help you assemble your group of supporters, let's have a look at the roles the members of your Fearbuster Team can play. Of course, if your members are familiar with the tenets of Fearless Living, so much the better. You'll be able to communicate more efficiently and profoundly when you're all speaking the same language. And don't be discouraged if you find yourself with fewer than three individuals on your present team. Building a powerful Fearbuster Team takes a willingness to identify what you need as well as an open mind to include people you have never thought of in this capacity. I challenge you to embrace any opportunity to connect with a potential Fearbuster Team member.

Support Buddies

There are times in your life when you need cheerleaders. You need unconditional love and support. You need to hear people who know you and care about you say, "You can meet this challenge because you're you. Give it everything you've got. And remember that I'll always love you no matter what." In other words, like devoted sports fans, Support Buddies will root for you because they believe in you, but they won't give up on you if you suffer a setback. They are not fickle. Whether you win or lose, they're your biggest boosters. They're always ready to encourage you to keep going. And when you do have a championship season, they go wild.

Remember that your parents may or may not be good at serving this function. The notion that parents (or grandparents, for that matter) are automatically capable of offering love to their children with no strings attached is a fallacy. This does not mean that your parents or grandparents can't be members of your Fearbuster Team. They may be superb sources of some of the other forms of help that we'll be exploring in this chapter. Just don't make the mistake of calling on them when you need Support Buddies if that's not their strength. In fact, this principle holds true for all of your team members. Recognize the ways they help you master your fear and don't expect them to do more than they can.

The people who are good at being your Support Buddies provide a safe environment for you to explore being you. They praise you to the skies when you need it most, but they never give you false encouragement. That's why you trust them when they tell you what your strengths are. They empower you, remind you of your gifts, give you the space to change and grow, and aren't upset when the cycle of friendship means that there are times when you are either less in need of support than you once were, or less available, or both. They may have seen you at your worst, and they love you anyway. They have also seen you at your best and they help you celebrate that without your having to fear being thought of as egotistical.

My sister Cindy saw me at my worst. We had every reason to despise each other after my parents died. She tried to take over as Mom but no one could take Mom's place. I resented Cindy's attempts to help me. Yet Cindy was always right there for me no matter what. Each time I sabotaged myself, she would buy me a book or send a card or call to see what she could do. With her consistent support, I was finally able to realize that she did believe in me, so in turn I began to think maybe I could do the same. Your Support Buddies believe in you when you don't believe in yourself. That is the greatest gift of all.

You can also vent to your Support Buddies about a genuine roadblock in your life and they'll help you remember that you're ready, willing, and eminently able to overcome the situation and be true to yourself. When they listen, you have time to process the fears that have been holding you back. And they will give you the feedback you need to help you gain clarity regarding any situation in your life.

Your Support Buddies will be proud of you with each baby step you take and help you up when you fall. And don't forget that you usually need to ask for their help. They're not psychic. If I ever feel myself slipping back onto my Wheel of Fear—that is, doubting my worthiness—I call on Marta, one of my most trusted Support Buddies, and ask if she has time to refresh my memory about the truth of who I am. If she does have time, I tell her what I am experiencing and then tell her what type of support I need. We have trained each other to ask what type of support is needed instead of assuming the other one knows. When feelings of worthlessness come up, that usually means I am forgetting that what I do has value and a purpose. In those moments, I ask her simply to remind me that I'm good at what I do. She will then ask me to choose one of the many letters of thanks I have received—I save them all—and read it out loud to her. Or she'll remind me of a time during one of my workshops when someone stood up and publicly thanked Fearless Living for changing his or her life for the better. Or she'll replay a speech I gave that woke the audience up to their fears and showed them a way out. Marta will go on and on until I tell her I feel better—until I am back on my Wheel of Freedom.

In the end, Marta usually has me laughing. After I talk with her, I am renewed and can face my day knowing that my doubt is not the truth of who I am. And in the process, she has helped me build new evidence to prove that, which is the main reason support is important. Support gives us the courage to have confidence in who we are faster than if we relied only on ourselves. When we are in our Wheels of Fear, it is difficult to remember for ourselves what our commitments are. Others will remember for us. They are our link back to ourselves. True, reaching out takes a willingness to be vulnerable, yet it also allows us to practice the art of trusting with the people who love us most.

For Meredith, her fourteen-year-old daughter proved to be a natural Support Buddy. Lucy, who was twelve when her parents' marriage ended, effectively came of age as her mother's personal cheering section. Watching Meredith grow and change had been inspiring for Lucy as she approached adolescence. In turn, Meredith had developed a respect for Lucy's judgment and evolving maturity. At a time when many of Lucy's friends were rebelling against their parents, Lucy and Meredith forged a relationship based on respect and admiration. That's why Meredith trusted Lucy when Lucy went into Support Buddy mode. Here are some of the ways Lucy encouraged her mother:

• Lucy saved up her baby-sitting money to buy a gold-plated necklace engraved with "#1 Mom," and gave it to Meredith on the day she signed the lease on the space for the antique store she was planning to open.

• Lucy made a habit of buying greeting cards with messages such as "What would you do if you knew you could not fail?" and gave them to her mother whenever Meredith needed comfort and motivation.

• Lucy wrote an essay in English class entitled "My Mom Is My Role Model" and then had it framed as a birthday present for Meredith.

• On an evening when Meredith came home distraught because an irate customer had ranted about having to wait to make his purchase while Meredith was talking to her landlord on the phone about the overflowing toilet, Lucy said, "None of that was about you. You're totally amazing and really good at running your business. Who knows where that guy was coming from? He probably yells at everybody. He could learn a thing or two from you about that Wheel of Fear you keep telling me about! And the Wheel of Freedom too. Anyway, let's talk about your plans for the coming year, the way we were doing last night. Are you really going to open a new location? That is so incredibly cool! All the other kids are jealous of me for having a mom who totally rocks!"

Remember when I mentioned that Marta and I "trained" each other to be good Support Buddies? You can do the same in order to establish reciprocal relationships that put everyone involved in a can-do, fearless frame of mind. The secret is to learn the language of support:

- Issuing orders doesn't work when someone is in emotional pain. Yet people often do just that. "Snap out of it," someone might say. "Get over it. Chin up. Stiff upper lip. Stop crying." People cannot will their negative feelings away. If they could, they would. There would be no fear and no depression and no grief. The person seeking support needs comfort, not sermonizing. You and your Support Buddies can practice saying such things as "I hear you. I'm sorry you're in pain (worried) (confused) (overwhelmed) (doubting your abilities). What do you need? How can I support you? Would you like me to remind you how valuable (smart) (amazing) you are?"

- Avoid trivializing the person's feelings. You know—and in fact the person knows—that the feelings are transient. That doesn't make them any less unpleasant at the moment. So don't say, "Tomorrow is another day. You've blown this whole thing way out of proportion. You're really overreacting." Instead, practice saying, "I'm honored that you feel comfortable talking with me when you feel this way. I'm here for you."

- Don't compare the person's pain with other people's, as in "There are plenty of people a lot worse off than you are." A person who has gone blind in one eye is not going to feel better when reminded that there are people who are totally blind. The same goes for emotional wounds and needs. Let the person feel the pain. Honor that pain. That's the only way we can own it and master it. Similarly, avoid jumping in with stories from your own life or stories you've heard about other people. You shut down the lines of communication when you cut someone off with "I know just what you mean! Why, when my aunt Ida was getting a divorce, she was a basket case." You are turning into a Complaining Buddy instead of functioning as a Support Buddy. Instead, use simple interjections that keep the person talking: "Really? Wow. Go on. Hmmm. Then what happened?"

- Ask the person if they want your opinion. Don't be offended if they don't. Often when feelings are fresh and raw, the person is not capable of hearing advice. And never, ever, even in a joking way, feed into the person's fear by suggesting revenge in the form of "If I were you . . ." Saying something like "What a jerk! If I were you, I'd strangle him!" is destructive, not supportive. Say instead, "You were obviously hurt by that. Why don't we talk about some of the times when people have appreciated you?"

- And if the person is ready and willing to take new action, ask them, "What are you committed to?" This allows them to remember what is important in their life and reestablish a connection to it. Your job is to be a reminder, whether just by your presence if they aren't ready to hear it, or verbally, if they are, that they are magnificent. Giving them the opportunity to remember what is important allows them the freedom to move beyond their fear with more ease due to your support.

As you and your Support Buddies get better at the language of support, you'll "catch" one another when negative phrases slip out of your mouths. Marta and I still do this and we usually end up laughing—which, of course, helps the healing.

Wise Council

Sometimes, of course, you need more than just encouragement. You need a chance to gain some perspective. That's when you call on the members of your Fearbuster Team who can act as Wise Council. The role is context sensitive. Meredith, for example, didn't rely on fourteen-year-old Lucy as Wise Council when Meredith was drawing up a business plan for expanding her antique store to a second location. Instead, she called her brother Ralph, who is a successful entrepreneur himself. Ralph proved to be an ideal sounding board and brainstorming partner even though he was facing some challenges of his own as a result of having lost two valuable employees to a competitor. Ralph's Wheel of Fear had been reactivated when that happened, but he was able to look at Meredith's situation objectively in spite of his own concerns. That is the hallmark of someone who is capable of acting as a member of your Wise Council. A Wise Council member who has a core fear of failure doesn't let that cloud his judgment when helping you sift through the pros and cons of taking a new job. He can play the devil's advocate in a productive way by listening as you sort through the possible results of what you're considering doing, and then encouraging you to assess how you would handle the various outcomes.

The reason that the people on your Wise Council are able to consider your agenda without imposing their own fears on it is that they have a fair amount of peace, freedom, and equilibrium in their own lives. They are big enough emotionally to be in a position to wish you well. And when you succeed, they really mean it when they say, "I'm so happy for you!"

You may also want to seek professional help to act as Wise Council. Just as you would have a surgeon perform your appendectomy, you can hire a professional to help you lose weight, make a career change, cope with a crumbling marriage, or cure an addiction. The money you allocate for sessions with a qualified nutritionist, personal coach, physical trainer, counselor, therapist, or social worker is money well spent. And usually there are sliding scales available to suit your needs.

Check your local Yellow Pages or use a Web search engine. Also pay attention to word of mouth. The recommendation of a satisfied customer still goes a long way. But keep in mind that the counselor who worked wonders for your aunt Sally might leave you cold. Hiring a counselor or coach is a very personal decision. And if you ever feel pressured to sign a contract, walk out. Reputable companies and individuals will want you to make this decision at your own pace and because you want to.

Another good source for referrals is professional associations. Go to your local library and ask the reference desk for books on associations. There are thousands. Look up your area of interest and contact the appropriate group. Representatives will be happy to help you find the information you're looking for.

I can't tell you what the techniques of all the various professionals could be. You'll need to evaluate potential coaches and counselors on your own. And be sure to ask them about their skills, experience, and educational training. Most will be happy to meet with you for no charge to help you figure out if they are right for you. Listen to your intuition. Trust it. If you feel intimidated or frightened, then this person—no matter how many degrees are hanging on the wall—is not for you. If you want a personal coach, find someone who will hold you accountable by assigning you "homework" that will make a difference for you. Be sure to check out http://www.FearlessLiving.org for numerous resources. Important: Remember to give both yourself and the professional enough time for change to take place.

Whether your Wise Council members are professionals or friends, their function is to help you think things through. When my client Leslie was considering moving from a smaller entrepreneurial company to large corporation, she called a successful colleague who had no reason to be threatened by her. Gary said, "I can understand your hesitation. You'd be making a lot more money, but you'd be giving up the autonomy you have at the smaller company. This is a very personal decision. You have to consider your ability to be creative, to think up and direct new projects, if that's what's important. A lot of people would go for the larger dollars, but if you'd be miserable with someone directing you, then would the switch be worth the extra income?

"Or do you want more money because your leisure time is what matters most to you? Also think about the fact that you would have the challenge of leading a larger work force. You could make quite a difference in that big company. It's all about a balance sheet. Get it down in black and white. Make columns on a piece of paper. Give yourself time to mull everything over. And by the way, in my experience, when you make the choice that aligns with your personal commitments, everything falls into place. You get ahead simply because you're doing what's really you."

Leslie did her homework and then set up another meeting with Gary to evaluate the data she had collected. The upshot was that the corporate challenge stirred up her passion exactly because she didn't know if she could do it. Fear had turned into excitement through the guidance of her Wise Council member.

Your Wise Council members ask open-ended questions, allowing you to come up with the answers for yourself as well as helping you investigate your options without comparing them to what they personally like or what they would do. Their own fears are put aside as, free of their opinions and personal agendas, they listen to you. They are wise enough to know that what would work for one person may not work for another. In the end, they know you are the only one who can decide. Each time you call on your Wise Council, you engage your Wheel of Freedom and are able to give yourself permission to risk.

FEARBUSTER EXERCISE

To get the most out of an encounter with a Wise Council member, be prepared:

- Make a written list of concerns you have about a risk you're considering taking. If possible, give yourself two or three days' lead time to do this so that aspects of the potential venture will have a chance to occur to you at odd moments. Trying to come up with a list in one sitting often isn't as effective as letting the topic stay in the back of your mind and allowing it to bubble up unbidden. Be sure to keep a notebook handy so you can capture your thoughts when they happen. I'd even have paper and pencil on the nightstand in case an idea wakes you up in the middle of the night.

- Treat your time with your Wise Council in a businesslike way. I remember one client, a young woman in her twenties, who learned to use her mom as a Wise Council member. Whenever Chloe, the daughter, was facing a scary new grown-up challenge, she called her mother and asked for "consulting time." They stuck to the topic at hand for fifteen minutes to a half an hour, either in person or on the phone. When the sessions were over, time permitting, Chloe and her mom had lunch and allowed themselves to talk about other topics. "It was like flipping a switch," Chloe remembers. "It worked great for us."

- Don't rely on memory alone. Take notes and/or tape-record what your Wise Council member has to say.

- Keep in mind that your Wise Council is not there to make decisions for you. You are accountable for your own life and your own decisions. You're not consulting with Wise Council members in order to get yourself off the hook. After each session, take some time alone to write down your conclusions, as well as any new questions that may have come up.

Voices of Experience

Let's say you've been cheered on by your Support Buddies, thought things through with your Wise Council, and made a brave decision to take a risk by trying something new. Whether you're going to change careers, have a baby, have elective surgery, move to Alaska, or get a divorce, you may want the guidance of Voices of Experience along the way. You're past the point of choosing your new Fearless Path. You're already on it. And sometimes along the way you're going to experience doubts and feel your fear. That's when the reassurance of people who have been down a similar route and encountered similar pitfalls can be invaluable. Meredith, for example, couldn't call on her daughter Lucy, her favorite Support Buddy, to help her through the specifics of her divorce. Her brother Ralph, the entrepreneur, was no expert in that situation, either, since he was happily married. True, both Lucy and Ralph were sympathetic, but when it came to concrete help—both emotional and practical—Meredith counted on Cathy, her ex-husband's sister. Cathy could relate when Meredith said she had recurring, painful memories of happier times past when she and Phil were young. Cathy had advice for Meredith about how to get a phone and a credit history in her own name after eighteen years as Mrs. Him. Cathy made Meredith laugh through her tears by telling tales of how she survived the ordeal of dropping her kids off at her ex's house for visitation and being greeted by a brand-new Other Woman. "You're not alone," Cathy would say. "You're not crazy. This is the way it feels. And you'll get through it just the way I did. And you'll be better for it."

You can also find Voices of Experience in organized support groups, both real and virtual. Support Groups such as Alcoholics Anonymous, Weight Watchers, Parents Without Partners, and the National Association of Women Business Owners can be invaluable supporting you on your path. There are thousands more, including faith-based groups, singles organizations, and gender or ethnic-based associations. I joined a writers' group when I first embarked on this new aspect of my career. And plenty of people find solace and advice on the Web during challenges and crises ranging from losing a job to losing a loved one to welcoming a second baby to caring for aging relatives. Mentors are also Voices of Experience. Because they are accomplished in the career you're aspiring to, they are inspiring and instructive examples of what being on the Wheel of Freedom can do for people. Remember, even if your regular Fearbuster Team doesn't include a member who has the experience you need in a specific situation, you can look elsewhere.

✳ FEARBUSTER EXERCISE ✳

The point of seeking out Voices of Experience is to get a green light, even if you also get some gentle warnings about how to cope gracefully with what may lie ahead. What you definitely don't need are doomsayers. As we have seen, Cathy was able to put an emotional arm around Meredith's shoulder during her divorce because Cathy felt she had achieved a positive outcome after her own divorce in spite of the challenges along the way. If Meredith had turned to someone who was sour and defeated as the result of a divorce, that would only have hurt Meredith's chances of mastering her fear. To make sure you choose Voices of Experience who will help you say, "Yes!" to the risk you're taking, use the following litmus test:

Ask your potential Voice of Experience whether he or she would do it over again. For example, "If you had it to do over again, would you (get divorced?) (have your rotator cuff repaired?) (take out a loan to start your own business?) (have a baby after age forty?) (refinance your mortgage?)

If the answer amounts to a lot of hand wringing, you've got a Fear Junkie on your hands. People who love to tell you the gory details, *even if the outcome was ostensibly successful,* are still on their Wheels of Fear. The person who landed on her feet after being dumped for a trophy wife but who still wants to dwell on what a skunk her ex-husband is won't help you at all. The fellow whose shoulder is now as good as new but who loves to tell you that he suffered the agonies of the damned after the surgery is not the man you need to listen to. Sure, it's nice to know something about what's in store, but right now your most pressing need is to hear that you're on the right track. You need a divorced friend who stresses the good times and gives you a thumbs-up, or a person who says that a little post-op pain will be just a memory and you'll be glad you got yourself put back together again. You're looking for votes of confidence, not horror stories.

Powerful Partnerships

Powerful Partnerships are relationships in your Fearbuster Team that involve a long-term commitment. They may play many of the roles we have already examined, but the added dimension is that at least some aspect of your lives is devoted to a joint goal or enterprise. Your Powerful Partner could be your spouse, your business partner, your agent, your manager— anyone with whom you team up, often legally with a signed contract, for an extended period of time. Commitment is paramount. Agreements and boundaries must be spelled out, as well as roles and responsibilities. Compliments are freely given and gratefully received. Powerful Partners also help one another face their fears without putting each other down. That can be challenging. The secret is that Powerful Partners ask before giving any coaching. Then the other person has an opportunity to admit if he or she is ready for it.

If you have a partner who understands that in order for the relationship to thrive, you both must thrive, you have a partner to be cherished. You and your partner can be a Fearless Living team, consciously and actively encouraging one another so that your sum is greater than your separate selves. You can accomplish more together, monetarily and emotionally, than either of you could on your own. You are pulling together, jointly putting fear in its place and rejoicing in your freedom.

If partnerships as ideal as the one I've just described are rare, that is only because most people enter into relationships based on fear. Both people are desperately seeking approval, yet trust is elusive when neither partner is willing to risk full disclosure. We offer a false front in an attempt to feel safe rather than taking a chance on achieving genuine intimacy by revealing the truth of our imperfections.

Sadly, most people can pour their hearts out to strangers on an airplane or pay their therapists to get an earful, but turning to their partners and telling them they are scared or lonely is unbearable. Yet how can we know true love, friendship, and support if we don't dare to show ourselves to one another? If you don't reveal yourself, aren't you always wondering in the back of your mind if your partner really loves you? The more we hold back, the more insecure we can become, just waiting for the other person to discover the very thing we have been attempting to hide. Powerful Partnerships override that tendency. When your commitment is to the partnership, you have permission to be yourself, knowing that other person is there to help you become even more of who you are—and vice versa.

Sam and Jacob are an example of a Perfect Partnership. They started a Web incubator in New York City's Silicon Alley in 1997, and three years later they were riding a crest. When an opportunity came for a takeover, Jacob got cold feet. He told Sam that he didn't want to end up working twenty-four/seven. Sam heard Jacob out with no interruptions. After a thoughtful silence, Sam said, "If we decide to acquire our competitor, that will mean extra hours at work. Do we want to do that? I know how important fishing is to your well-being, so we could make an agreement. If you cut back on your fishing for one month while we integrate their system to ours, I will have no problem if you want to take a long weekend to go to your favorite spot. And during the holidays this year, I would appreciate if you could help me out so I could spend some time with my family back in Seattle. Do you want to go for it?"

As Sam and Jacob prove, Powerful Partnerships work because you and your partner appreciate each other's strengths and respect each other's needs. With mutual support, getting off the Wheel of Fear and moving toward the Wheel of Freedom is easier. You both benefit. A business partner might say something like "I don't want you to feel you have to stay stuck if this business is no longer your dream. I can see you are ready to move on. Let's take a hard look at the numbers and figure out a plan so that you can make a change. Either I will buy your share of the business, we will find a new investor, or something else will come along. My commitment is to help us both achieve success." A husband might say something like "If you want to volunteer to read to the blind, that's terrific. The kids and I will be fine the evenings you're gone. That'll be our quality time." A wife might say something like "Sure, I'll miss you if you spend a month in Maine at that summer artists' colony, but honey, you can't miss this. You're this close to showing your paintings. This is just the opportunity you have been looking for."

✵ FEARBUSTER EXERCISE ✵

If you're on the verge of forming a partnership, put your agreement in writing. You can include a clause that says you'll renegotiate as time goes on and circumstances change. But don't shy away from getting everything down on paper, even if you're madly in love. Perhaps especially if you're madly in love. Many a marriage was destroyed, or at least damaged, by hidden agendas. Whether the issue is as seemingly unimportant as who is going to take out the garbage or as major as whether the children will be brought up in the husband's religion or the wife's, make sure it's on the table. The same, of course, is true for business partnerships. Any kind of Powerful Partnership works only as well as the contract between the two of you. When it's clear, your chances of living fearlessly together are very good indeed.

Now you have discovered where your friends fit in your life and how to best serve each other. To expand your Fearbuster Team, I challenge you to make the following an ongoing commitment: connect with one person with whom you would like to reestablish a bond, thank one Fearbuster Team member for his or her support, and reach out to one new potential supporter. With this as your base, your Fearbuster Team will always be filled with supportive, loving individuals who think you are the greatest.

Now that you have your network of friends in place and poised to help you, you're ready to begin the really deep work of the Fearless Living program. First, we'll eliminate the unrealistic expectations that have been keeping you afraid that you're not good enough.

Part Two

THE FEARLESS LIVING PROGRAM

Avoiding danger is no safer in the long run than outright exposure.
Life is either a daring adventure or nothing.

Helen Keller

No Expectations

On a January evening in the southern city that was my new home, I was getting ready to go out with Daniel. We had fallen crazy in love the previous March during an idyllic spring break in Florida. After I went back to finish my sophomore year at the University of Minnesota and he went back to the southern college where he was a senior, we kept up a long-distance romance. Our phone bills alone totaled upward of six hundred dollars a month, and he treated me to a steady stream of flowers delivered to my door plus occasional surprise visits. When summer came, we agreed that I should switch schools and move down to be with him. I rented my own apartment and settled in, but I fully expected the fairy-tale ending to be marriage. I would be safe in Daniel's love, never abandoned and afraid again.

However, things weren't going exactly as I thought they should. While I fussed with my hair and picked out a nice outfit, I made up my mind to talk to Daniel that night about how disappointed I was that I hadn't seen more of him since I had arrived six months earlier. I had talked with him several times about this but I just wasn't getting through to him and I was not happy about that. After all, I had left a college I liked and relocated a thousand miles away from my sisters. Sure, Daniel's schoolwork was demanding, but hadn't I moved here for him? He owed it to me to try harder.

What I didn't know was that Daniel had a scenario of his own in mind for that night. After dinner, during which I made my speech about not getting enough attention, we ended up at our favorite bar where we had a few drinks with some friends. I joked about how I had gotten a case of the prewedding jitters when Daniel and I had looked at engagement rings a couple of weeks earlier. Daniel chose that moment to let me know it was over between us.

He nodded and said, "Yeah, I had the same reaction. It's a good thing we didn't buy a ring. Because actually I don't think I love you anymore."

My whole body froze. I couldn't breathe. I was fourteen again, back in Michigan on that rain-streaked June day when my father's gunshots instilled the powerful fear that I didn't deserve to be alive. I was a loser. I was worthless. I was unlovable. I had been publicly dumped by the man who was supposed to make all the pain and fear go away. This couldn't be happening.

And then the self-loathing gave way to rage. Not again! Hadn't I been through enough? How dare he! Daniel knew about my past. Couldn't he understand that I was doing the best I could after what I had been through? Shouldn't he try harder after I had pulled up my roots, said good-bye to my family, and followed him on the promise that we'd be together always? My initial paralysis loosened its grip. Fear drove me beyond the limits of my fragile control and I snapped, unleashing a hailstorm of hostility toward him, a shoe-pounding shower of broken mirror behind the bar. The owner deemed my departure necessary for the safety of the other patrons. The bouncer showed me the door. Daniel made no move to come with me. Instead, he asked his roommate to drive me home.

Alone in my apartment, I paced like a cat in a cage. I decided I had to get out of town. Maybe that would hurt Daniel. I reasoned I couldn't just hang around waiting for more rejection and humiliation. I had to make him miss me. What should I pack? Wandering around my apartment in a stunned panic, I gathered whatever was in front of me and stuffed it in my suitcase. I grabbed some marshmallows and Band-Aids, matches and a cushion, a cassette tape and some pencils. I made some hot chocolate. I stopped to dust a table. I sat down to dial the phone. I had no direction or balance. I was losing it.

I left countless unanswered messages on Daniel's machine. Then when I dialed, the line was busy. I called the operator to break through and was told that his phone was off the hook. I couldn't believe this was happening to me. Not with Daniel. Not now after I had given up so much to be with him. Why wouldn't he talk to me? In the silence, with my cup of cold cocoa, I refused to accept the reality that the man who once couldn't bear to be away from me didn't want me anymore.

Then the fear that I was worthless surfaced again. Obviously, I shouldn't have been surprised when he dumped me. I'm sure I deserved it. I called my sisters to try to connect with someone, anyone. I told them how awfully I had behaved, but hung up when they began their litany about thinking positively. Both of them were instinctively reacting as members of what I would later identify as my Fearbuster Team when I developed the Fearless Living program. But at the time, I was not open to their love and support. Cheerleading wasn't what I had in mind. Punishment was. I desperately wanted someone to hurt with me, not help me. At that point, I was terrified Daniel was gone for good, which meant more evidence that I was worthless. I came to the conclusion that if I took my life, Daniel would forever regret his decision. Alarmed by my own thoughts, I reached for the phone.

"Suicide Hotline. This is Nancy. May I have your name please?" the upbeat voice said.

"Rhonda."

"Hello, Rhonda. Thanks for calling."

I told the overly nice woman that I wanted to kill myself, thus eliciting what was surely a standard question-and-answer routine. I gave her my phone number, a phony address, and sketchy details of my relationship problems. Nancy then proceeded to read—or so it sounded—a script that was meant to keep crazy types like me off the tenth-floor window ledge. Everything about her delivery bothered me. Her canned rhetoric and nauseating tone only made me feel more alone. I ended the call by telling the volunteer that because of what she had said, I was going to kill myself for sure.

In search of sympathy, I turned to my last hope, Woody, my best friend of the month. I called and told him I had taken some pills. The realization that I hadn't thought this through very well hit me when he announced that he was on his way over. Now I either had to take the pills or confess to Woody that I hadn't told the truth. I couldn't bear to be a liar. Daniel was a liar. I was not going to be like him. In my confused state, making good on my word seemed to outweigh the risk to my life. I didn't have anything exotic on hand, but I swallowed every over-the-counter pill I found in my medicine cabinet and purse—an entire bottle of aspirin, the rest of the Tylenol, some antacids, my vitamins, a packet of Midol, even the calcium supplements.

Woody had called 911 before he left. To my dismay, he and the ambulance arrived at the same time. I would have preferred to be passed out by then, but no such luck.

After the drama of the emergency room, where I was forced to drink something that smelled like rotten eggs to make me vomit, I woke up in the psychiatric ward. Once you land there, you don't get to tell them you were just upset with your boyfriend and then check out. I was "observed" for a few days. After that, the assigned therapist told me with the utmost sincerity, "You have no real friends here, no family, no support. Just go back to Minnesota."

That was not what I wanted to hear. How could he be so cold? This was not the treatment I expected from a professional therapist. But secretly, I knew he was right.

Most of us expect certain things to happen a certain way. We've planned for it. We've visualized. Maybe we have even lit candles at church, just to be sure. We want to do more, have more, and be more. We not only want to have it all, we expect to get it. Our family and friends are thrown into the fray as we expect as much from them as we do from ourselves. And, when we've done all we "should" do, "paid our dues" and "gone the extra mile," we want guaranteed results. Haven't we worked hard and earned a little place in the sun—or a big place, depending on what we think we deserve? Disappointment is inevitable if things don't turn out exactly as we had planned, which is usually the case. And when that happens, our worst fears are confirmed. You expect to be loved forever. You get dumped and your fear that you are unlovable surfaces. You expect to get the raise you're asking for. You don't get it. Your fear that you're incompetent takes hold. You expect to be rewarded with your children's respect and appreciation after all you've done for them. They get lives of their own and forget to call on your birthday. Each failed expectation only confirms your worst fear. Your actions are colored by your frustrated expectations. The fear of being rejected grips you. In the end, expectations breed fear and discontent. And our unfulfilled expectations are the catalyst for acting out the rage, self-pity, and victimization that stem from our fears.

If You Loved Me, You'd Know What I Need

That is why expectations can stunt your growth and potential. That is also why they can poison your relationships, both personal and professional. When you expect something from someone else but never express that expectation, you are asking the other person to be a mind reader. Of course almost inevitably, the other person will fail to guess what it is you expect. It can be tough to act on the "right" assumption. Wayne, for example, expected his wife to be literally just like the girl who married dear old Dad. His mother had been the consummate homemaker, the classic woman behind the man. Yet Wayne's wife, Lynn, was now going back to school just as she had planned once their youngest turned ten. He had known that when he married her, and the year before she started, he bragged about her to all his friends. Still, he was upset that Lynn didn't have dinner on the table every night at six. He was hurt because she sent his shirts out instead of laundering and ironing them herself. And he was angry when she spent the evening studying instead of snuggling up next to him on the couch to watch TV.

He never told her, though. He simply expected her to know what he needed in order to feel loved. The fact that she didn't seem to know, or worse yet that she appeared to him to be purposely ignoring his wants and needs, triggered Wayne's Wheel of Fear. Wayne was afraid of being rejected and he ended up feeling utterly inadequate. His father had succeeded in being the kind of husband who merited a devoted wife. Why, Wayne thought, couldn't he measure up to Dad's standard? Wayne sought relief by heading rejection off at the pass. This was his pre-emptive strike. He turned his back on Lynn in bed. He pretended he didn't hear her when she was speaking to him. He stayed out late without telling her where he had gone. After all, he reasoned, Lynn couldn't reject him if he rejected her first. And with the twisted logic common to people on the Wheel of Fear, Wayne also thought that by giving Lynn a dose of her own medicine, he would show her that she had hurt his feelings by not guessing correctly how he wanted to be loved. All that happened, however, was that Lynn became even less available to Wayne as a result of his behavior. The day after Lynn first slept on the couch instead of in bed with Wayne, he came to me for coaching. He had heard about my work from a colleague, and he told me he wanted "the courage to get a fearless divorce."

After I had heard him out, my intuition and my experience led me to believe that Wayne desperately wanted to heal his relationship with Lynn. We started by identifying his Wheel of Fear—fear of being rejected, followed by his fear of feeling inadequate. Then we moved on to identifying his Wheel of Free-

dom. At first, thinking as most people do that his Wheel of Freedom would be the opposite of his Wheel of Fear, Wayne picked
"loving" as his essential nature. However, his five heroes were:
Jack Nicklaus, one of the greatest golfers in history; Wayne's
most admired college professor, a woman who had dedicated
her life to decoding DNA; jazz musician Duke Ellington; baseball Hall-of-Famer Babe Ruth; and legendary tiger-tamer Gun-
ther Gable Williams. Wayne picked "focused" as the essential
nature for Nicklaus, the professor, and Ruth; "creative" for
Ellington; and "courageous" for Williams. Then he said, "Ellington and Williams were pretty darn focused, too, when you think
about it."

You know by now what happened next. I revealed to Wayne
that his essential nature was not "loving" but "focused." He
blushed. "Well, maybe once upon a time," he said. "Back in
high school, I was determined to be a golf pro. But right before
I got my B.A., some recruiters came to the campus—I was at
Princeton—and one of them dangled a six-figure salary in front
of me for a job as an investment banker. This guy said he didn't
care what my major was. My GPA was 3.9 and I was 'good material.' At twenty-one, I was afraid to pass up the opportunity. I
took the job, fully expecting to be caught up in the excitement
of the world of international high finance.

"Well, it turned out to be just a lot of hard work, most of it
pretty tedious. Still, I got used to the money and the lifestyle
that went with the banking job even though my heart's never
been in it. Once, a couple of years ago, I considered joining an
amateur league just for fun but it always seemed the kids had
some weekend activity that I didn't want to miss. So I figured,
hey, my family will be my life. As I said, however, that's not working out either."

As Wayne's story shows, expectations that are unspoken, unrealistic, and unmet can cause us to do such things as take the
wrong fork in the road and punish the people we love. That is
heartbreaking. It destroys dreams. It destroys marriages. It
keeps people stuck on the Wheel of Fear. Worst of all, nobody

involved has a clear idea of what went wrong. When things don't turn out the way we want them to, we simply feel baffled and powerless. When our expectations are a primary factor in the way we think, speak, and listen, disappointment becomes a way of life. Expectations seem to change with each individual situation, yet in the end, it is just our fear manifesting itself in endless ways. And expectations make everything seem personal. But no one is doing anything to you. You are reacting to your own Wheel of Fear.

☀ FEARBUSTER EXERCISE ☀

Negative language is a dead giveaway that unrealistic and unspoken expectations are keeping you from living fearlessly. I gave Wayne a list of words most commonly used by people when a situation or a relationship is fraught with expectations. You may have used them to describe yourself or somebody else. The more often they are present, the more likely it is that expectations are spinning your Wheel of Fear out of control. Ask yourself if any of these words determine your daily actions or solidify your belief systems. These words will give you a clear indication of how often you are expecting things to be different from what they are.

Do you:

deny	hide	whine	judge	suffer
wait	blame	deflect	isolate	assume
settle	defend	deserve	wish	struggle
control	pretend	hesitate	condemn	compare
manipulate	complain	compromise	procrastinate	worry

Do you feel:

bitter	entitled	guilty	irritated	victimized
annoyed	confused	powerless	resentful	inconsistent

disappointed   ambiguous   irresponsible   ignored   self-pitying
self-centered   dissatisfied   perfectionistic   indifferent

Wayne's negative action words turned out to be "settle," "blame," "defend," "deserve," "compromise," and "compare." His feeling words were "bitter," "disappointed," "entitled," "dissatisfied," and "ignored." I asked him to write these words down in order to begin to accept them without shame. I want you to do the same. For the next three days, write down any of the words of expectation that you think or say.

After that, write down the words that pop up whenever you suspect that unspoken or unrealistic expectations are triggering your Wheel of Fear. Which of the words on the list come up most often for you? Are there any that made you cringe or feel particularly uncomfortable? Perhaps you noticed that you have already let go of some that were once common for you. That's great. Always be aware of your progress. Do any of these words remind you of certain friends? If so, the company you keep may be contributing to your fear. Jot down the words that have the most power over you and the ones you want to let go of. As we build awareness, I am asking you to be vigilant, because expectations are an opening for discovering and transforming your Wheel of Fear. Once we identify how expectations are infiltrating your life, we can get you on the Wheel of Freedom where there is only one thing left: you. A powerful, fearless you!

That's precisely what happened for Wayne. I taught him that the next step after identifying the words of expectation is to look once again at the list of one hundred proactive and self-affirming behaviors on pages 79–81 and identify those that might work in your current situation. Wayne picked "Do something kind for someone else," "Be willing to be wrong," "Eliminate silent contracts," and "Practice the art of conversation." He effectively did all of those things when he expressed his expectations to Lynn, using "I" sentences instead of "you" sentences as I had taught him. ("I feel ignored when I have to spend the evening watching TV alone." Not "You ignore me almost every evening while you're doing your homework.") This opened the lines of communication. Wayne and Lynn ended up having heart-to-hearts almost every day at first and then about once a week. The result was that when Wayne verbalized his expectations, he was able to begin to genuinely appreciate Lynn for her drive and enthusiasm. She in turn eased up on her nightly study habits and instead, whenever possible, she did her homework during the day while Wayne was at work. Once again being around Wayne in the evenings became a tempting pleasure. The next step was that Wayne hired a top-notch golf pro with his eye on a local tournament. They also agreed that Lynn's next school break would be spent together in Cancún without the kids. Wayne came back to me after that saying, "You sure were right. Once I got focused, I got my wholeness: confidence. My golf game is better than ever. I am not a duffer after all. And I got all the rest of it too. The creativity came when I jammed with a jazz band while we were in Mexico. I used to play a mean sax, and even though I'm a little rusty I haven't lost my touch. Now I'm practicing again just for fun. Then there's the intimacy. I don't have to tell you how much more intimate my relationship with Lynn has become now that I'm being true to myself after all these years."

The Blame Game

One of the biggest temptations you face when you are in expectation is to point fingers. Wayne had been blaming Lynn for their marriage problems. And I used to find a way to blame someone else for almost anything. Why would I want to face my own issues when in my mind I had suffered enough? For starters, my father "should" have loved me. That's what parents are supposed to do. My mother "should" still be alive, because she deserved to be. And, Daniel "should" have been waiting for me at the hospital, asking for my forgiveness. That's what love and loyalty are supposed to look like, right? Instead, Daniel had his roommate pick me up at the hospital and drop me off at the front door of my apartment, where I was face to face with the consequences of my prehospital rampage. Rather than look inside of myself for answers, it seemed easier to blame my father, guns, or Daniel. If they were the bad guys, I didn't have to be.

A longtime client of mine named Jennifer is a good example of this same false logic at work. Even though she was excited to get the job promotion she had been working for, Jennifer was now in foreign territory. In her new position, she didn't have her familiar allies around her, she wasn't quite sure how things were done, and she felt out of place in her role in senior management. Her boss came to give the ground rules on Jennifer's first day and he laid down the expectations he had for her performance. It was quite a list. Jennifer expected that he would mentor her through the transition, but weeks went by and he didn't offer any help. Jennifer never asked for help either. Consequently, she felt left out and unsupported. She began to have doubts about whether the job was right for her. And she blamed her boss for her predicament.

"How am I supposed to know what to do if he doesn't tell me?" she asked when she came to see me after landing her new job. "He just leaves me to figure everything out on my own. I don't think he likes me. He wants me to fail."

Because Jennifer had not communicated her expectations, she had made a snap judgment motivated by fear. When we feel uncomfortable because expectations are not met, fear makes us think things such as: "They don't know what they're doing." "You don't belong here." "You shouldn't have taken the job." "The money isn't worth the harassment." "What is wrong with you?" "You should have seen this coming." Jennifer's expectations had turned on her, becoming negative self-talk. Soon she was building up piles of evidence to prove why her coworkers weren't as efficient as the previous ones, and why they were undermining her attempts to improve upon outdated systems. She had a vision of how a boss "should" behave and was resentful when hers "didn't know how to be a boss and he didn't even attempt to be a mentor." Since he was in a position of authority, he was an easy scapegoat.

Even though Jennifer had already made great strides in living fearlessly that had enabled her to land this new job in the first place, expectations came up when she took the risk to step into management. That is common. Whenever you step into unfamiliar territory, your Wheel of Fear will be triggered. When Jennifer took on the new job, her fear of being thought of as stupid and her feeling of helplessness kicked in. Spinning in her Wheel of Fear, she could think of nothing but the expectations she had for herself and for the way the job should be. The good news is that once you begin to identify the expectations that trigger your Wheel of Fear, you will be able to take proactive, self-affirming actions to help you get onto your Wheel of Freedom. Life is a continuous process of change, with challenges at every level of growth. Fear will always come up, but you'll get better and better at eliminating the kind of expectations that prevent you from mastering your fear.

✸ FEARBUSTER EXERCISE ✸

I had Jennifer answer the following questions, which was very powerful for her. I want you to do it as well.

- Name a particular situation. In that situation:

    What are you expecting from yourself?
    From others?

Jennifer had a hard time answering at first. She wanted to deny her part by reacting with anger and blaming others. When we are reactive, we expect the impossible.

Are you reactive? Answer the following questions:

1) Is "should" part of your vocabulary or your criteria for decision making?
2) Do you do things for others because you have to?
3) Can somebody else's bad mood bring you down?
4) When you are criticized, do you become defensive?
5) Do you seek approval from others before moving forward?
6) When someone yells at you, do you automatically yell back?

If you answered yes to any of those questions, you are reacting. The more numerous the yeses, the more frequently reactive behavior occurs, which means the more expectations you have placed upon yourself or others. Most people believe they are making choices when they are really just reacting. That is what Jennifer thought.

When you build up a case against yourself (or someone else), it takes courage to admit that perhaps there is another point of view. It takes a commitment to the truth to face the reality of your fear. Jennifer isn't alone in her initial denial of her expectations. They seemed so reasonable. She could easily justify each one. Most of us do it. I explained that her expectations didn't make her wrong or stupid. They made her human. We all want things a certain way. No one can escape the blame game altogether.

Jennifer confessed that she had expected to get it together faster, feel confident, and feel powerful, now that she had "made it." She expected her team to welcome her new ideas and work at a higher production rate. She thought her office assistant would certainly be friendly and efficient, her friends would be supportive, her father would finally respect her, and her new boss would be the boss she had always dreamt of.

It sounded to me as though Jennifer just wanted to be understood, respected, and loved. Pretty much what we all want.

Ironically, when her Wheel of Fear engaged, expectations actually separated her from the positive experiences she could have helped to foster. Everything seemed confused and exaggerated. She felt as though she had ruined her shot at a good start. She now knew she was reacting to feeling stupid and helpless. Was it too late? Of course not.

I explained to Jennifer that she had forgotten to share "Jennifer's Rules" to prevent ineffective office behavior by her co-workers before she started her new position. She laughed. Seriously, I told her that she needed to be honest with herself. She realized she was pushing responsibility away from herself (where she had power to change things) and onto someone or something else (where she had no control). Jennifer came to see the base problem: Her fear of feeling helpless and being thought of as stupid had manufactured her expectations and limited her success. Who said she would have an efficient assistant? Who said she should know everything? Regarding her assistant, if she wanted things done in a particular way, communication was in order. Everyone else working with Jennifer had their own expectations too. Mix it all together and you have a recipe for disaster. No wonder so many people are frustrated in their jobs. Expectations will always build evidence for you and against others. Without clear communication and an authentic commitment to personal accountability, no one has a chance.

Jennifer's homework was to eliminate all of the silent contracts she had with others and communicate her needs, wants, and desires clearly. Silent contracts are those agreements we have made with others that they know nothing about. Jennifer's most glaring silent contracts were with her assistant and boss.

When Jennifer understood that it was no one else's responsibility to know, or to provide, what she needed, conflicts lessened. And when they did come up, solving them was easier. Because of her fear of looking stupid she had also expected herself to know everything. When that is the case, it is difficult to actually learn anything. She had to accept where she was before she could move forward.

Jennifer moved onto her Wheel of Freedom by taking responsibility for her state of mind. She went through the list of words on pages 144–145 and identified "wait," "blame," "complain," "judge," "assume," and "worry" as the fearful ways she was behaving. Then she picked "disappointed," "entitled," "powerless," "resentful," and "ignored" as the ways she was feeling. Then Jennifer looked at the list of one hundred proactive and self-affirming behaviors on pages 79–81. She found some that worked in this situation even though they were not on the basic list she had already identified and put on her laminated card. That might happen for you as well, in any given situation. Jennifer picked "Say, 'I don't know,' when you don't," "Be honest," "Initiate a conversation," "Ask for something you want," "Risk embarrassment," and "Ask questions." The next day at work, she broached the subject of her responsibilities by saying to her boss, "I'm eager to do a great job for you and for the company. Could we schedule a time for me to ask some questions that I have about the job description you gave me?"

To her surprise, her boss said, "Of course! I have one hour available between three and four P.M. Does that work?"

Jennifer agreed and showed up right on time with a written list of questions in hand. After exchanging pleasantries about the weather and filling their coffee mugs, Jennifer and her boss settled down to a very productive interchange. He turned out to be a good teacher, obviously enjoying letting Jennifer in on his expertise.

"Thank you so much," Jennifer said when 4:00 P.M. rolled around. "I feel much more confident that I can do what's required here."

"You're most welcome," her boss said. "Frankly, until we started talking today I had no idea how many parts of the job are company specific. I just took it for granted you understood the jargon. You know, I should probably make up a list of terms and acronyms and give it to new people."

"What a great idea!" Jennifer said.

"I have you to thank for it," he said with a smile. "I hate to think of how many people have struggled to get the hang of things around here but were afraid to speak up and admit they needed help. Listen, if you ever have any more questions, feel free to let me know. It takes confidence and courage to ask for help. I admire that. Oh, by the way, we've got somebody in your department who's starting tomorrow. Would you mind taking him under your wing?"

When Jennifer made her success dependent upon her boss's behaviors, she had been unconsciously avoiding control over her career. By choosing to take back control through requesting mentorship, she was choosing to be fearless. Jennifer was promoted again within a year due to her proactive, go-getter attitude.

When was the last time you blamed someone for something? Did you think you had the "right" to blame? How did it feel justified? Did others agree with you? If you're like most people, several instances will come to mind. Perhaps your spouse did something that upset you. Maybe your best friend let you down. Maybe you are unsure if you blame. A good indication is if you use "If only . . ." in your vocabulary. But one thing is certain: In order to blame someone, you must have had an expectation that the person "should" have done something differently. Unfortunately, expectations will always leave you feeling out of control and on your Wheel of Fear. That's guaranteed. When you assume others can read your mind and know what you need, you are setting them up for future blame. In truth, no one else is responsible. You are the only one who is responsible.

Wishing, Waiting, and Hoping

After picking me up from the hospital and driving me home, Daniel's friend wished me luck and left. I turned the knob and opened the door. The scene stopped me cold. My apartment looked as if a burglar had ransacked every drawer, cabinet, and corner in search of hidden treasure. There was no rhyme or reason to the chaos. Cotton balls were in the candy dish. Flour and cocoa powder were spread on every countertop and table. Ants marched from the doorway to the kitchen garbage can. All of my emergency medical supplies were laid out as if I had been about to perform surgery in the foyer. The gravity of the situation hit home. I had lost control. I was afraid I had become my father. I forced myself not to think about that.

Left having to clean up my own mess, I was heartbroken. If Daniel hadn't cleaned up after me, it meant he really didn't care. I felt deserted and betrayed. Couldn't he have at least spared me walking into this? I was dying inside to be seen as special, something extraordinary, and this scene was telling me I was anything but.

As I stood in my ravaged apartment, I realized that something was very wrong. Thoughts of how worthless I was haunted me. Depression consumed me. Unable to function, I called a friend whose parents took me in. I lay in their guest bed for three solid months, all the while hoping Daniel would call to make up. I had expected him to love me forever even if I acted unloving. I had expected him to save me even if I couldn't save myself. I had expected love to last even though I didn't know what love was. I cried out: "What is wrong with me? Why wasn't it my turn?" Secretly, I was afraid it would never be my turn for happiness. My mom had never got hers. Why should I?

I had become a prisoner of the wishing, waiting, hoping trio of expectations. Wishing, the first stage of this mechanism for avoiding reality, involves immature and magical thinking reminiscent of a child blowing out candles on a birthday cake and really believing that the silent request will come true. Waiting, the second stage, is when you sit back and assume that your desires will be fulfilled even if you do absolutely nothing to make that happen. Hoping, the final stage, is a desperate, aching kind of inner pleading that kicks in when you have to admit to yourself that time is slipping by and your wish isn't getting any results. And while you hope, you just keep on waiting.

Even after all that happened with Daniel, I kept a fierce hope alive that we would reconcile. Those three months I lay in bed weren't spent being proactive. Believe me. They were spent hoping that Daniel would call. Every time the phone rang, I would jump. Every time there was a knock on the door, I would hurriedly fix my hair, just in case. Of course Daniel didn't call or visit, but that didn't stop me from waiting for him to come to his senses. I told myself that I would wait as long as it took for him to remember that he loved me. I was a classic victim.

FEARBUSTER EXERCISE

- In what areas of your life are you still wishing, waiting, and hoping?

- Choose one main area where you have been on hold, expecting things to change magically.

- Brainstorm how you can turn things around. Fearbuster Team members are great brainstorming buddies.

- Name three actions that you are willing to take that would enable you to move forward. Be sure to refer back to your proactive and self-affirming behavior lists. Maybe the actions are as simple as writing a note to someone or making a phone call. Remember, it's better to start somewhere. If doing so makes you feel uncomfortable, get some support.

- List the benefits of taking those actions.

- Choose one action that you will take *within the next twenty-four hours* and do it.

No Guarantees

I was expecting to get my turn at love. I wasn't facing the fact that the world does not owe us anything. That is contrary to all of the happy-ending scenarios we grew up believing in. You are especially vulnerable to resisting the reality that there are no guarantees if you have a secret desire to be seen as special or extraordinary. In my seminars, this concept is one that elicits the most startling breakthroughs. Many people are dying to be plucked out of their pain by a secret admirer who sees their worth and value. That applies to relationships as well as careers. The truth is we are unique as we embrace our essential nature and express our wholeness on our Wheel of Freedom. Yet, for some of us, the overwhelming desire to be seen as extraordinary actually separates us from the love we crave and keeps us from doing the work necessary to be free. Whenever we want to be seen as extraordinary, we want special treatment. We are putting ourselves above others. We believe we deserve something extra and we definitely feel entitled.

❋ FEARBUSTER EXERCISE ❋

Have you ever had thoughts like:

> I am entitled to more money because I have devoted my life to this job.
> I deserve love in my life because I give so much to others.
> I have earned success because I work hard on myself.
> After all I have been through, life should be easier by now. Haven't I paid my dues yet?

Did those thoughts resonate with you? What else came to mind when you read them? Did you recognize any of the prevailing beliefs your parents or grandparents had? I've had clients tell me that when they focus on this exercise, they can practically hear the voices of the past echoing the fears handed down generation to generation.

When we believe we have earned, deserve, or are entitled to things, we are in for a letdown if life doesn't go our way. Entitlement is a seductive expectation. It feels as if what we desire should be true. If it weren't, that would mean that life (or God) isn't fair. When was the last time you felt entitled? Usually people who feel entitled are waiting for life to come to them. They want success to happen to them to prove that they are a gifted, extraordinary talent. Otherwise, they would just be like everyone else. Most of us fantasize that someone will notice our specialness just the way actress Lana Turner was discovered by an agent while she was sipping a malt in Schwab's Drugstore. And if something like that doesn't happen, we become disillusioned. Our own expectations set us up for the fall.

To make matters more complicated, we protect what we expect. Chances are, you will stand up for your expectations, defend and fight for them. Even when this means losing, expectations usually tell us it is better to be "right" than to change our minds. Expectations move you, motivate you, and too often destroy you. They set you up for failure even when you think you are doing everything "right." The more expectations you have, the more disappointment is assured. Expectations keep your Wheel of Fear in motion.

Eliminating Expectations

Simply put, you cannot live fearlessly if you continue to count on things turning out just the way you expect them to turn out. If you attempt to take a risk—a new job, a new relationship, a new way of doing something—with only one acceptable result, you're going to be crushed if things don't pan out the way you expected. Not only that, but you won't be open to serendipity. If you're determined to be the dictator of your own story, you'll miss the thrill of chance meetings, the breathtaking excitement of unanticipated plot twists, the rush of joy that comes with pleasant surprises. Worse, when there are nasty surprises—and there almost always are, as anyone over the age of ten has surely noticed—you'll beat a quick retreat, justifying your backtracking by saying to yourself, "See? I should never have taken a risk. It's scary out there. You never know what's going to happen."

No, you don't. And that's true even if you squander a lifetime trying to stay safe. You might as well give up the notion that you can foresee the future. Until you eliminate expectations, you'll still be on your Wheel of Fear, not your Wheel of Freedom. Yet because expectations are so accepted and feel so safe and justified, learning not to rely on them takes great strength. I understand all too well. When I broke the mirror in the bar, I did it not only because I had expected Daniel to be there for me forever, but because I felt entitled to his love after I had moved a thousand miles to be with him. When I thought about taking my own life, I was overreacting because I didn't want to be seen as a liar. When I got out of the hospital, I blamed Daniel for not taking care of me so I wouldn't have to face my fear of unworthiness. Secretly, I was afraid my father was right: I just wasn't worth loving. My Wheel of Fear had me convinced that the more I acted out, the more I needed to be taken care of. Therefore, Daniel would have to take care of me, I reasoned.

Yet leaving me with my mess was the best thing that Daniel could have done for me. It didn't feel good, but his refusal to make my problems his problems eventually left me with no choice but to own them once and for all. I had to take responsibility for my life. I was forced to see how my expectations could never be met. It wasn't anyone else's job to make me happy. It was now up to me. Was I going to keep being a victim or be accountable for the mess called my life?

Finally I came to see that Daniel hadn't lied to me. Neither had the therapist. In the past, if I could accuse someone of lying, I was off the hook. That was me reacting out of fear. It's true that Daniel had told me he would always love me, but was it all his fault that we didn't work out? No one can deliver one hundred percent of the time. It just doesn't happen. Basing your life on the promises of others puts you in the victim position. You are then expecting others to put your needs, desires, and wants before their own, even if circumstances change. People are usually telling the truth, yet many times someone can make a promise based on a situation in the present moment, and then circumstances change and the promise cannot be kept.

Daniel got tired of being held up to my impossible-to-meet expectations. I was tired of forcing myself to be perfect. Daniel was tired of keeping promises that no longer rang true for him just because they had at one time. We were reacting from our fear. Both of us were pointing to our expectations as if they proved we were right. Daniel broke up with me the best way he knew how. True, doing it in front of others may have seemed callous, but I imagine he thought that I would be less likely to lose it in public. Yet I broke down nonetheless because I had expected him never to leave me. My Wheel of Fear produced the expectation that kept getting in the way of us finding the love we were both looking for.

Does this mean we drop our obligations? No, but many of us stay in situations or relationships we are unhappy in just because we once thought that's where we needed to be. Expectations limit our focus and lead to condemnation, judgment, frustration, and disappointment. Expectations separate us from our truth and the love that could heal us.

✻ FEARBUSTER EXERCISE ✻

Remember that your journey toward Fearless Living is a process. Although the changes start immediately, it will take time to release all of your expectations. Let's begin breaking the hold expectations have on you.

Review daily the words of expectation on pages 144–145. Notice which ones continue to be signposts for identifying your Wheel of Fear.

Now it is time to name all of your unfulfilled expectations. I want you to list anyone and everything that comes to mind, no matter how petty or ridiculous it may seem. Write until you cannot think of anything else.

To get you started, begin by filling in the blanks:

My parents expected me to _____.

My siblings thought I should _____.

My teachers believed _____.

My grandparents wanted _____.

My boss thinks I am supposed to _____.

My spouse needs me to _____.

My friends expect me to _____.

My children always want _____.

I expect myself to _____.

I think I should be more _____.

In my career I should _____.

I should treat my body _____.

I have never finished _____.

I have worked hard and deserve _____.

People think I am _____.

During the holidays, my role is _____.

I am indebted to my community because _____.

I want my friends to _____.

Why can't my spouse _____?

_____ owes me a favor.

I deserve _____.

I feel guilty because I didn't _____.

The reason I am tired is _____.

When I _____ I will finally be happy.

If only that would happen I could _____.

If I were a good person, I would _____.

My greatest disappointment is _____.

My church thinks I should _____.

God expects me to _____.

Turning Expectations into Intentions

Once you have identified your expectations, there is a much greater possibility of attaining freedom. I'm going to teach you how to do that by reframing your expectations as something I call "intentions." Expectations are what you think ought to happen as a result of what you do, say, or plan. For example, "I expect to get a raise and a promotion if I buckle down, work really hard, and bring in new business for the company." On the other hand, intentions are your approach to life based on your essential nature and your wholeness. For example, "I intend to acknowledge my talent for creating persuasive sales presentations and to enjoy the day-to-day process of putting that into practice on the job." What's so wonderful is that when you act out of intention instead of expectation, you are more likely to experience positive outcomes such as a raise and a promotion. Working doggedly with grim determination solely because you want a certain result isn't nearly as productive and powerful as working because you take pride and pleasure in what you do.

Similarly, when you approach your relationships with intention instead of expectation, you expand the possibility for mutual delight and support. Expectation made Wayne—the client who came to me thinking he wanted a divorce from Lynn—say, "I expect Lynn to play the role of wife exactly the way my mother did." Intention allowed him to say, "I intend to make a priority of focusing on my sense of purpose in life. I also intend to allow the confidence that comes from that focus to guide me while Lynn and I discover ways to redefine the roles of husband and wife to suit ourselves and our partnership."

Intention is living purposefully. On purpose, with purpose. Proactively, responsibly, and intuitively. When we intend, we erase "should" from our vocabulary. There is a commitment to the process versus the results. Rather than the little details of life dictating your every decision, choices are aligned with your essential nature. When intention is our mode of operation, we give up the idea that our past dictates our future. Intention is living in the present, actively choosing the future while being aware that in each moment your state of mind is up to you. Your mood no longer becomes dependent on how other people treat you or their opinion of you. Judgment of a situation or how another person "should" be, and, in fact, how you "should" be, ceases to exist. You learn how to accept what's really going on and how to handle it. In the same way that your Wheel of Fear uses expectation as its grease to keep you spinning out of control, your Wheel of Freedom uses intention to keep you focused on your commitments. Intention is the pathway to shift your focus from fear to freedom.

 FEARBUSTER EXERCISE

- To keep yourself on purpose through intention, keep track of the proactive behaviors you are choosing to help you move onto your Wheel of Freedom. Write down a minimum of three per day and build up to five.

- Make a note of your Wheel of Freedom's life-affirming actions that are appearing in your life on a daily basis. Again, write down at least three and build up to five.

Don't be discouraged if in the beginning you take the proactive behaviors and notice the life-affirming actions fewer than three times a week. One is better than none. Two is better than one. You get it. So whenever you notice them, write them down. The point is to build your awareness so you can choose with intention.

A Clean Breakup

Seventeen years after Daniel ended our relationship, I was faced with having another man leave me. This time it was Carl, my husband of seven years. It was once again January. As we sat in the therapist's office attempting to reconcile, it became painfully clear to me that despite the words my husband was saying, he was no longer in love with me the way he had once been. He wanted out. I wanted to ignore that uninvited insight, so I frantically began to search for evidence to the contrary. I mean, he was telling the therapist he didn't want to get divorced. And, he was promising to work on our marriage. His holding my hand while I cried surely meant he loved me. I thought about my expectations of what a marriage should be: a bond forever.

I meant those words. I am sure he did too. I told myself that I would calmly explain to Carl that this was not what I expected and of course he would wake up and realize how wrong he was. I would just appeal to his sense of reason and then surely he would try harder. Even though I am a coach who understands intellectually that this method won't work, I wanted to believe more than anything that it would. I'm human, after all. But

Carl's behavior over the previous few months was hard to brush aside. After we left the therapist's office, I knew I had to face the fact that another man I loved was walking out the door. Once again, I felt worthless.

My Wheel of Fear was the reason I thought the end of our relationship was all my fault. This time I made a conscious decision not to believe that. Through developing the Fearless Living program, I had learned it was not about finding anyone to blame for my feelings of unworthiness, and that included myself. I carried those feelings around whether my husband stayed or left. My sense of worthlessness and my fear of being a loser were mine and mine alone.

I'm not saying that getting off my Wheel of Fear was easy. A divorce is a huge and shattering event in anyone's life, and mine was no exception. I had the urge to gather evidence that Carl was wrong and I was right. I thought about reconnecting with my old Complaining Buddies and convincing them that Carl had made a mistake. But I knew better than to give in to my fear. That's not how I wanted my relationship to end. This time I was not going to be run by my fear-based, unconscious expectations. I was not going to deny what was happening between us. I was not going to put my head in the sand as I had tried to do with Daniel. I was not going to punish Carl or myself for our present situation. There were no temper tantrums. No hate-filled words. No manipulation or guilt. Just a deep sense of loss. And, yes, my heart was broken. Yet the rage and denial that had characterized my breakup with Daniel were absent. This time around there was only overwhelming sadness.

It was time to grieve the ending of a marriage. It was clear I was not going to handle this separation the same way I had handled my breakup with Daniel. With Daniel, I was living in expectation. And expectations make our Wheel of Fear turn around and around. Our complaints, excuses, and the way we beat ourselves up all stem from expectations. This time around, I would live with intention.

The Freedom in Accountability

When living in intention, accountability is paramount. Our life is in our hands. No one else's. My life was not Daniel's, Carl's, or my father's responsibility. It was no one's but mine. Sometimes that is a hard truth to accept. It is so much easier to blame, yet that is a symptom of expectation. And trust me, there were days I prayed that there was another woman just so I could point my finger at Carl and have a sufficient reason to make his life miserable in retaliation for my present pain, but to no avail. We have learned that blaming another is just frittering our time, energy, and creativity away. This leads to regret and resentment, which leads to losing our power, our choice, and our courage to shine. Remember, if fear is deciding how you are going to react, and expectations are in control, then you aren't living your life anyway.

On that January afternoon, facing the man I had vowed to love forever, I realized that my future happiness would be determined by my intentions. Just because we weren't going to be together didn't mean I had to regret having married him in the first place. Those seven years were instrumental in my own personal transformation. Plus we weren't divorcing because we hated each other. (Hate is always a cover for fear.) Carl was leaving because somewhere along the way our paths had gone in two different directions. Who knows for sure how it had happened, but it had, and I was now ready to face the hurt, anguish, and disappointment that seemed, at times, unbearable. Not go around them or to the side of them but straight through the heart of my feelings. I knew if I wasn't willing to feel the pain of my divorce as I was experiencing it, that pain would lodge inside my heart and make an appearance anytime I tried to love again. It would become an unconscious reaction to intimacy. In fact my present pain was doing just that by calling up my past fears that had never been healed. That was not okay with me. I wanted to fulfill my potential. I wanted to love again. I wanted to be free.

To recover from my divorce, as well as the old negative feelings that were swelling up within me, I also had to accept the situation for what it was rather than what I hoped it would be. When Carl left, all my fears of being a loser and feelings of worthlessness descended upon me. I knew it was up to me to accept that those were just feelings and not facts, in order to embrace, honor, and release my attachment to them. I knew I could no longer try to avoid feeling worthless. I needed to accept that it was just how I felt, not who I was. The miracle is that when we allow ourselves to have negative feelings (but not act on them), they run their course naturally, eventually becoming powerless when we embrace them and choose to heal them by taking actions that are proactive and self-affirming. Therefore, we learn when we deny our feelings, we are pushing ourselves farther away from our essential nature.

I had to be willing to feel the very feelings I had been running away from when Daniel left me, when my father abandoned me, and all the times I had deserted myself through alcohol and my suicide attempts. If you allow yourself to feel and accept your feelings, you will stop the self-judgment the Wheel of Fear needs in order to keep spinning. Otherwise, all we are doing is running away from ourselves, and the feelings that make us human.

During my divorce, I cried, laughed, hurt, cried some more, and vented—a lot. I asked for help and love. I accepted my feelings and experienced them. One after another they would come up. Depression. Rejection. Stupidity. Resentment. Abandonment. I was willing to feel them all. But more important, I was keenly aware that they had no power over me unless I let myself believe those feelings added up to me. When my feeling of worthlessness came up, instead of sighing, "Oh, no, not again," I would say to myself, "Well, I am obviously in a new situation. Good ol' worthlessness is back." As I moved through the painful proceedings of my divorce I would feel it again, yet I would resolve to take actions based on my Wheel of Freedom, my essential nature. I knew that was the way for me to reach self-acceptance. No matter what, I kept my eye on my commitments and lived with intention.

Intentions Make You One of a Kind

People who live on purpose with purpose are not interested in standing out in the crowd. That may happen, but it is not why they do what they do. When you live with intention, your primary focus is the process rather than the end result. Expectation-driven people go for the goal no matter what. No matter how frustrating it gets or how out of sync with their Wheel of Freedom. The achievement of the goal becomes the priority because they think that determines their value and worth.

The same is true for people who attempt to be extraordinary. Remember my sister Linda, the math teacher who dreamt of working for NASA? Her expectations got in her way. She became frustrated and figured she would never contribute anything to changing the world, so what was the point of teaching full time? She had plenty of evidence to prove her point. We have all heard the stories of how brutal the classroom environment is and how meager the pay is. So she decorated her house and bought some fish. Then a school called that had an emergency. Could she substitute-teach a high-school math class for two months? They were desperate. Well, she reasoned, she could use the money. She started to teach. And that is when everything changed. All of a sudden, instead of waiting for something big to happen where she could help change the world, she began to embrace the work right in front of her. Linda is a gifted math teacher with an amazing ability to help the tough students learn with ease. An ordinary job, yet she realized her ordinary job was exactly what made her feel special. She contributed without thought of return. Instead, her reward was seeing a child understand a concept that had been Greek to him just the day before. As my sister Linda claimed her ordinariness, she stepped out of her fear and began to contribute in an extraordinary way. She was in intention.

What happened to Linda is what happens when you are willing to own the power of ordinary. Yes, I said ordinary. Because we all share many of the same qualities, we are at some level ordinary. It is our ability to be ourselves that allows our uniqueness to shine. To live with intention and be ourselves, we must be ordinary. I know that is the only way I have achieved what I have. Before I owned ordinary, I kept success at bay judging what it should look like and where it would come from. Nothing was good enough or perfect enough. And I didn't want to do the menial labor necessary to succeed. It is that same attitude of wanting to be extraordinary that keeps someone from working at a fast food restaurant when they desperately need the money. They would rather starve than work at something that they think is beneath them. But that's the point; no job is better than any other. It is only in your mind. I waitressed for over fifteen years and, let me tell you, that job taught me everything about running my own business. It was anything but beneath me. It gave me the skills I needed to operate a thriving enterprise and the confidence to speak in front of a crowd. Break your addiction to extraordinary and get in touch with the power of being ordinary.

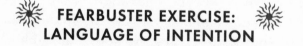

🎇 FEARBUSTER EXERCISE: 🎇 LANGUAGE OF INTENTION

The language we use affects how we are perceived in the world. It advertises what we think and believe. When we live in expectation, we discover that the language we use disempowers us. On the other hand, when we live in intention, the words we speak empower us and the world at large. Our vocabulary determines whether we accept ourselves, believe in who we are, and walk our talk. It is the accumulation of our conscious and unconscious thoughts.

The following are some of the words of intention I would like you to incorporate into your vocabulary on a regular basis replacing the fear-based words of expectation. See how often you empower yourself. Also notice which words are constants within your Fearbuster Team.

- Eliminate as many "supposed to's" "should's" and "need to's" from your vocabulary as possible. They limit your thinking, taking away personal responsibility. Replace them with the words of intention and accountability "I choose," "I want," and "I decide."

- Cut down your usage of "but." Often we express a feeling or thought and then follow it with "but." I am sure we have all heard the saying that "but eliminates the statement before it." An example is "I love you, but . . ." We all know what that "but" means. Replace it with "and" and "yet." Those are the inclusive words of intention.

- Instead of talking about the fear-based future or past, which is where comparing and competition lives, as often as possible only speak about the freedom-centered present. Also actions only happen in the present. The present moment is where life happens.

- Refuse to be outer focused. That means your life is decided by reactions to the outside world versus inner focused where intuition and intention are the guiding forces determining your future. Using the words "they think" or "they say" puts the power into the hands of individuals outside of your control. Instead say what do "I think."

- Give up saying "I can't." Those two words are straight from your Wheel of Fear. Substitute "I can" or "I could" or "I will," which gives you freedom to believe in limitless outcomes.

- Speak about commitments when you are making a decision. Intention uses your essential nature and quality of wholeness as the foundation of any commitment. Without commitment, emotional boundaries are impossible, yes and no have little power, and integrity is elusive. "I am committed to . . ." lets your intention be known.

- No more "what's wrong?" Instead ask "where is the opportunity in this situation?" This allows for creative brainstorming. It also teaches you how to reframe the way you look at the world from a negative fear-based viewpoint to a positive, proactive, powerful one.

- "Difficult," "hard," or "problem" are words that immediately make the situation appear to be too exhausting, too overwhelming, and impossible to overcome. Instead replace those words with "challenging" or "challenge." Challenges allow the opportunity of solution, inspiration, and guidance. It is easier to confront a "challenge" head on than a "problem."

- No more "impossible." We only have our limited fear-based filtering system in place if "impossible" is our word of choice. Yet we have all heard of miracles occurring in regard to health challenges or money situations, and that is where intention comes into play. "Possible" opens up our minds to seeing things differently, and that is where opportunity lies.

Changing your language will set your intention firmly in place. And that will alter your filtering system from one based in fear to one that thrives in freedom. False perceptions are eliminated and truth and integrity fuel your intentions.

Fearless Intention

When I got divorced, I made a choice. I didn't want to handle rejection as I had previously with Daniel. Rather I wanted to take conscious actions and love my way through it. Remember, when we get into a jam or take a risk outside our comfort zone, the Wheel of Fear comes up automatically. It exists to keep you safe, so it will do what is necessary to alert you to any dangers coming your way. When you live within your Wheel of Freedom, the Wheel of Fear will come up when you risk, but the difference will be it will no longer throw you into anxiety, worry, and doubt. It will be recognized for what it is: fear. It will have no power. You will be able to see it for the higher purpose of fear, a sign that you are growing, risking, and changing. Carl and I are friends, and that is due to our commitment to honor our marriage by ending it with intention. It is good to know love is what is real between two people rather than our backlog of excuses and regrets.

So what does a day in intention look like? Your best friend forgets your birthday. You love her anyway. The package you needed for your presentation does not arrive. You work around it. You lose your car keys and instead of wasting energy beating yourself up, you call the car dealership and have another set made. All of this may sound simple, but how often do mishaps and disappointments like these ruin your day? Without expectations, anger, resentment, frustration, and jealousy cannot thrive.

Living in intention through acceptance, responsibility, proactive choice, and the willingness to be ordinary, will move fear aside and allow intuition to surface. All of those skills teach us to be inner focused and aware of who we are becoming. That is powerful. That changes lives.

There are no guarantees when living in intention except one. Intention gives you the gift of being centered in your self, being able to pick yourself up no matter what. It's relying on the qualities of being that you have claimed as your own through your understanding of the Wheel of Freedom. With intention, love still may not last forever, but you now see that when you move out of judgment, there seems to be more love around you than you had previously thought. Success is no longer a byproduct of what you do, but rather it is determined by who you are.

✳ FEARBUSTER EXERCISE ✳

So how do you stay aware of your intentions? Having an Intention Statement is helpful and can be added to your laminated card for ease of use. As we have discovered, intention is the operating system of your Wheel of Freedom. It puts your essential nature and quality of wholeness in the forefront of your mind and actions.

Your Intention Statement is similar to a vision statement, yet the foundation is not in your personal commitments to your career or family life. Rather it answers the question of "how" you will walk through life. Using your Wheel of Freedom as the base, your Intention Statement is simple and easy to remember. Just fill in the blanks.

I am committed to living my life using (your essential nature page 77) _____ as the foundation for my decisions and my success criteria. I am committed to expressing (your essential nature) _____ more and more each day. In doing so, I am expanding my ability to accept and express (your quality of wholeness page 77) _____ in my life. When I am true to myself, others are given permission to do the same. When I live from my Wheel of Freedom, I am free to fulfill my potential and live fearlessly.

Speak and read your Intention Statement daily and be sure to list it among your proactive behaviors. Carry it with you and repeat as often as necessary. Other good ways to claim it as your own is to use it as the statement for your screen saver, or to write your Intention Statement down and place it somewhere that is convenient and easy to see—perhaps on the bathroom mirror, or in a frame on your desk, or inside the cover of your day planner. Your Intention Statement is here to remind you what is important when fear comes to visit. It centers you back to the truth of who you are, giving you permission to stand for yourself and express your brilliance.

You have learned how to live with intention, a powerful proactive path that is centered in your Wheel of Freedom. Now, let's keep breaking the hold your Wheel of Fear has over you. In the chapter that follows, you'll find out how to stop letting fears from the past dictate your future.

No Excuses

Kara came to me, as so many people do, saying that there was nothing ostensibly wrong with her life. By society's terms, Kara was successful. "I'm my own boss because I own a Mail Boxes Etc. franchise," she said. "I make fantastic money. My oldest, Mickey, is the assistant manager. He's going to college part time in business administration. The younger kids, the two girls, are still in high school, but they work in the store summers and holidays. Susan wants to be a physical therapist and Shannon is looking at getting into an Ivy League college and then going to med school.

"People envy us. I know that. We don't answer to anybody, we have the means to live the good life, and we all essentially get along. But when I heard you speak at that conference, and you were talking about being fearless and expressing your essential nature, I felt like you were talking to me. Nothing is really wrong, but I got a feeling that something is not quite right. But I don't even know what it is."

Clearly, the persona Kara presented to the world was that of a quintessential hard worker and a model mom. I suspected that underneath that persona was a woman who was afraid and had an excuse for why she wasn't being true to a hidden dream. We talked for a while, and eventually she said, "I'm really glad Shannon wants to go to med school. That was my original goal. I was the big star in downhill snow skiing in high school and all the scouts from the top colleges wanted to give me scholarships. I planned on making a name for myself and turning pro. But during a practice run, I blew out my knee. I mean, the whole megillah—the anterior cruciate ligament, the medial collateral, the meniscus, everything. Nowadays, they have arthroscopic reconstruction options available. Back then they used to cut you open and kind of patch you up. But you were never the same after that.

"I came from a big family, eight kids, and there was no way my parents could pay for college, let alone med school. I had good grades, but I wasn't scholarship material without skiing. So I figured it wasn't meant to be. Sure, I was bummed. And not just about missing out on the scholarship. I hated being permanently sidelined. I loved the sport. I felt like something in me had died.

"I tried to talk to my mom about how I felt, but all she said was, 'There are a lot of people worse off than you are. There are quadriplegics.' And my father was just not a talker. He worked hard and I know he loved us, but he didn't think a man should show his feelings. He caught me crying once after the surgery and just the look he gave me shut me up fast. Then there was my older brother. He had these subtle ways of making me feel I got what I deserved. I had always been the one with the athletic ability. So I felt like I was being punished.

"Anyway, I lowered my sights. I worked my way through a community college for two years and got my A.A. degree. I met my ex-husband in one of my business administration classes and we hit it off right away. We divorced when our youngest was just three. It was tough raising my kids as a single mom, but that is the way it goes. I have tried to date, but it seems too hard with the kids and everything. Anyway, I don't have a bad life. And it's probably way too late at forty-seven to change anything now. I've toyed with the idea of going back to school and studying something in the medical field, but who has the time? The store keeps me hopping. And I need to build my client base even more, so that the kids can go to college. Besides, I am the only one I can count on to take care of myself after the kids are gone, so I am saving for my retirement.

"But you know, it's funny. I'm not really looking forward to retirement. The knee has kept me from being very active—I have felt out of shape for years—and it is tough to ski anymore. I've got joint mice, these little random pieces of cartilage that have formed, so I'm in a certain amount of pain all the time. I would love to travel to Europe when I retire. But there's no way I could walk all over Paris and Rome.

"I have so much to be grateful for that I feel guilty wanting more. But I guess I'll never stop wondering what the script would have been if I hadn't lost control on that mountain and fell just the wrong way. I have always had a secret fear that the real Kara got derailed that day and I've just been making do."

Letting the Past Predict the Future

Kara's excuse for not being true to her essential nature was not a figment of her imagination. She really had suffered a serious knee injury. That really had created some limitations. It really had affected her ability to make certain choices. The vast majority of excuses are like that, which is precisely why they are such potent forces for keeping you from moving forward. You may point to the fact that your father was a raging alcoholic, or that you grew up in poverty, or that you are dyslexic, or that you never got the training that could have made you a concert violinist, or that you were an army brat who never got a chance to make any friends. I could (and in fact, I used to) point to the fact that I was orphaned at fourteen after having witnessed my parents' murder-suicide. Whatever the excuse is, it did actually occur. In that sense, it is true. But the problem is that it is only true in regard to the way it shaped your life *in the past*.

The only thing keeping you from getting beyond your excuse is that your Wheel of Fear has you believing that some version of whatever happened in the past will happen again. This takes away any sense of personal responsibility, accountability, or power. Excuses also give you permission to ignore your own values, beliefs, and commitments, thereby setting aside any sense of personal integrity. You probably don't articulate the fear in that way, but that's what's going on. For me, my excuse was that I had failed to save my mother, and my fear that I was worthless convinced me I would fail again. I was sure of it. That was my excuse for not risking. I was the queen of surviving, but then I had a ton of evidence to back up my really good excuse for not thriving, and nobody had the courage, awareness, or permission to call me on it. I didn't have a Fearbuster Team. I had successfully kept everyone at bay. And I was positive I was not responsible for the way my life was turning out.

In Kara's case, the fear was that if she went after a dream, something would happen—just like before—that would make sure her dream wouldn't come true. The lesson she had internalized from the injury that took away her chances for med school and the pleasure of skiing was that it is risky to have big dreams and that it hurts almost unbearably when something beyond your control puts an end to your dreams. From there, she concluded—albeit subconsciously—that she would only be disappointed if she took a risk. And it became a self-fulfilling prophecy. The Wheel of Fear was spinning.

Excuses excuse you from fulfilling your potential. Kara used her excuse as the reason for everything from her weight problem to her vague dissatisfaction with her life in general to her inability to find time for continuing ed courses to her difficulty imagining an enjoyable retirement. Excuses can stem from our unfulfilled expectations. Kara's Wheel of Fear compelled her to think, "Don't dream. Don't try to take charge. Don't go for anything. You might get hurt again. You might end up disappointed again. Better take the safe road. Just be satisfied with the status quo. It's not great, but it's better than risking pain."

The phenomenon Kara was experiencing is the same one that makes people afraid to look for love after they've been through a divorce. It's what makes people afraid to get back on a horse, literally or figuratively, after they have fallen off. Yet if we are to live fully, we must love as though we've never been hurt, dream as though our hopes have never been dashed, and take steps toward the future as though life has never given us pain.

Listen to the words of the playwright George Bernard Shaw: "People are always blaming their circumstances for what they are. I don't believe in circumstances. The people who get on in this world are the people who get up and look for the circumstances they want, and, if they can't find them, make them." Yes. No excuses. Authentic transformation comes from accepting wherever you are in life and going on from there. As the great choreographer Agnes DeMille once said to a group of aspiring dancers who were bemoaning their physical limitations, "Dance in the body you have." And I say, live in the life you have. Wasting it with excuses and regrets amounts to rejecting your essential nature. And that is the worst crime of all.

The Badge of Honor

Of course, plenty of people have more than one excuse for why they are afraid to go forward. I know I did. I was right there with all the others who kept repeating the refrain "If only . . ." We continue to collect regrets as we go along, as though that gives us the right to adopt an overly cautious and therefore limited approach to life. If only I had gone to Interlochen as a voice major the summer I was fourteen, I would say. If only someone in my family had stepped in as a mentor after my mother died. . . . If only I hadn't been raised in a tiny town in northern Michigan where opportunity is scarce. . . . If only I hadn't left the college I loved to follow a guy who dumped me. . . . If only I could have had a baby. . . . If only . . .

Sharing our regrets with someone who understands creates a powerful connection. This can be healing but it can be seductive as well. The last time you shared your regrets with someone, how did you feel afterward? Heavy, down, depressed, or light, up, joyful? The answer lets you know whether expressing your regrets is keeping fear at work or letting you break free from the past. Pay attention.

There is no denying that my life would have been different if some or all of my "if onlys" had occurred. Yet, would it have been a brighter or better life than I am living now? I will never know for sure, yet I believe the answer is that those things I wished for would have actually been detours, and in truth, I am exactly where I am supposed to be. Sure, I could regret lost love, missed opportunities, and wasted time. Yet, maybe love was not lost, maybe I didn't miss an opportunity, and maybe I didn't waste a minute of my life. Yes, there has been love in my life that didn't last, yet because of each of those relationships I have acquired the skills to love with greater depth than I ever dreamt was possible. Yes, it seems I missed opportunities, and maybe they weren't mine in the first place. Yes, I could point to seemingly wasted years, yet during that time I learned how to heal my pain, move beyond my fear, and love myself and others without regret. That gave me the courage to live a life that is mine and mine alone, and to make my contribution to the world.

In order to find that courage, I had to choose to give up what I call my "Badge of Honor." Most people have one. It is a figurative award we bestow on ourselves for all that we've endured. It is all the excuses for the way our life is or isn't. We are perversely proud of this badge, a kind of Purple Heart that we believe proves our valor in the face of life's inevitable difficulties. The badge tells the world we have been wounded in action. No wonder we're not doing better than we are. We compare war stories, verifying that it's dangerous out there and that we shouldn't take chances without a guarantee of success. We give each other permission to stay safe instead of being courageous enough to go onward. We understand each other. We nod sympathetically. This feels like friendship, but all we're doing is confirming one another's fears. And so that Badge of Honor is really a Badge of Fear in disguise. When I took responsibility for mine, I then had the power and the freedom to move beyond it. When I stopped repeating my litany of excuses, I started focusing on what I can do now instead of on what happened in the past. And that has made all the difference.

※ FEARBUSTER EXERCISE: FORGIVENESS ※

In order to move beyond your Badge of Fear, you must be willing to get past your past, let go of who you thought you were supposed to be, and forgive all that you believe has kept you down, including yourself. Each time we validate our Badge by using an excuse, we are announcing how we are attached to our fear as well as making clear what and who we need to forgive. When we have regrets, forgiveness is in order.

My former college roommate, Kathryn, asked me recently if I have truly forgiven my father for killing my mother and himself. I wanted to spit out my usual answer: "Yes, of course." Yet I hesitated. How do you answer that question when you finally admit that the answer is not black and white but shades of gray?

One thing I have observed in myself and others is that forgiveness is not a one-time-only event. It is a process. The first stage typically happens very soon after we are wounded by another person's behavior. At that point what feels like forgiveness is usually nothing but *denial*. Remember how I sang "Thank You" at my father's funeral? I had told myself that I had instantly forgiven him. Yet why, when I looked at him in the casket, didn't I shed a single tear? I had a great deal more healing to do, even though I wasn't conscious of that at the time. Denial is a fine temporary mechanism that helps us cope with the most unspeakable of assaults on our souls. But eventually we need to acknowledge it and then release it.

The next stage of forgiveness is most often *anger*. This is a self-absorbed feeling that allows us to use the event as an excuse. How could he have done this to me? Why did this happen to me? We feel like an innocent bystander who has caught the bullet from a drive-by shooting. Life isn't fair! People who stay stuck in this stage never truly forgive and they allow fear to rule their lives. If this horrible thing happened through no fault of my own, the bogus logic of fear goes, then I must not be a worthy person. In fact, maybe it was my fault after all. Self-pity, resentment, and blame are the most commonly expressed feelings of fear at this stage. And depression is most often anger internalized. This is when we may become convinced that we have been betrayed and scarred by the event.

The third stage of forgiveness can be extremely challenging. It is *acceptance*. The event happened. Life does not have a rewind button. You have to go on from here. Harboring anger only poisons you, not the other person. You cry. You vent, but you understand now that the person has power over you only if you allow yourself to focus on the feelings of the past. You stop searching for meaning and reasons. You stop blaming. You release the other person or group of people and ask for a healing. You accept the situation as is and move forward the best you can.

Finally, you will reach stage four of forgiveness, *compassion*. You are able to see the event from the other person's perspective. Now, so many years after the murder-suicide, I am able to see my parents for who they were: two scared people who couldn't get past their own insecurities and fears because they didn't have the skills to do that, but who desperately wanted to be loved. Not unlike most of the population. My father didn't know how to handle my mother's rejection so he killed my mother and himself for fear that living without her would be too painful. For him, death appeared to be the only alternative.

I have forgiven him for his false thinking and for his lack of self-acceptance. I have been able to reach this stage of forgiveness because I have accessed my essential nature and claimed my wholeness, thereby connecting to life around me.

I have forgiven my father, as well as my mother, in the sense that what happened no longer affects my daily life. I am able to share my story in my talks, tapes, and books. I have forgiven my father for loving my little sister best. I have forgiven him for putting his hands around my throat and squeezing. I have forgiven him for taking my mother away from me. I have forgiven him for leaving us with no money or caretakers. I have forgiven him for his selfish act because I now know he was scared. I have forgiven him.

That doesn't mean, however, that I'm "over it." The tragedy is an integral part of the fabric of my life. I can't will it away. And now, I wouldn't even want to. Forgiving my father doesn't mean relinquishing the tender and bittersweet moments when I long for my mother. When I became engaged years ago, I cried. It just didn't seem right that my mother wasn't there to help me pick out my wedding dress. When I got divorced, I cried again. Where was she when I was in so much pain? Have I forgiven my parents? Yes. But that doesn't mean I don't sometimes imagine their smiles and ache for their affection. It doesn't mean that I live in stage four all the time. In fact, the stages are interconnected and, depending on how I approach life, will determine where I am.

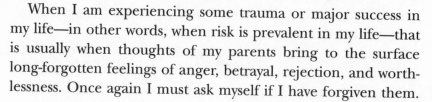 FEARBUSTER EXERCISE

When I am experiencing some trauma or major success in my life—in other words, when risk is prevalent in my life—that is usually when thoughts of my parents bring to the surface long-forgotten feelings of anger, betrayal, rejection, and worthlessness. Once again I must ask myself if I have forgiven them.

Instead of expecting myself to give a simple yes or no, I ask myself the following questions:

What did I want from the person, group of people, or situation that I didn't get?

How often do I think about this encounter? Monthly? Daily? Hourly?

When I think about this event, what negative feelings come up for me? What is the intensity of the emotion?

What satisfaction or benefit do I receive for not forgiving in this situation?

Am I willing to forgive the other people involved?

Am I willing to forgive myself for harboring judgment, ill will, or any other negative feeling against this person, group of people, or situation?

When I ask myself those questions, I can see how much my Wheel of Fear is in control and evaluate how my unwillingness to forgive steals my positive energy away. It brings to light whether I am holding myself accountable for any past hurts or still wasting time blaming them on someone else. It helps me find out if there is something to forgive. Myself? Another? The circumstances? I must remember that forgiveness doesn't mean I approve of the behavior that was or is being exhibited. Rather it is an opportunity to set myself free from the negative connection that binds me to something over which I most likely have no control. I am actively choosing to remove regret from the forefront and move into appreciation of what was or is. Forgiveness is not about condoning the behavior or situation. Forgiveness overcomes the past, allowing you to move on, break free, and live in the present. Forgiveness takes our regrets and excuses and transforms them into lessons learned and skills acquired to help us achieve self-mastery.

If I think about my excuses and they still bother me, more forgiveness work must be done. If I find myself contemplating clever answers and smart quips to defend my position, more forgiveness must be done. If I have a negative attitude regarding my excuses, then they are still affecting my behavior and more forgiveness work must be done.

Forgiveness is never for the other people involved or for the situation itself. It is always for you. Forgiveness allows you to accept, release, and make peace with the people and circumstances that perhaps have been keeping you up at night. It is a willingness to get over what you think should have happened and an acceptance of the reality of what actually happened. Yes. I have forgiven my parents. Yet more importantly, I have forgiven myself.

 ## FEARBUSTER EXERCISE: FORGIVENESS CONTRACT

When I teach my workshops, I ask my clients to use the following Forgiveness Contract. Repeating it daily helps you deepen your willingness and commitment to forgive yourself and others. Much of what holds the Wheel of Fear together is our lack of self-forgiveness and continued judgment of our thoughts and feelings. I urge you to have a Fearbuster Team member witness this agreement as you make it with yourself. This person can support you through the process as necessary. Forgiveness heals. Be open to the freedom that is released when you are willing to forgive.

I, (your name)_____, am willing to forgive myself.

I am willing to forgive any individual or group I believe has hurt, harmed, or betrayed me.

I forgive myself for all the times I let myself down or ignored my own needs, wants, and desires.

I forgive any judgments or unrealistic expectations I have made of myself or others.

I am willing to see the good in myself and others.

I am willing to restore my essential nature through forgiveness.
I am willing to claim my sense of wholeness as I forgive.
No longer do I waste precious time or energy staying stuck in
an unforgiving mindset.
Instead I am willing to forgive for my sake.
As I forgive my fear is dissolved.
As I forgive I am free.

Your Signature: _____

Witness: _____

Date: _____

When we finally see how excuses have been controlling our
life, that is not the time to berate ourselves for what we've been
doing. It is a time to celebrate and say yes to healing the pain of
regret. Now we can let go.

A Letting Go Ceremony

To take responsibility for my Badge of Honor (really, my
Badge of Fear) and at the same time release myself from its
grip, I performed a Letting Go Ceremony. This worked so well
for me that I'm going to share with you my experience and then
give you guidelines about how to create a similar experience for
yourself.

Over the course of several years, I began to face the power
my parents still had over me. They had been running my life
longer in death than they had when they were alive. I was stuck
in my Wheel of Fear, going around and around, continually
reliving my fear of worthlessness. I had never let go of my
dream of walking arm in arm with my mother on a Sunday afternoon . . . of the desire to understand what went on between my
parents . . . of the searing pain that I had been left with. On the
twentieth anniversary of my parents' deaths, I knew it was finally
time to let go.

Letting go was one of the most challenging things I have ever done. Because it was a risk, letting go brought up my fear of being worthless. I thought that if I let go, that would mean my parents' deaths had been in vain. If I let go, I would no longer wear the Badge of Honor (really, the Badge of Fear) that helped me avoid confronting my fears and living a full life. My biggest fear of letting go was that it would mean I would forget my parents. I interpreted letting go as a betrayal that would somehow make their lives meaningless.

If I refused to let go, then my attachment proved how much I loved them, right? Wasn't I willing to be miserable for my entire life to honor them? Wasn't I willing to sacrifice relationships so I could continue to live in blame and shame? Wasn't I willing to put my mother on a pedestal so I could make her the innocent victim? All of this kept me attached to them, and somewhere in my mind I thought that was what a loyal daughter did. For twenty years, I wouldn't let go.

Then, on that twentieth anniversary, I asked Marta to accompany me to a lake in the hills above Los Angeles. I wanted to be in a comforting surrounding. For me, that meant trees, water, and birds. I brought with me a copper pot, a white sage stick, paper, and a pen. I asked Marta just to be there with me to support me by witnessing the event. She stood behind me and slightly to the right as I began my Letting Go process.

First, I sat down and wrote a letter filled with the pain I had experienced for twenty years. Next, I cut some paper into dozens of little strips and wrote down the thoughts, feelings, and behaviors I wanted to release, one on each piece of paper. After that I wrote a love letter to my mother, and finally, a letter of love and forgiveness to my father. I told them about all the gifts I have received from them. I wrote until I could write no longer. Tears were streaming down my face for over an hour. Exhausted, I smiled. I knew I had put it all down on paper. I had left nothing out, nothing behind, nothing sacred.

I filled the copper pot with sand and placed the letters and strips of paper inside one by one, lighting each one on fire in turn while I spoke out loud the feelings in my heart. First came the letter of anger, hurt, and sadness. Then, I added all the thoughts, feelings, and behaviors I wanted to release. And last were the letters of love and forgiveness. I told my mother and father that it was time for me to let go and become who I was meant to be. I spoke with an inner conviction even though my voice was quavering. I told them who I was and what I had learned because of them, and in spite of them. As the letters burned, a deep stirring occurred within me, signaling some movement, some internal acceptance. Something was happening. I couldn't name it yet, but I knew. I was finally taking responsibility for my life. My letting go was what my parents had been wanting all along. They didn't want me to continue to suffer. They wanted me to live. They loved me. They didn't want me to live in fear.

I took the smoldering sage stick and swirled it around myself to symbolize that I was clearing away the past. I then fanned the letters with the sage, to symbolize that I was releasing any residuals of hurt and accepting the healing. As I looked upon the letters now turned to ashes, I suddenly knew I had to bury them in the earth. I grabbed a rock and dug a hole beside the lake, then carefully placed the ashes within. I covered them with some earth while affirming: "I forgive you. I forgive me. I am willing to let go. I accept love in my life." With the remains of the letters buried, I picked up my now empty copper pot and said good-bye. Good-bye to shame and guilt. Good-bye to blame and resentment. Good-bye to the Rhonda who had been afraid.

When I let go, I was letting go of my need to understand, have the answers, and be a martyr. Letting go meant I was willing to embrace the gifts my parents had given me while they were alive and even after their deaths, and was releasing all that no longer empowered me. Letting go meant I could no longer blame my father or my mother for the negative things that had happened to me. Letting go meant I had to be responsible for myself. Letting go meant I had to claim myself with all of my faults, imperfections, and pain as well as all my strengths, talents, and potential for joy. Letting go meant I was giving up my excuses. When I let go, I found me.

Emancipate Yourself from Your Excuses

You, too, can forgive, let go, and find you. Make a list of everyone who can still make you angry, frustrated, and resentful even though you haven't spoken to them in days, years, or decades. Even if they have already died. Also, if one of your main excuses is an event—such as Kara's knee injury—write down the people who handled the situation inappropriately for you. Kara, for example, wrote down her mother because she had told her to minimize her pain by comparing it to the pain of others. She also wrote down her father, for putting importance on keeping a stiff upper lip, and her brother, for believing that the injury served her right. She had difficulty at first giving herself permission to list her family because she felt it wasn't nice to own up to the fact that she blamed them. I reassured her that she would also have an opportunity to thank them for all the good things they had done. You will do the same, so don't leave out somebody simply because you've never before allowed yourself to admit that you have negative along with positive feelings about the person. And if you can, include your name on the list.

Pick one name from your list. You might choose the one that has the strongest hold on you. However, if you sense that might be too challenging, that's fine. Pick someone else. Where you begin doesn't matter. Your willingness to start is what counts.

Write two letters to your chosen person. The first one is about your hurt, rage, and pain. Put all of it down on paper. Don't be kind. Don't hold anything back. In the next letter, write down all the reasons you care for the person and all the lessons you learned from the person. Add, if you can, your desire to forgive the person. In between writing the letters, you may choose as I did to write on separate slips of paper the thoughts, feelings, and behaviors you want to release.

Writing those letters, those thoughts, those feelings, and those behaviors can be challenging because the process has a tendency to bring up old emotions you have hidden away. Uncovering them takes courage and willingness. But those are the very qualities you are seeking to incorporate into your life from now on. This is as good a time as any to start.

Next, find a safe place to burn the letters and slips of paper— perhaps in your fireplace or in a bowl filled with sand, or outside in an open area surrounded by sand or rock. If you are in a high-risk fire zone or don't feel comfortable burning the papers, tearing them up has the same effect.

Now, as you light them on fire or rip them up, speak your intention to let go even though you may not feel you are able or really doing it. State the person's name and say you are letting the person go. State your name and claim that you are releasing yourself from this situation.

If you want support, as I did, ask a trusted Fearbuster Team member to come with you. Ask that person to stand or sit with you, but not to interfere. He or she is there in case you need comfort or support. You determine that, not the other person. Boundaries must be spelled out before you begin. After I completed my process, I asked Marta to hug me. On the drive home I realized I needed to talk about what had just transpired. She gave me permission to share my feelings, which allowed me to process them, thereby owning the shift that was occurring within me.

When you have completed your Letting Go ceremony, be attuned to subtle changes. You may not experience a dramatic change. Just trust that the process is working whether you feel something small or something seismic or nothing at all. Kara, for example, told me that she felt peaceful when she burned the letters. Nothing more. But that in itself is a big leap forward from fear to freedom. And later, Kara used the memory of her Letting Go ceremony to trigger further changes. I use the memory to reinforce my changes whenever my Wheel of Fear threatens to take over again.

FEARBUSTER EXERCISE: YOUR LIFE LOG

Once you have let go of your excuses and the people involved in them, you are ready to take responsibility for your own life, fully and fearlessly. This is an exciting and, yes, a scary and challenging task. But this is where you will begin to see that fear can work for you instead of against you. We've established long ago that you won't eliminate fear. However, you can use that rush, that tingle of apprehension, to set yourself free. Psychologist Mihaly Csikszentmihalyi calls this "flow"—the perfect emotional equidistance between boredom and anxiety. And Maslow maintains that, precisely like a psychologically healthy child, you can grow if you "gratify basic needs for safety, belongingness, love, and respect, so that [you] can feel unthreatened, autonomous, interested, and spontaneous and thus dare to choose the unknown."

How can you accomplish that? The technique I have devised is what I call your Life Log. When you write down in black and white exactly what you do all day, you end up with a clear picture of whether you are frittering away your life on low-priority activities out of fear, or whether you are bold enough to use your time wisely and well in order to go where you were meant to go. The Life Log also lets you know whether you are consciously and proactively living by the values and principles that make up your essential nature or whether you are living in a constant state of emergency, simply reacting to whatever comes up. It holds you accountable. No more excuses. The way you spend your time defines your life. Look at your Life Log as if you were a stranger. What would you say about that person? Is family a priority? Work? What does the person value?

The Life Log also shows where your Wheel of Fear can trap you. What are the things you do during your day that sabotage your intentions? Excuses such as "I don't have enough time," "I don't have enough energy," and even "I don't have enough money" will be exposed for the shams that they are. With it spelled out in black and white, you will be empowered to improve your circumstances as you take responsibility for how you are spending your time.

Most of us don't really know how we spend our time. We think we do, yet most people fritter away minutes, hours, and even days simply finding ways to avoid their Wheels of Fear or trying to figure out how to live up to their expectations. Add to that the amount of time spent complaining, making excuses, and beating ourselves up, and it's a wonder we accomplish anything at all.

Debbie is one of the many Life Log success stories. She had a job with a telemarketing company and her personal goal was to make two hundred sales calls a week. When Debbie began to work the Fearless Living program, she scoffed at the Life Log. She swore she knew exactly how her time was spent. I told her to do it for one week and if she was on target she would no longer have to repeat the exercise. She took the challenge.

After the first week Debbie walked into my office with a long face. Her Life Log proved she was not living the life she had thought she was. Her phone calls totaled a little more than half of the goal she had set for herself. Debbie discovered the power of the Life Log. It captures all your fear-based efforts as well as actions generated by freedom. The hard truth was that Debbie would make her phone calls but after a particularly good or bad one, she thought she deserved a break. And that break would last as long as it took her to go around the office sharing the results of her latest call because she was afraid that if everyone didn't know what she had done, they would think she was lazy. The hours she spent on her Wheel of Fear kept her from fulfilling her potential and making her quarterly bonus. Once she recognized the pattern, she saw how talking about her calls was keeping her from performing up to her standards and reaching her goals. Now Debbie is happily making 350 calls a week and shattering all sales records.

In your Life Log, I want you to jot down what you're doing, every half hour. Maybe you, like Kara, Debbie, and many of my other clients, think you don't have time for that. My answer is that I have seen results with thousands of people, and I know you don't have time *not* to do this. By doing the Life Log, my clients actually find more time, usually anywhere from four to eight hours a week. Just think of what you could do with that amount of time. Kara did come around after a little stalling and started to keep her log. She couldn't be happier that she did. She has become a veritable emotional efficiency expert. She has made time to go to night school, where she is thrilled to be studying to become a medical technician. She has had surgery, which has vastly improved the functioning of her injured knee, and reduced the pain. She has asked a Support Buddy to become her "health partner," sticking with a regular walking program and switching to a sensible diet. Kara has trimmed down and has started to date. She says she feels younger than she has in years. And she has decided not to wait until retirement to travel. She is taking a three-week singles tour of Europe and leaving the kids in charge of the store.

Kara took back her life. You can too. Follow these simple rules for keeping your Life Log:

- First, write a list of what you believe are your commitments in order of priority. Put it aside.

- Then for one week, at each half-hour interval, write a quick explanation such as "Watching TV" or "Surfing the Web" or "Daydreaming" or "Sitting in the dentist's waiting room" or "Talking to my mother on the phone" or "Playing Candyland with the kids" or "Working on the Wilson account." This is for your eyes only, and part of the reason you're doing it is to learn to recognize when you're on your Wheel of Fear, so be brutally honest. If you ate a whole bag of potato chips after the boss yelled at you, write that down. If you slept most of the weekend after a demoralizing Friday night at a singles party, write that down. If you spent most of the morning schmoozing in the office break room instead of answering your e-mail, write that down.

- Warning: Keeping track of every half hour for the first week can be daunting. If you find that to be the case, start by keeping track of time you spend in the area you are currently focusing on. If you are working on career, be vigilant about how you spend your time while doing anything related to that. If your focus area is relationship, do the same thing. Then keep adding more and more areas until you are up to twenty-four hours, seven days a week.

- At the end of that first week, create categories such as career, relationship, parenting, extended family, self-nurturing, physical fitness, personal growth, recreation, spirituality, friendship. Make up any categories you need to describe your life. Put commuting time under the appropriate category such as "career" if you are on your way to the office or "physical fitness" if you're driving to the gym. If you are effectively doing two things at once—say, socializing at a party but also exchanging business cards—divide up the time into two categories.

- Next, add up how you spent your time in each category during the past week.

- Now get out your list of priorities and compare what you actually did with your time to what you feel is important. If your top priority is opening up the restaurant you've always dreamt of, but you didn't do anything to further that goal, take a look at your log and figure out how you could have behaved differently. Where in your busy life was there an hour that you could have spent researching the rent per square foot in the area of town where you'd most like to have your restaurant located? Where were there a few minutes when you could have calculated how much of your nest egg you could reasonably use as venture capital? Where was there a little downtime when you could have simply indulged in some creative thinking about the decor and the menu and the wine list of your dreams? If there was time, and you didn't use it to get closer to your goal, then fear was holding you back, not lack of time after all. If there was time, and you used it in a counterproductive way such as making an expensive impulse purchase that ate away at the resources you've been meaning to use to open up the restaurant, then fear was causing you to work against yourself. Remember, as long as you simply say you're yearning to open the restaurant but do nothing about it, you're safe. You can't fail. But, of course, you can't succeed either. And as long as you say you want to open a restaurant but you sabotage your efforts, you are guaranteed to fail.

The same goes for any area of your life. Did you spend time with the one you love because a top priority is strengthening your relationship? Or did you go to bed early rather than put the energy into communicating? Did you spend time with your children because one of your priorities is to be a more involved parent? Or did you park the kids in front of the TV while you did something you "had" to do like clean the bathroom? Did you put in a little extra time at the office because one of your priorities is to become more proficient at some new skills you just learned? Or did you knock off early because you're secretly afraid you'll never master those skills and you'd rather not try than to find out the truth about yourself? Did you take a morning walk because one of your priorities is to stay fit? Or did you "forget" to set the alarm for a little earlier than usual? Ask yourself questions such as those, and you'll see whether you are letting fear run your life.

- Pick one area of your life to work on. You may want to keep it the same as the one you chose in Chapter 1 or perhaps some other area seems more important to you now. Again, any area works.

- Commit to increasing your time in that particular area a minimum of five minutes a day. Your Wheel of Freedom proactive behaviors list is a good place to choose new actions to take in any area of your life. This small five minute shift integrates the new behaviors into your daily life, guaranteeing success. Most of us look at the list, pick five areas and want to change them all tomorrow. That's a surefire way to fail. We are setting ourselves up to be overwhelmed. Instead, I want to set you up to succeed, to win, to integrate the behaviors permanently. If you shift one area of your life for five minutes a day, the alterations will be felt throughout your entire life. When you take charge of five minutes day after day, you are building the skills to do that in any area of your life. You begin to count on yourself.

- Each week, increase your time by five minutes. If you choose to do more than five minutes, that is just a bonus.

- After you feel you are on solid ground in that one area, you can add a second area. When you feel masterful there, add another. Add only one area at a time. I want you to master, not manage.

- Keep your Life Log for a minimum of twelve weeks. Fear is not overcome without awareness, and the best way to account for your shifts is the Life Log. In this way, the Life Log becomes a written history. You will have a permanent record of how you have altered your life, five minutes at a time. When you look back over that, your confidence will rise. You will know you can count on yourself.

Living in fear is wasting your time and your life. If you are truthful with yourself, you'll see that there are enough hours in the day to live fearlessly. Fear gives you excuses to do this or take care of that before you can get on with the important things in life. Yet you'll never get to the important things if fear keeps you busy. So fill in your Life Log day by day and week by week and study it. Soon you will release your excuses, take back your time, and become responsible for the minute-to-minute decisions that determine your life and set you free.

When you have begun to do that, we are ready to examine the most common way fear shows up in your daily life.

8

No Complaining

Doug plunked himself down on the sofa in my office and let out a huge sigh. "I'm giving this a shot because my buddy Jason told me how great your program is, but I don't think it really applies to me," he said. "I mean, you call this 'Fearless Living,' but I'm not walking around afraid of anything. My only gripe is that all the good women are taken. I'm thirty-two years old and I feel like I missed the boat. I see somebody I'm attracted to and she's either got a ring on her finger or she tells me two sentences into the conversation that she has a boyfriend.

"Well, okay, maybe that's a little bit of an exaggeration. A lot of times I see somebody and I don't even bother to start a conversation. I just figure somebody that hot is already taken. Oh, sure, I could read the personals or get into chat rooms, but everybody knows that only losers do stuff like that. So that's my deal. Like I said, this fearless stuff probably can't help me find anybody decent for a relationship."

Doug might as well have been wearing a sandwich board with the slogan "I'm afraid I'm an outcast and can't bear to be rejected, so I can never get up the nerve to ask a woman out on a date." As I have told scores of clients and audiences, complaining advertises your fears. Doug had built enough evidence to keep his fears firmly in place and he used complaining to cover his core fear. That is how complaining keeps you spinning in your Wheel of Fear. And if you are complaining, then you are expecting things to be different than they are. As we discovered in Chapter 6, expectations lead to disappointment. That disappointment is frequently expressed as complaints. And complaining only exacerbates the problem by focusing your attention on what is wrong in your life rather than focusing on taking actions to solve it or accepting the situation as is and finding peace with it. Judy complains that her job as a receptionist is so exhausting that she never has the energy to go to her evening acting classes or update her pictures and her résumé or go to any auditions. She is broadcasting her fear that she is sure to be a disappointment, not only to everybody she cares about but to herself, if she takes the risk of trying to make a go of her acting career. Gene complains that his wife is a control freak and that her parents are the same way, and in fact his parents are as well. He is letting the world know that he is afraid he's weak. Claudia complains that the only people her professors pay any attention to are the rich kids whose parents endow the college. She is publicizing her fear that she feels invisible and afraid that she'll never measure up. Sharon complains that her teenagers take her for granted and ignore everything she says. She is announcing her fear that she is insignificant.

Yet most of us accept complaining as a form of conversation. I had a client in one of my seminars confess that she didn't know there was anything else to talk about but complaints. Sad, but true. I used to be a professional complainer myself. Not only that, but I hung out with Complaining Buddies who would commiserate with me. In fact, I was such an expert complainer that I developed what I have come to call my "Story of the Day" routine. I kept everybody in stitches as I distracted them with what amounted to a stand-up comedy routine about poor little me. "You will not believe what happened," I would say. "First, my alarm clock died or something. No, seriously, it worked fine yesterday and then it picked this morning to have a total meltdown. Just my luck! The day of the power breakfast with the boss, and I ended up oversleeping. So anyway, once I finally got up, things went from bad to worse. My blow-dryer started to spark and then burned out completely. Oh, great! Wet hair is definitely not one of my best looks. Then, I stepped on the scale and saw that I had put on three pounds. When I passed thirty, my metabolism slowed to a crawl. It's so unfair! I have a friend who can eat like a truck driver and not gain an ounce, but all I have to do is look at a piece of chocolate and I gain weight. So I was pawing through my closet going, 'What the heck can I wear that will make me look thin?' You know what I mean? Man, that really puts you in a great mood, doesn't it? Then . . ."

Does this sound familiar? When you have a Story of the Day, your complaints keep you preoccupied. You don't have to face the real issues of your day or interact on a meaningful level with other people. You also almost certainly fail to notice whatever is positive in your life. Your day revolves around the attention you get for your entertaining story. Like all confirmed complainers, my Complaining Buddies and I actually got a kind of perverse joy out of what we were doing. And my Complaining Buddies backed up my belief that whatever I was complaining about was a hopeless situation. We'd agree that there are no decent jobs in our field. We'd say with conviction that men have commitment issues . . . that some people have all the luck . . . that the boss wouldn't give anybody a compliment if his life depended on it. And I was leading the pack when it came to complaining. Yet all along, what I was really doing was advertising that I felt worthless.

Complaining Can Become a Habit

Unfortunately, when we routinely make fear-based complaints, we often also branch out from there and simply complain about anything and everything—the weather, the traffic, the crowds at the mall, the lines at the bank, the fact that we're getting older. A veteran complainer bemoans the fact that a thunderstorm spoiled plans for a Fourth of July barbecue, as though the rain were falling only in his backyard. He personalizes every irritation and setback, proving to himself that he is being singled out for trouble and bad luck and convinced that this just proves it permeates every area of his life. Therefore, he can't possibly take a risk and succeed. You've heard the description of a pessimist as the person who sees the glass as half empty, while the optimist sees the very same glass as half full. The pessimist is simply a fearful complainer. "It's always something," he says with a melodramatic shrug when the airplane sits on the tarmac for forty-five minutes, or the Internet connection cuts off in the middle of downloading a thirty-page report, or the tickets to the big game are sold out, or there's a half-hour wait to get a table at the restaurant.

Yet if that complainer were on his Wheel of Freedom instead of his Wheel of Fear, he'd read or nap while the plane's takeoff was delayed. He'd remind himself that before the advent of the Web, he used to have to trek to the library to do his research. He'd make plans to go to a sports bar to watch the game. He'd chat with someone while waiting to be seated in the restaurant. And if he were truly evolved, he would consider the seemingly negative events as opportunities, not problems. Maybe he'd choose to be grateful for the forced downtime on the airplane while the takeoff was delayed. Maybe he'd realize that he ought to switch to a more efficient Internet service provider. Maybe he'd strike up a conversation with someone at the sports bar and end up with a new friend. Maybe he'd make a mental note to call for reservations the next time he wanted to go to the restaurant, thereby taking control of one small area of his life instead of remaining a "victim."

Notice that the evolved person, the person who is free from fear, does something. He makes conscious choices. He is proactive rather than passive. He doesn't let life happen to him. He makes his life happen. He doesn't complain. He captures the moment and makes the very best of it. He sees everything as an opportunity to learn something new, share something about himself, or make a request.

And many times that is all a complaint really is: an unfulfilled request. Questions we haven't asked, issues we don't confront, and problems we refuse to face come out as complaints. Look at your complaints. Are there any that could be solved tomorrow if you took actions consistent with your Wheel of Freedom instead of your Wheel of Fear?

❋ FEARBUSTER EXERCISE ❋

- Keep a log of your complaints for one week.

  What are your most frequent complaints?
  What would you lose if you no longer had that complaint?
  What is the satisfaction you receive by keeping your complaints?
  Which ones seem unsolvable?
  Which are real concerns?
  Which are long-term problems?
  Which can be solved easily?
  Which ones can you take care of now?
  Which will you need help solving?

- Keep track of the feelings you experience when you are complaining.
  Are they the same as when you are on the Wheel of Fear?

- Reframe your complaints as challenges.

    For example, not "My boss is a tyrant" rather "I either need to find a way to work more comfortably with my boss or I need to look for a new job."

- Reframe your complaints as requests.

    For example, "I would like to learn how to communicate better with you. I'd like to discuss the differences in our styles. Would Monday at eleven work for you for a meeting?"

- How would your life be different if you had no complaints?

Venting Is Valuable

There are, of course, times in your life when you need to talk about a truly upsetting situation and get some comfort and advice. That's when you can vent, which is much different from complaining. Enlist members of your Fearbuster Team as venting partners. You'll all benefit. Venting, unlike complaining, is a positive and productive process. Complaining just keeps you stuck in the complaint. Venting honors your feelings and gives you a chance to clear your head or release an expectation, which eventually helps you come up with a solution.

You may already have some trusted confidantes who you know will be there for you and who can count on you as well, yet formalizing the validating process makes it even more effective. Next to my sisters, Marta is my top-choice venting partner. We've trained one another to listen and be present during the process.

As you learn the venting process, it is easy to fall back into old patterns such as complaining, gossiping, enabling, or dissecting the problem. To get back on track, gently remind each other about the rules of venting. Teaching your venting partners may take a few tries, but the effort is well worth it. To help Marta and me stay on target, we both keep a printout of the venting rules by the phone, just as a reminder. You and your friends might want to do the same.

Here are the Fearless Living rules for venting:

1) Pick a venting partner who is supportive and trustworthy.

2) Explain that you need to vent about something, and ask your chosen ventee whether he or she is free to talk. If the person is busy, respect that and find another mutually convenient time. However, if you are extremely distressed and panicky—maybe you just canceled your wedding, or you were given the boot at work, or the biopsy was bad news—then contact other members of your Fearbuster Team until you find someone who is available to help you move beyond your fear right away.

3) Honor each other's time by setting a limit, saying something such as "I really need to vent. Do you have fifteen minutes?" This isn't time to chitchat or make plans for a future event. This is focused time that you are requesting from your venting partner to help you get to the other side of a challenge you are experiencing. The time limit will also remind you to express yourself as clearly and concisely as possible rather than rambling. Sometimes, though, you have to ramble to clear your head. That, too, is part of the venting process. If you have to ramble, do it consciously. Say something like "I had a really bad day. Do you mind if I try to sort out what went on?" Being free to talk about your fears in a nonjudgmental environment helps you to let go of the shame that can be associated with them. If your venting partner has time to listen, go on and say something such as "It all started when I was calling roll and this one kid didn't answer. Honestly, that kid has been a troublemaker since the first day of school! I don't know how the other teachers handle him. Usually, I'm good with teenagers, but

this one has attitude like you wouldn't believe. I've been meaning to talk to the counselor about him. So anyway, when he didn't answer I said, 'What's your problem?' Well, this kid went and told the principal that I was rude and that I embarrassed him in front of the whole class. Now I'm in hot water. I don't know how to handle this."

4) Explain that you need a safe environment in which you can tell what happened, and that you don't want the ventee to offer solutions. ("I think if I just talk about this, I'll be able to figure out what to do. Right now I'm so rattled that I can't think straight.") The ventee's job is to listen. Period. Venting is not about a quick fix or rescuing you or finding someone to agree or disagree with you. Venting is a process that honors your feelings and transforms negative thoughts into ones that are expansive, life affirming, and positive. The very act of venting eliminates the urge to resort to your Wheel of Fear's self-destructive behaviors as an emotional painkiller. Venting also keeps you from dwelling on the problem and losing sleep over it. It creates a safe space that helps you discover what is important to you, what no longer works, and ultimately, to reveal more of who you are.

5) Get everything out, within your allotted time frame. In other words, if the part that's troubling you the most is also the most embarrassing, don't keep it a secret. If, for example, you did sound pretty sarcastic when you spoke to the student, tell your ventee that. This is your opportunity to share your feelings, so don't hold back. Yes, you may feel vulnerable, yet remember, you chose this person because you felt safe enough with him or her to express yourself fully.

6) Breathe.

7) If you need to be reminded that you are okay and that you'll get through this, ask for support. Tell your venting partner what you need in order to help you move

beyond your fears. Sometimes when we are venting, we just need to be told that we aren't crazy, stupid, or a loser. Other times we need to remember what we are committed to. Marta and I usually end every venting session with the following: "Tell me what you are committed to." That gets us back to our essential nature and our feeling of wholeness, which is always bigger than the present problem. ("You're a wonderful, generous, smart teacher and you've touched countless young lives. You'll figure out how to handle it. I've seen you cope plenty of times before, like when that mother chewed you out in front of the whole PTA. You were so calm and so rational. We all learned a lesson from that. Tell me again why you are a teacher. What are you committed to?")

8) Thank your ventee for his or her time and support. Your partner just gave you a gift. Honor it by saying something as simple as "Thanks for being there for me. I really appreciate that."

9) When you are finished, change the subject or simply hang up. It's time to shift your focus. This signals your subconscious that you have processed your feelings and are now ready to take actions consistent with your Wheel of Freedom.

For certain situations, such as divorce, death, or other traumatic events, you will probably need to vent more than once, twice, or even three times. That is absolutely fine. Just be conscious of your process and if you can, spread your venting around rather than putting it all on one person. Constant venting can be draining for your loved ones. If you find yourself venting more than you would like, or more than your venting partners can easily handle, professional counseling may be appropriate. Therapists are perfect venting partners. They have been trained to listen and provide the safe space you need.

One reason for having trusted venting partners is that they

know you well enough to understand your basic commitments and they won't hold you accountable afterward for feelings that they know will be transient. If you say you hate your husband, your venting partner won't bring this up later when the trouble has blown over and you love your husband again. Marta is great at this. She knows not to take what I say during the venting process as gospel. I am venting. That means anything goes, so I may not necessarily be empowering or pleasant. Yet, when I am able to share what is really going on inside of me, we both know I will move through the difficult situation faster. Then I will be back to my empowering self in no time at all.

Venting partners are also there to validate your feelings. Because ventees can be objective, they can remember the old saying that goes "This too shall pass." They know that the emotional pain you're experiencing, however agonizing at the moment, will not last forever. But—and this is very important— they don't throw that in your face while you are in the midst of your turmoil. They allow you to explore and process the feelings you are currently experiencing without squelching you or judging you.

I am reminded of Abigail, a young woman whose best friend committed suicide because of a broken heart. On hearing the news, Abigail immediately blamed herself for not having picked up on her friend's signs of desperation when they were together the night before the tragedy. Everything that had ever made Abigail fear she is not good enough was crystallized in that moment. She couldn't even find a word strong enough to describe her self-hatred. She said to her mother, "I will feel this way forever."

Her mother, a friend of mine, reports that all she said to her daughter was "Go ahead and talk about how you feel if you want to. Or you can just cry and I'll hold you." Abigail began to sob, and her mother rocked and crooned softly as she had done when Abigail was a little girl. The mother did not contradict her daughter or diminish her pain by saying, "That's silly. You won't feel like this forever." But the mother knew that in time, her daughter would come to terms with the feeling and that it would at the very least recede, if not dissipate altogether. In fact, Abigail experienced the feeling with great immediacy for many years on the anniversary of her friend's death, just as I did on the anniversary of my parents' deaths. But even that reaction began to lessen when Abigail wrote a poem about her feeling and read it out loud each year. This is an example of the fact that feelings that stem from fear are not the truth. Abigail is not worthless, no matter how worthless the friend's suicide made Abigail fear she was. Abigail felt guilty, yet it wasn't her fault that her friend had taken her life. Yes, Abigail's feelings were to be honored, but those feelings were not the truth about Abigail. Again, honor feelings by venting but don't give them power by acting on them. When her mother gave her the space to grieve, Abigail's healing process had begun.

Many times it gets down to this: Our feelings lie. I'm talking about the feelings that are derived from fear-based thinking, and sad to say, that's most of our feelings. Yet the majority of people believe their fear-based feelings define who they are. They do not. Feelings move through you in the same way that a head cold or a thought does. Feelings do not sum up who you are. Think of the feelings you experience on a daily basis. You love your job. You hate your job. You love your spouse. You hate your spouse. You want to start your own business. Starting your own business would be too much work. You get the point.

Unfortunately, people tend to act on the feelings that are the strongest at any given moment whether they are true or not. That is why venting is so important. It keeps you from reacting based on fear. Abigail was in effect venting to her mother. If she had kept her feelings to herself, or if her mother had dismissed them with something like "You shouldn't feel that way," then Abigail might have acted on her feeling that she was worthless. The outcome might have been defensiveness, depression, isolation, or, worse, a copycat suicide attempt—all of which I experienced in my attempt to push away my feelings of worthlessness.

In less dramatic situations, people act on feelings every day even though they know they shouldn't. They can't help themselves. You dial the number of your ex late at night when you're lonely. You give up on your spouse because you're tired of dealing with the issues. You react to the latest office gossip and make decisions regarding your future based on the rumor mill. You dash off a hotheaded e-mail to the boss and regret it the minute you click "Send."

The way to prevent acting inappropriately as a result of feelings is to vent. If you don't have the time or opportunity to contact a venting partner, you need to vent to yourself. Grab a piece of paper and write down all of your feelings as fast as you can. Get it all down on paper. Every comment, thought, and feeling. When all is expressed, rip up the paper. I prefer to rip it up into tiny, tiny pieces. Repeat the writing and the ripping until you no longer feel heightened emotions. Through that process, you have done a compacted version of venting using yourself, and that piece of paper, as a venting partner. And you can always do the good ol' standby of hitting a pillow or screaming into the wind. Complete the process by writing down the next proactive step you will take or a positive empowering statement, or just by thanking yourself for having the courage to honor your feelings rather than acting on them.

To honor who you are yet allow yourself to be human, remember the four A's:

1) Acknowledge you are having feelings. ("I am livid because of the way the boss treated me in front of visitors from the other branch.")
2) Allow yourself time to process the feelings. Honor them through the venting process but don't act on them. (Don't send that angry e-mail in the heat of emotion.)
3) Ask yourself, "What am I committed to?" ("I basically

like this job and I value my reputation in the industry as
a cool head who is a team player.")

4) Act on your commitments. (Schedule a time when you
can calmly discuss your point of view with the boss, making suggestions about how a similar situation might be
handled in the future. Go to the boss with a solution, not
a problem.)

When you master those four steps, feelings will no longer dictate what you do. Rather your commitment to your essential nature will allow you to decide consciously who you are becoming.

How to Stop Feeling Sorry for Yourself

Another way you and your venting partners can help one another to stop complaining is to remind each other gently during the course of any conversation—a formal venting session or
just anytime you're talking—that you need to replace "Why?"
with "How?" "Why?" keeps you inside the problem. "How?"
makes you accountable and puts you into action.

Here's what I mean. When I was stumbling my way through
adolescence and young adulthood after I saw my father kill my
mother and himself, I asked, "Why?" every single day. Why did
my father do such a horrendous thing? Why was I the one who
was on the scene? Why didn't I do something to stop my father?
Why didn't my father kill me? Why did God let my parents, especially my precious mother, die? Why was I born?

As long as I kept asking why, and getting no answers, I was
stuck in that freeze-frame moment when the crack of a rifle
taught me to be afraid that I didn't deserve to be alive.

My solution, years later as I began to develop my program,
was to stop asking, "Why?" and start asking, "How?" How can I
turn my experience into a force for good that will help not only
me but other people as well? How can I stop obsessing about my
pain and begin instead to recognize all that is right and beauti-

ful in my life? How can I forgive myself for not being able to save my parents and learn to acknowledge myself for my fine qualities, my abilities, and my accomplishments? How can I forgive my father? How can I let go of the fact that my sisters, even though they were orphaned, were not singled out to witness our parents' grisly deaths? How can I spend my time and energy on the here-and-now rather than on trying to fathom why God allowed the tragedy to happen?

Switching from "Why?" to "How?" can give you, just as it has given me, a more productive and joyous life than you ever imagined. Even if your whys are less dramatic than mine, they are equally capable of keeping you on your Wheel of Fear, unable to move to your Wheel of Freedom. In the course of working with clients over the years, I have heard a lot of whys, and they all boil down to one universal question: "Why me?"

- Why didn't my parents teach me about money?

- Why can't I find anyone to love me?

- Why did my parents get divorced?

- Why can't I be more disciplined?

- Why didn't my parents spend more time with me?

- Why did my boss pass me over for that promotion?

- Why can't I get more organized?

All of these whys have just as much power over the people who ask them as do more extreme whys such as "Why am I blind?" or "Why did I become a paraplegic after that car accident?" or "Why was my mother a homeless drug addict?" The magnitude of the misfortune isn't the issue. When you feel that life has dealt you a bad hand for whatever reason, and when you keep trying to figure out why, you only perpetuate your fear that you are unworthy or useless or powerless or destined to amount to no good.

The fact is, we can never truly know why. Sure, I can come up with a reasonable explanation for why my father killed my mother, but I will never really know why. Only my father knew that and in truth, he probably wouldn't be able to tell me the core reason even if he were alive today. Yet asking why can feel very good. When you ask why, you can actually rationalize that you are working on yourself when, most likely, you are just spinning around in your Wheel of Fear. Of course, in some types of therapy, examining why is useful, but that is with a trained counselor who is doing the probing for a specific reason. Your asking yourself why, why, why, only keeps you in the why—and why does not promote action. It promotes self-analysis, and I don't know about you but thinking any more than I do about all of the challenges I have had only increases my fear and lowers my self-esteem. And even if you try to get some perspective by reminding yourself that there are people worse off than you are, that doesn't make your plight any better. In fact, comparing your pain with another's only belittles yours and will probably make you feel guilty for your self-pity, which once again feeds your fear.

Asking, "Why?" keeps you stuck in the problem. Asking, "How?" moves you into proactive solutions. Pledge to yourself that you will stop asking, "Why me?" Instead, ask, "How can I be aware of and find the opportunities that are all around me?"

❋ FEARBUSTER EXERCISE: GRATITUDES ❋

If you want to give up complaining, you must learn how to reframe any experience at will. Just think of the power and mastery you would have over life if you could change any negative situation into a positive opportunity. I'm going to share with you a potent technique that has helped literally thousands of my clients and seminar participants to do just that. They trained themselves to see that proverbial glass as half full instead of half empty. The technique is deceptively simple. Yet that is the beauty of it. You don't need any more than five or at most ten minutes a day to put this strategy to work. And the effect is cumulative. By the end of a few weeks, if not days, you'll have built positive emotional muscle in the same way you would gradually build physical strength if you worked out regularly. Promise yourself that you will take this assignment seriously and stick with it.

Here's how it works. Every day, I want you to write a list of "Gratitudes." This exercise is not unlike the age-old advice to "count your blessings," yet it's bigger than that. Or rather, smaller. Most of us think of blessings as the major positive factors in life—good health, freedom from want, love, a chance to make a difference. Gratitudes, on the other hand, are myriad and exquisitely specific. As such, they do more than make you feel good for a little while. They literally change the way you think from negative to positive. They reframe your language from negative to positive. They change the way you listen and the way you see the world. They put you on your Wheel of Freedom effortlessly. Gratitudes shift your focus so that you are aware of what you have instead of what you don't have. When you make Gratitudes an integral part of your day, you are increasing your ability to see opportunities and possibilities where perhaps none existed before.

Here's an example of how Gratitudes helped one of my clients when she was in unfamiliar territory. Betsy was attending a party where she knew absolutely no one. As she walked into the crowded ballroom, she immediately felt uncomfortable. She told herself this wasn't her type of gathering. Everyone was much older. As she turned to leave, a gentleman asked her to dance. Not wanting to be rude, she accepted. Up to this point, fear had been making her feel that the situation wasn't safe. "These people aren't my type of people," she thought. "I don't think I should be here." Yet when she got on the dance floor, she was in her element. Betsy had been taking ballroom-dancing lessons, and she had assumed that no one in this crowd could dance. How wrong she was. As the gentleman whisked her around the floor like an old pro, she was grateful for the lessons she had taken. When the music ended, he complimented her on her style. Again, she was grateful that he noticed and appreciated her effort to keep up. Watching him walk away, she surveyed the room and instead of complaining about the crowd, she realized she had been about to walk out of an event that could perhaps be a lot of fun. Betsy silently said another Gratitude about being thankful she had been invited. By the time midnight came, she had taken every opportunity to dance with the best ballroom buffs in the room. It was like getting free dance lessons. Another Gratitude. The event could have been a disaster. But instead of getting stuck in complaining, Betsy had expanded her opportunities by being willing to see the possibilities rather than focusing on the seeming limitations. Limitations only exist if we decide they are limitations. Betsy also was doing something very powerful: she was reframing her thinking from negative to positive in the process. In the end, by expressing gratitude, she was able to put aside the preconceived notions activated by her Wheel of Fear and embrace the essential nature and the wholeness of her Wheel of Freedom. And she had a lot of fun.

Here are the rules for Gratitudes:

- Five Gratitudes a day are optimum. However, you may begin with fewer and add more per day as you get better at this.

- Gratitudes must be written down. And Betsy did just that when she returned home that evening. In the same way, if you choose to say your Gratitudes out loud or to yourself when you can't write them down—driving to work, perhaps, or in a meeting—that's fine as long as you do write them down later. By writing them, you are in effect creating an archive of your shifts and changes that becomes imperative whenever you need a reminder that you are indeed moving forward.

• Use the present tense. I use "Today, I am grateful for . . ." This keeps you awake and attuned to what you are experiencing at any given moment.

• Eliminate the word "not." Rather than writing, "I am grateful that my hairdresser did not cut my hair too short this time," reframe that as "I'm grateful that my hairdresser got the length of my hair just the way I like it today." This will help you learn to phrase your thoughts positively and that will have a beneficial effect on the way you speak, think, and listen.

• Be as specific as possible. Instead of "Today, I am grateful for the blue sky," which is a general statement, bring out more details. "Today, I am grateful for the sun shining through the clouds landing on the daisies coming up through the broken sidewalk." One major benefit of being specific is that it is easier to relive a positive experience in the present moment while at the same time building a memory.

• Gratitudes are not about your accomplishments. They are about events, about things other people do, about the beauty of the world, about serendipity. Examples: "I am grateful for the excellent job Russell did fixing my car today." "I am grateful that the parking spot at the mall opened up this afternoon." "I am grateful the sale started today." "I am grateful Sofia asked me to join her for lunch."

• Gratitudes don't have to be grand and important. Any little thing counts—a child's smile, the perfect pair of earrings for a price you can afford, the fragrance of lilacs on a spring breeze, the sweetness of a fresh orange, the chance to take a refreshing nap, the antics of a pair of kittens, a chance encounter with an old friend, a table by the window at your favorite restaurant, the string of traffic lights that turned green for you when you were running late.

- Gratitudes can be more significant events, as well: the opportunity to help a loved one through an illness, finally getting your divorce papers in the mail, finding out you don't need surgery after all, getting a tax refund.

- Pick an area. The perfect way to start is to list five Gratitudes in the area of your life you are presently focusing on. As you expand your awareness, attempt to have each Gratitude be on a different subject. In other words, if you write that you are grateful that the sun shone during your morning walk, then think of four other Gratitudes that are about something besides the weather. Use your Gratitudes as an opportunity to be thankful for each time fear is diminished and freedom is expanded.

- Be aware of your feelings as you write your Gratitudes. Are you uplifted? Moved to bittersweet tears? Powerful? Confident? Full of love? Amused? Awed? Inspired? Excited? Optimistic? Glad to be alive? If you would like, write down the feeling next to the appropriate Gratitude as a method of connecting the positive feelings you have to experiences in your life. This will be meaningful when you need an additional boost in self-confidence, which is one of the more powerful effects of Gratitudes. When you keep an ongoing list, it gradually shifts your filtering system. That changes your perceptions and alters how you build evidence. With each Gratitude, your Wheel of Freedom is gaining power.

Gratitudes can help you feel the way Piglet does.

"What day is it?" asked Pooh.

"It's today," squeaked Piglet. "My favorite day."

Here is the list of Gratitudes that I wrote today:

1) Today, I am grateful for the opportunity to speak in front of a group of leaders for an international corporation.
2) Today, I am grateful for getting a massage from a gentle therapist.
3) Today, I am grateful for crying during a movie, reminding myself how deeply touched I am by humanity.
4) Today, I am grateful I was in my hotel room when a long distance call that I had been anticipating rang through.
5) Today, I am grateful for the snow falling on the ground during the conference lunch break. I love snow.

Back when I was still a complainer, I would almost certainly have overlooked the precious moments when things were going my way, or I'd have been blind to the beauty of the snow. I would have framed everything in the negative: Why did I have to get a run in my hose right before my speech to all those important people? Why is massage therapy so expensive and why isn't it covered by my insurance? Why did I have to ruin my eye makeup crying over a silly movie? Why did I have to be in a hotel far away from somebody I love? Why didn't I have time to take advantage of the snow and go skiing? Complaints like those are a way of saying: "I'm afraid I'm not good enough to be giving this speech. I'm afraid I'm never going to have enough money. I'm afraid I'm weak and foolish because I cried. I'm afraid I'll lose the person I love. I'm afraid my life will always be all work and no play."

The Gratitudes, on the other hand, dispel the fears. They are a way of saying: "I wouldn't have been asked to give this speech if people didn't think I'm good enough. I'm fortunate to have enough money to be able to afford a massage. I'm mature enough and sure enough of who I am to be honest about my emotions. The person who called loves me enough to want to hear my voice. Watching snow fall, even for a little while, is one of life's great pleasures when I allow myself to appreciate that time fully."

That is the magic of Gratitudes. The very act of writing them down triggers the process that helps you master fear and release what Maslow says is "a fundamental characteristic, inherent in human nature . . . a tendency to do anything creatively . . . more easily and freely with less blocking and self-criticism . . . without strangulation and without fear of ridicule." Gratitudes are actions you can take that refine your ability to distinguish between the world of fear and the world of freedom, between fear-based feelings and your freedom-based intuition. Judgment of yourself and others is reduced as your ability to see the good in all things increases. When you consciously choose to see the good that is already present in your life, you immediately open up the floodgates for more good to come your way.

Intuition Doesn't Lie

Gratitudes put you in touch with your intuition. Feelings, as we have seen, cannot always be trusted. But intuition is never wrong. It is subtle. It is clear. You just have to learn to distinguish it from the voice of fear. When a fear-based feeling comes up, you may feel as though there are two of you arguing about what to do next. For example, Jean wanted to ask for a raise. One voice told her she wasn't good enough to get a raise while the other voice told her to go for it. Maybe you've had a similar experience. Those two voices have very different jobs. The first is the voice of fear while the second is intuition, the voice of freedom. Which one do you listen to? The voice that limits and constricts the voice of your essential nature, the you that is absolutely amazing, magnificent, and a privilege to be?

How do you know which voice is motivated by fear and which one is your freedom-based intuition? The voice of fear is always in a hurry, relies on evidence from the past, wants you to believe there isn't enough for everyone, diminishes possibilities by pointing out why things won't work, uses your logic and feelings to convince you and in general, makes you feel bad about yourself. When Kathy received two job offers on the same day, fear told her to take the one with the biggest salary. Intuition told her to take the one that made her heart leap at the prospect of going to work every morning. Fear told her to take the job that she knew from experience how to handle. Intuition told her to go for the one that held the promise of new challenges. Intuition tells you to invest in yourself, believe your thoughts and ideas, and trust your own process. Intuition expands possibilities, knows there is more than enough time and money, and has the patience of a saint. Intuition is available twenty-four hours a day, seven days a week, yet very few people take advantage of its amazing decision-making abilities. When you use Gratitudes to master your fear, the subtle, peaceful voice of intuition becomes your primary guiding force. Intuition shows you the path to your purpose while accessing the passion you need to take the risks necessary to live fearlessly.

Gratitudes are a gateway to your Wheel of Freedom—an action you can take that will immediately change your focus by attuning you to your intuition. And they worked extremely well for the clients I mentioned earlier in this chapter. Doug, the lonely guy who swore that all the good ones are taken, listed the following Gratitudes on a certain Saturday in June after working on the technique for several months: "I am grateful that the bus driver saw me running and was kind enough to wait for me to board. I am grateful that the weather was sunny for the company picnic. I am grateful that I found a brand of bug repellent that actually works. I am grateful for the way hamburgers smell when they're broiling on a charcoal grill. I am grateful for the way grass feels between my toes when I'm barefoot." By Doug's own admission, his pre-Gratitudes view on those same events would have been the following complaints: "Why didn't they have the picnic on a workday? I hate getting up early and trying to catch a bus on the weekend. It was so hot that I wished I were in the air-conditioned office. Must be the greenhouse effect. The whole planet is going to melt. Why is bug repellent so smelly and greasy? Why did they only serve red meat? And cook it over charcoal? Are they trying to give us cancer? Why wasn't the park in better shape? I pay my taxes! Somebody should mow the friggin' lawn once in a while!"

"Looking back, I can't believe how I used to gripe about absolutely everything," Doug said. "No wonder women didn't want to be around me. But that has changed. On the day of the company picnic, I was thinking up my Gratitudes and just feeling so darn good and so relaxed, and up comes this pretty woman from accounting. She said, 'Hey, whatcha smiling about?' And I said, 'Oh, just everything. I'm just feeling grateful to be here.' So we hung out for the rest of the day and I asked her for her number. We've been dating for two months now. I guess all the good ones aren't taken after all!"

Similarly, Judy, the one who moaned about how her day job was keeping her from pursuing her acting career, started listing Gratitudes and ended up with a whole new attitude. She became grateful for her day job, realizing that it allowed her to pay for her acting classes. She was grateful for her excellent acting teachers, her photographer, and for the résumé service she used. Before long, she got up the nerve to go to some auditions and, sure enough, she landed a job.

Gene, who whined about how his wife and other family members were all control freaks, learned to be grateful for the love and support of his family, for the laughter in their lives, for their comfortable circumstances, for his wife's cooking, for his parents' good health in spite of their advancing age, for his in-laws' readiness to baby-sit for the grandchildren. Gradually, he sorted out the difference between the "control" he resented and the

help he appreciated, and he gained the courage to bypass his fear of being weak so that he could discuss the control issues in a nonemotional way with everyone involved. To his surprise and delight, the issues were resolved easily and with no ill will.

Claudia, who was sure her professors were playing favorites, found out through listing Gratitudes that when she looked at life in a positive way, she was capable of doing much better academic work than she had ever thought possible. She had the courage to ask for additional mentoring and discovered that her professors noticed her after all.

Sharon, who said her kids didn't pay any attention to what she said, built up her sense of joy through Gratitudes, and with it her self-esteem. She was able to distinguish between healthy teenage rebellion and inappropriate behavior. As a result, she began to put her foot down when the kids needed some discipline. They were actually relieved that she was performing as an adult, and they all grew closer.

☀ FEARBUSTER EXERCISE: ☀

- Write down a minimum of three Gratitudes for the first week. Build up to five.

- Ask a Fearbuster Team member to be your venting partner.

- For each complaint you wrote down in the Fearbuster Exercise on pages 200–201, write down a gratitude to replace it.

- If you catch yourself verbally complaining, either vent instead or immediately replace the complaint with a Gratitude.

- Pick one of your most frequent complaints and remove it from your conversations for one week.

- Eliminate three complaints this week either by reframing, requesting, or solving.

I know you are on your way by now to becoming an ex-complainer and that you're ready to tackle one of the most challenging and at the same time the most exhilarating stages of the Fearless Living program. Come with me and find out how to stop being your own worst enemy, how to start bolstering your self-esteem, and how to unleash the spontaneity that fear has been keeping in check.

9

No Beating Yourself Up

'm going to tell you something about myself that I was ashamed of for years. Before Fearless Living, I would have died if you had discovered this about me. Here it is: I'm the kind of person who waits until the last minute to accomplish most everything. That's right. In the past, I would have called myself a procrastinator or lazy. Not many people suspect that I'm an eleventh-hour type, of course, because all that the world sees is the satisfactory end results. Nevertheless, back when I was a regular on my Wheel of Fear, I was afraid that people would think I was a loser if they knew that I frittered my time away by decoupaging or potting plants instead of working hard on a project, any project. I felt that I always had to work hard, efficiently, and perfectly and this last-minute thing was really pulling me down. Even though nobody saw me potting those plants, my fears had me convinced that this was something to be avoided at all costs. Each time I didn't plan ahead, I felt ashamed and guilty, certain I was doing something wrong. Then I would either force myself to buckle down and try to work on a project months before it was due, fidgeting all the while and getting nothing accomplished, or—and now I'm really going to confess—I would get really creative and find even more ways to avoid being at my desk. I would have this strong urge to find light-switch plates to decoupage or I would look at my dying plants and conclude that in order to save them I had to drive to Home Depot for the perfect fertilizer right that minute. Or worse yet, I would take myself out to lunch, since I was already feeling bad, and top the meal off with a slice of chocolate-chip cake, heated and smothered in whipped cream, thus undoing two weeks of healthy eating.

Whether I was attempting to accomplish the task at hand or avoiding what I thought I had to do, the consequence of any of those actions was that I would feel worthless. Nothing I did seemed good enough. The entire time I was actually sitting at my desk I would berate myself for not getting everything done and fast. When I visited Home Depot, I accused myself of procrastinating. And when I went to lunch, my Wheel of Fear gave me reason to call myself lazy, stupid, or worse. And then I would vow that next time I would figure out ways to manage time better and prepare in advance, which is what I was convinced all winners and worthy people do.

This lasted for years . . . and I mean years! Then as I began to develop my program, I realized that what others called procrastination was actually the way I worked best. For me, it wasn't procrastination at all. I work well under pressure. It turns me on. It gets my creative juices flowing. It heightens my mental functioning and helps me learn better and retain more. It works for me. I get things done. And I also realized that the time I spend decoupaging or potting plants or puttering around the house is not wasted at all. Because of the way we process information, our mind needs time to sort through our thoughts, piece them together, and then rearrange them into something that becomes our perspective on life. For me, that happens best when I'm not straining to get everything just right. Ideas literally pop into my head at odd moments, such as when I have my hands around a root ball while transplanting a geranium or when I'm cutting pictures out of a magazine to decoupage a light switch.

Plenty of research has shown that cramming at the last minute is not beneficial to the learning process. And every teacher I ever had took me to task for not working in a slow and steady fashion. But as I began to develop my program, I gained the courage and confidence to question the research and the admonitions of my teachers. What if pacing myself according to their "rules" is not the best way for me to learn and create? What if I am one of the exceptions to the rules? What if there are no rules? What if I am not a loser? What if I'm not a worthless procrastinator with no self-discipline? What if I am a perfectly fine person who happens to have an idiosyncratic learning and creating process? What if I stopped beating myself up and instead empowered myself in any situation?

At that point, I told myself I would not beat myself up for three months about the way I work. Instead, I would praise myself for what I did, however small. If I produced one paragraph, great. If I finished a whole project, great. But no longer would I judge myself on the process. During those three months, I realized that I do love the pressure, the tension, the stress. They give me a high. They prime the creative process for me. My anxiety decreased and my guilt disappeared. I wrote my first workbook in a matter of weeks and did the same for the second one. Those were projects I had been yearning to complete for a long time, but my habit of beating myself up because of the way I work had been keeping me from accomplishing those very ambitions. When I began to embrace my late nights and afternoon mocha breaks, I found my natural rhythm, freed myself from fear, and began creating in the way I was meant to create.

No More Negative Self-Talk

Since then, I have helped many clients overcome fear-driven, self-limiting behavior by showing them how to reframe their experiences and eliminate their need to beat themselves up because they "think" they should be working differently. However, I also want to emphasize how important it is never to beat yourself up even if you really have done something self-destructive or inappropriate. Beating ourselves up with negative self-talk is the single most damaging thing we do while spinning on the Wheel of Fear. When we do it, our confidence, courage, and self-esteem are obliterated. Beating yourself up will never motivate you to change. I have never met anyone who has achieved high self-esteem and therefore the courage to make positive transformations as a result of saying to herself, "You are an idiot! How could you do something like that? What the bleep is wrong with you? Won't you ever learn? You should know better by now!" When you talk to yourself that way, you become more fearful than ever that you not only don't but can't measure up. That voice is not your higher self. It is not your conscious. It is your Wheel of Fear. All the voices of past judgment, inherited hurts, and faulty belief systems. The voice is not you.

Remember Frank, the real estate salesman who had a fear of failure? He proved that you can accomplish a great deal with fear's whip at your back. Yet, what we are talking about here is much more than accomplishing "stuff." We are talking about Fearless Living, accomplishing life on your terms while igniting your passion, and embracing your essential nature. And to that end, there is never, ever a reason to disempower yourself by beating yourself up. Never!

The solution, then, is to begin the process of altering the way you talk to yourself and the way you talk about yourself to others. First, though, I'll briefly explain the process that occurs when you become aware of how and when you beat yourself up. Learning to let go of the ingrained habit of beating yourself up takes commitment. I urge you to give yourself, as I did, at least three months to experience significant progress. These are the stages you may experience as you learn to stop beating yourself up. Use the following as a map toward freeing yourself from the critical voice of fear.

Once you commit to becoming aware of your negative thoughts I am convinced the following will play out with slight variations: After understanding the negative effects of beating yourself up, you decide to earnestly release this detrimental habit from your daily life. You decide to notice your negative thoughts but realize you usually become aware of them only long after the fact—minutes, hours, or even days later. And the only reason you notice them at all is because of the effects, such as lower self-esteem, lack of possibilities, anger at the world, etcetera. You notice that beating yourself up usually follows your personal version of not being good enough. During this phase, you may begin to see a pattern, as I did when I noticed that I was beating myself up for my work habits. Then it gets worse, you discover you beat yourself up for beating yourself up. You note how clever your Wheel of Fear can be. With your heightened awareness, your negative thoughts about yourself and others become easier to see. Awareness is being expanded and refined. After increased awareness, you now hear your negative self-talk immediately after you utter it. The good news is you are catching it more quickly. The time between action and awareness has decreased. When you are in conversations, you hear how other people talk negatively about themselves. It isn't attractive. You decide to become more vigilant. Next, you notice you are beating yourself up while you are in the process of actually doing it whether it is done silently or out loud. This is a critical moment. It is proof that your awareness has been heightened. Soon, you stop the negative self-talk in midstream. The fact that beating yourself up is lowering your ability to reach out to others, take risks, and be true to yourself is becoming more evident. You vow to stop. You don't want to do it anymore. Slipping back into your old habit, you begin to beat yourself up about beating yourself up. You do it again and again and feel powerless to stop it. You remind yourself that learning to stop beating yourself up is a process. First you must know you are doing it before you can choose differently. Compassion enters the picture. You give yourself a break.

As you quit trying to be perfect, you notice the negative self-talk before the thoughts actually form fully in your head or come out of your mouth. This is an important step. You now have the awareness to stop the behavior in its tracks. You observe how fear attacks when you are at your most vulnerable, like when you are taking risks. You begin to differentiate between thinking the thoughts and speaking them. Then, you think negative things about yourself yet you don't say them anymore. This is a powerful sign that you are mastering the voice of fear. You begin to hear your negative inner dialogue and instead of beating yourself up, you do nothing except listen. When you say something bad about yourself, you immediately counter it by telling the voice the truth, "That is a lie. That is not the truth about me." Next, you are able to stop yourself in the middle of a thought and immediately reframe it in the positive. Not "I'm raiding the refrigerator again. Jeez, I'm a human garbage pail!" Instead, "Something must really be up for me today. I must be taking a risk in some area of my life. I acknowledge myself for noticing my overeating." You take out your laminated card and choose an action from your list of proactive behaviors. Then you acknowledge yourself for the behavior.

Or you might thank the voice of fear for caring about you so much that it wants to keep you safe; then you remind it that you are doing great and don't need help right now. The voice decreases in frequency and intensity. Your thoughts are more positive than negative. You are paying attention to how you speak to yourself at every turn. The criteria for empowering self-talk becomes "Is what I am saying loving, compassionate, kind, empowering, or insightful?" It feels odd when you do beat yourself up. It doesn't feel good. When you are around others, you feel uncomfortable when they beat themselves up. Rarely do you beat yourself up, and when you do, you switch to an empowering statement right away. You have mastered reframing. Others notice a difference in you and ask you what you have been doing. You feel less fearful, and you're able to achieve much more than you previously thought you could.

As you can see, there are many places that people could be stopped when they begin to master their Wheel of Fear. I've spelled out the moments for you to encourage you to keep moving forward. It is normal to be pulled back, but it's only temporary and it usually happens just before you are about to take a quantum leap. It is a process and once you've mastered it, your mind has space to create and expand into areas that you choose.

Nobody's Perfect

When you make it through the various stages, you will have accomplished a great deal. Yet sadly, at the very moment that you begin to master your fear and let yourself grow, you are likely to beat yourself up because your metamorphosis is not complete and permanent. As Maslow laments, people seeking growth and what he has termed "self-actualization" have a tendency to think of these goals "as if they were Nirvana states of perfection. Once you're there, you're there, and it seems as if all you could do is to rest content in perfection." That's not life, of course. Life is about being, but it is also always about becoming. And sometimes it's about going back a bit without meaning to do so.

Even so, if you're like many of my clients, you will have the urge to judge your growth as if it were possible to be perfect. Yet, your judgments only perpetuate your fears. It brings up all our faults and tempts us to compare ourselves to others, making us fear more than ever that we're not keeping up and that fosters more insecurities.

In fact, we tend to be such harsh self-critics that accepting compliments about our transformations is often difficult. Someone congratulates you on landing a great new job after years of talking about leaving the old one and you think, "Sure, I got up the nerve to send out my résumé, and I aced the interview, but it will probably end up being the same mess I was in before."

Maybe you even say that, instead of simply saying thank-you. Either way, you don't accept the compliment. You don't relish it. Yet accepting what others see as your strengths is crucial to your continued growth. Compliments are a gift. They are an opportunity for you and another person to connect in a powerful, positive way.

A major shift happened in my life when I decided to accept other people's compliments about me unconditionally. One day, the man seated next to me on a plane watched me pull some plastic envelopes out of my briefcase and stack them on the tray in front of me. The envelopes were my portable filing system for the drafts of my first Fearless Living workbook. As the man watched me work, he whistled appreciatively and remarked, "You're very organized." Right then, my Wheel of Fear was activated, making me feel I wasn't capable of writing a good workbook. So I blurted out, "Well, you don't really know me."

Quickly, he shot back, "Well, I'm sorry you won't accept my compliment. I meant it." Of course I was startled, embarrassed, and didn't know what to do. So I thanked him and went back to working on my manuscript. The words blurred before my eyes, however, as I started thinking about all the compliments I had belittled. I wondered whether maybe the people who had complimented me knew something that I didn't. What if they could see something in me that I was blind to? In fact, as I thought about what the man had said, I had to admit that I am indeed very organized and always have been. What's so interesting is that when I owned that, I also stopped telling myself I wasn't capable of writing the workbook. The words came back into focus and I was proud of them. They said what I wanted to say. They would help people. I picked up my pen and started editing myself with a newfound surge of confidence.

From that moment on, I decided to see myself through the eyes of people who give me compliments rather than from my own limited point of view of myself. I wanted to see myself as they saw me. When I did, I began to embrace those qualities that I had previously discounted or ignored. If others saw them in me—especially if more than one person saw them—I chose to own them as true.

As I practiced accepting compliments, I realized that the minute you judge another person's compliment, you have discredited and minimized him as well as yourself. Maybe a colleague says, "I definitely learned something from the way you gave that presentation to the sales staff this morning." If, instead of saying, "Thanks! I'm glad you got something out of it," you say, "Really? It wasn't exactly my finest hour. I left out a lot of what I had planned to say," you have effectively told the person offering the compliment that he is wrong. You have refused his gift. Your judging disempowers the person giving the compliment. The connection is broken. Trust deteriorates. There is no partnership, only belittlement. On the other hand, your willingness to see a compliment for what it is would have allayed your fear, enhanced your ability to accept your accomplishments as good enough, and empowered the other person in the bargain. That is a classic win-win situation. An inability to accept a compliment only feeds your fear of accepting yourself for who you really are, and criticizes someone else's opinion at the same time. You both lose the opportunity to connect and to be seen for the gifts that you are.

Another thought about compliments: Resist the temptation to compare yourself to the best you ever were. For example, I was a size four in college. I am no longer a size four. Let's face it, I will never see four again. When someone compliments me on my figure, I could either think to myself—or worse yet, say: "You didn't know me when I was a size four. I don't look all that good at this weight. I was much more attractive then." Or instead I could honor the compliment, thereby honoring myself, with something like the following: "Thank you for the compliment. That is very kind of you and I appreciate it." Notice that I didn't have to agree with the compliment, yet I didn't disagree with it either. I simply accepted it. Accepting a compliment is a step toward mastering your Wheel of Fear and learning to accept yourself.

❀ FEARBUSTER EXERCISE ❀

Keep a compliment journal.

- Write down every single compliment you receive with no judgment or evaluation.

- After each compliment write, "I accept this to be so," or "I choose to believe that is true about me."

With each compliment you are expanding your ability to see how amazing you really are.

What's So Funny?

Another way we beat ourselves up is through jokes. I'm not talking about the healthy kind of humor that lets us see the absurdity of our fear. Laughing about the way you rushed around straightening up the house and dusting the tops of the pictures just because the service guy was coming to fix the dishwasher is terrific. You've caught yourself in the act of letting the fear of not being good enough run every little aspect of your life. But poking fun at yourself for your shortcomings is another matter entirely. That habit does nothing but disempower you. So does calling yourself names as a way of making people laugh. When you accidentally knock over a lamp and then say, "I'm a total klutz, in case you haven't figured that out," the ensuing laughter only makes you wonder if you really are inadequate. So the next time you call yourself a name or make yourself a brunt of a joke, ask yourself: "Did that empower me or disempower me?" Be sure you aren't beating yourself up.

When we beat ourselves up we are putting ourselves down, giving up on ourselves, and comparing ourselves to someone or some standard we have come to expect we should be like. When we beat ourselves up, we think we are being honest by pointing out our faults before anyone else can. Yet, all we are really doing is reinforcing our Wheel of Fear by telling ourselves over and over why things are the way they are. That makes us feel powerless, unable to change our circumstances.

Beating ourselves up can also be a misguided form of modesty. We think we'll have a better chance of being liked if we're not too accomplished, not too threatening, not too powerful. We put ourselves down so others don't feel uncomfortable. We're afraid of being seen as vain, so we downplay our strengths. We can't be too bright or too gifted or too together out of fear that we will antagonize people. So to ward off this fear, we reason that as long as we announce our shortcomings louder and more frequently than any accomplishment, no one will be offended or think poorly of us. We would rather minimize ourselves by calling it luck or giving the credit elsewhere so that we don't hurt anyone's feelings or show anyone up.

We may also play dumb so we won't scare off a potential mate. Women are especially prone to this, and are afraid that men are threatened by smart and accomplished women. Yet, there are plenty of men—and women—who are searching for mates who can keep up with them. Obviously, a woman who minimizes herself in order to attract a man is not going to attract the right man for her. We hold ourselves back for the good of the whole, yet that isn't good for anyone. In Maslow's words we are engaged in "a denying of our best side, of our talents, of our finest impulses, of our highest potentialities, of our creativeness. . . . [This is] the fear of *hubris*." The italics are his, and that word means arrogance. Yet if we would all stop beating ourselves up and start celebrating what is special about each of us, the fear of hubris would be mastered at last.

FEARBUSTER EXERCISE:
ACKNOWLEDGMENTS

I have discovered an amazingly effective antidote to the habit of beating yourself up. The technique builds your self-esteem and your ability to count on yourself. I call it "Acknowledgments." It is a specific way of giving yourself credit—credit that is no doubt long overdue. Acknowledgments are a way of fueling and refueling your emotional engine with self-confidence. If you do them regularly, you won't run out of gas.

You may have already heard about "affirmations." They are extremely valuable, yet their power is limited by your ability to believe that they could come true. You can say to yourself, "I have the right to speak my mind," or "I am qualified to do this job," or "I can reach my goal," and you may be empowered. That is great, yet I know that, for me, affirmations were difficult at times because I didn't really believe I could accomplish anything near what I was affirming. So I would affirm, then beat myself up, affirm, beat. You get the point. I hadn't built up a backlog of results to prove I could do what I was affirming. I hadn't praised myself for *something I actually did.* Acknowledgments do just that. They record the fact that you did walk a block. You did say hello to the cute girl at the coffee shop who smiled at you last week. You did make an appointment for a mammogram. You did do those things.

Acknowledgments are about every baby step you take. They are about each and every small act of courage. They rest on the premise that, as legendary football coach Vince Lombardi said, "Inches make a champion." Absolutely everything counts. If you were on the verge of beating yourself up and instead you distracted yourself by taking some action—secretly flexing and pointing your feet under the desk, getting a drink of water, scratching the dog behind the ears, polishing your glasses—that counts. And if acts as seemingly unimportant as those count, then acts with even a little bearing on something you hope to accomplish really count. Think of affirmations and Acknowledgments as business partners. As you embody your Acknowledgments, affirmations will be effortless to incorporate and believe.

Here's a perfect example. One day, before I got good at Acknowledgments, I am embarrassed to admit that I walked into a room, spotted a woman with a body to die for, and immediately had a fit of envy. She was thin and toned, with perfect proportions and a certain athletic grace. At the time I was far from overweight by medical standards. But by my own standards, I was pudgy and out of shape. I'd been "too busy" to eat right and exercise for a while. I had moved up to my fat clothes. My thin clothes were too tight. Nobody really noticed the extra weight, but I did. So I hated the woman with the gorgeous body, standing there in a skinny pair of jeans with her perfect abs and her cute little butt. I avoided her and quickly got into a conversation with some people who weren't such a reproach to me. I also vowed that the very next morning, I would join the gym and start working out.

What happened the next morning? I found lots of reasons why I was still too busy to get over to the gym. Then I beat myself up for not going to the gym. I looked into the mirror and beat myself up for the way I looked and the clothes I wore. I became very ashamed of how I hadn't taken care of myself. I told myself I was a loser for not going to the gym. And when I didn't keep my promise to myself the following day, I felt worthless. I lost my resolve and desire to go to the gym altogether. I lamented, "What's the use?"

Fast-forward to a time when I had learned the power of Acknowledgments. Again, I walked into a room and saw a woman with an enviable body. I realized the reason I was envying her was because I wanted what she had. Again, I made up my mind to join a gym. No negative self-talk. Rather, I became keenly aware that envy is based in my fear of being unworthy, so I resolved to get on my Wheel of Freedom and take an action. The minute I got home, I got out the Yellow Pages and opened to the list of gyms. That's as far as I got. I didn't even read the ads or pick a gym near me. But I wrote down in my journal, "I acknowledge myself for beginning the process of choosing a gym by opening the Yellow Pages."

The next day, I bought a good pair of sneakers and some gym clothes. I didn't put them on. I didn't pick a gym. I didn't get any exercise. Yet I acknowledged myself for what I had done rather than beating myself up for what I hadn't done.

Step by step, I got to the point where I finally joined the gym. Then one fine day, I actually went to the gym. I got on the tread-mill. As I explained in the Life Log exercise, five minutes is all you need to move from fear to freedom. It is the first step in integrating a new behavior. I resolved to walk for five minutes. Now, I know full well that you need twenty minutes on a treadmill to get all the cardiovascular benefits. I have also read those magazine articles that extol the benefits of strength training in addition to walking. Yet, I knew I would be sore for three weeks if I overdid it, and that I'd probably give up as a result. Forcing myself to do what I "thought" I was supposed to do would have surely set me up for failure. I stuck with freedom. I stuck with my commitments.

So there I was at last, starting to break a sweat on the tread-mill. Two and half minutes down, two and a half minutes to go. And who should show up and start walking on the treadmill right next to mine but the self-same goddess with the flat abs and the cute butt who had made me feel like a slob when I first saw her. She was a treadmill pro. She was up to using weights. Just by the way she got going, I could tell that ninety minutes would be no problem for her.

For a moment my fear got the better of me. "Don't be a wimp!" I found myself thinking. "Don't quit after five minutes! You can keep up with her. You can show her! Anyway, how embarrassing would it be to stop after such a short time? She's probably glancing over here and thinking, 'Holy cow, look at that jiggly behind!' "

And then I got ahold of myself. I remembered my Acknowledgments, that personal-best list of the steps I had taken that had gotten me on the treadmill in the first place. I stopped beating myself up. I realized that if I stayed on that treadmill longer than five minutes, I would be doing it as a reaction and not out of a conscious decision based on my commitments. I would be staying on because of her. If I did that, she would be running my life. That was not acceptable to me. At the end of five minutes, I got off the treadmill. I acknowledged myself for completing the five minutes as well as for sticking to my commitments. There was time enough, I reminded myself, to build up to more minutes and even to using weights. And you know what? That's exactly what I did. By the end of twelve weeks I was up to forty minutes on the treadmill and lifting weights three times a week. I lost ten pounds and was walking around in my skinny clothes. Lesson: Acknowledging yourself for what you do will help you master your fear and motivate you to keep taking positive actions. Beating yourself up will keep you fearful and either immobilized or prone to doing things that aren't good for you.

Getting to Know You

Another powerful aspect of Acknowledgments is that they are about you and your process, your way of working and playing, your style of interacting and dreaming. They become an incredible tool for self-discovery, giving you the ability to increase your awareness of who you really are and at the same time validating your achievements. That, obviously, is invaluable as you grow and begin to take risks.

A thirty-something woman named Amy is a good example. She lives in New York and has a telecommuting job as a graphic designer for a Web site with offices in California. Mostly, she communicates via e-mail and sometimes the office phones her or faxes her. So Amy, who works out of her apartment, has put herself on West Coast time. She stays up late and wakes up around noon when her colleagues are getting to the office for their nine-to-five stint. And when she does get up, she doesn't bother to get dressed. She makes a cup of coffee, butters a bagel, and props herself up in bed with her laptop.

So? Amy, whose mother had drummed Ben Franklin's early-to-bed-early-to-rise credo into her head, was afraid of appearing foolish. The fact that the neighbors across the hall could see that Amy's copy of *The New York Times* stayed outside her door long past the 6:00 A.M. delivery time made her feel incredibly guilty. She beat herself up about that, and vowed to set the alarm just to get up and bring the paper in, but she never did and then she beat herself up even more. She also had this weird feeling that the people she was talking to on the phone could see that she was in her PJs and hadn't put her contact lenses in or her makeup on. She vowed to start getting up earlier and dressing as if she were going to an office, thereby improving her sloppy lifestyle. She did do that for a while, but she spent so much of her morning getting ready that her productivity started going down. She beat herself up for that. Then she drifted back into her old routine, but by this time her Wheel of Fear was on a roll. She was sure her neighbors thought she was a complete fake and she felt completely foolish.

Amy heard me speak at a seminar while she was on the West Coast for one of her face-to-face staff meetings. We began to work together shortly thereafter, via phone and e-mail. Among other things, Fearless Living taught her the technique of Acknowledgments. Little by little, Amy stopped beating herself up for working in bed and started acknowledging herself for coming up with her most creative ideas just as her eyelids fluttered open in the morning. Then she acknowledged herself for capturing the ideas right away. She acknowledged herself for putting off the pleasure of reading the paper until after she had done a good few hours of work each day. She acknowledged herself for having the discipline to do a job with no supervisor breathing down her neck. She acknowledged herself for having a gift for imaginative designs. She acknowledged herself for finding a job that suited her personality and one she really enjoyed. She claimed each acknowledgment by writing it down.

While all of this was going on, Amy was making her own acquaintance, so to speak. She was meeting for the first time a talented, dependable, resourceful, creative person—herself.

She stopped worrying about what the neighbors and the building superintendent thought about her hours and her work habits. In fact, she realized with a touch of chagrin that since she is not the center of the universe, those people probably hadn't been paying attention to her lifestyle anyway. She also came to understand that enjoying the life she had made for herself was her inalienable right. Acknowledgments had helped Amy stop monitoring her every move as though she were being watched and judged. They had helped her stop judging herself and they taught her to reframe negative thoughts as positive ones. Amy realized that her Wheel of Freedom thrived on creativity, which gave her the inspiration to do the work she loved. She acknowledged her rhythm and her essential nature and her gifts. In so doing, she was well on her way to mastering her Wheel of Fear and was free to be all that she really is.

Surely not only Amy but everyone whose life she touches is better off for that. Finding your contribution is not about self-indulgence. When you are invested fully in your life, you actually like to work. Work is no longer drudgery. It energizes and excites you. And the work you do affects others positively. Whether you're making flower arrangements or putting siding on a house or figuring out people's taxes or performing brain surgery or running a day care center or training dolphins or delivering Meals On Wheels or harvesting oysters, you are giving of yourself. Now that you have mastered fear, you finally have enough of yourself to give. Once you stop functioning out of a sense of duty based on fear of reprisal, you begin to take the next step forward because it is, in Maslow's words, "more delightful, more joyous, more intrinsically satisfying, than that [with which] we have become familiar." And the world is better off for that.

Fear of Acknowledgments

Yet writing down Acknowledgments can be a daunting challenge. That is partly because, as Amy discovered, Acknowledgments can be about revelations and insights as well as about actions. Learning who you are can make you uncomfortable at first. For example, you might want to write, "Today, I acknowledge myself for realizing that envy is another way to see I am feeling incomplete in an area of my life," or "I acknowledge myself for seeing how fear limits my choices about how to use my time." Both are insights that will alter the way you live. And if that is too much for you at the beginning, then choose absolutely anything that is moving you forward. I don't care if it is as small as congratulating yourself on *thinking* about writing Acknowledgments, or just writing down one. The secret is to begin.

Another reason most of us have a difficult time coming up with Acknowledgments is because we think the act of giving ourselves credit implies we are bigheaded or selfish. We are afraid of being perceived as egotistical or superior. Worse, we are afraid of actually becoming conceited and puffed up. Yet without a strong sense of self, we are unable to take the risks necessary to move beyond fear. Your unique constellation of gifts and qualities makes you who you are. Their sum is what can be your contribution to the people you love and the world around you. When you acknowledge yourself, you free yourself to do yourself proud. That is a joyful and generous way to live, not a self-centered and stingy one.

People also have a hard time expressing Acknowledgments because they believe they will become self-satisfied and rest on their laurels. In fact, just the opposite happens. As our self-confidence soars, we are infused with more energy and creativity than ever before. We become curious and eager to risk the unknown instead of feeling threatened by it. When our fear subsides, we look forward to each new challenge.

How to Make Acknowledgments Work for You

Here is the technique for putting Acknowledgments to work in your life:

- Every day, write five Acknowledgments, using the present tense, as in "Today, I acknowledge myself for . . ." That may not be easy at first. Nothing seems good enough, does it? You finished the report but you should have started a week ago, so you rushed it. Therefore, you are not perfect and you can't acknowledge what you did. I used to feel that way too. Yet Acknowledgments are not about what you were supposed to do. They are about what you did. Whether you hesitated or quit before you had planned to or made some mistakes is not important. The question is, did you do it? Or did you make a step forward toward it? If the answer is a yes, write down what you did.

- The perfect place to begin acknowledging yourself is in the area of life you have chosen as your focus. Also another great starting point is to acknowledge yourself whenever you notice you are on the Wheel of Fear. Remember, this isn't about perfection. It is about any movement that you made that was a stretch, out of the norm, not your usual, thereby giving you the confidence to risk.

- Just as you did with Gratitudes, frame Acknowledgments in the positive. Ask yourself, "Is what I am acknowledging loving, compassionate, kind, empowering, or insightful?"

- Like Gratitudes, the more specific you are the more impact Acknowledgments will have by setting them in a solid foundation of details. The more specific they are, the quicker and easier it will be to claim the power of Acknowledgments.

- Keep track of what is easy to write down and what is hard. Maybe you're comfortable writing, "I acknowledge myself for doing the research for the next issue of the newsletter."

But maybe you squirm when you try to write, "I acknowledge myself for finding something constructive to do after my wife canceled our date night. I acknowledge myself for spending those hours starting a book I've been wanting to read." If so, you've just gained some insight into the fact that you are less fearful in the area of career than you are in the area of your relationship.

- Speak your Acknowledgments out loud to yourself, and then try saying them to someone you trust. What can you write down yet would have difficulty sharing with another? What is the difference? Maybe you can acknowledge yourself to another person for what you perceive to be worthy achievements, but you can't bring yourself to say, "I acknowledge myself for paying my bills on time this month avoiding any finance charges." That's fine. You don't need to expose your vulnerabilities until you have gotten to the point where your self-confidence is more solid. Right now, keep certain Acknowledgments private. They are your secret strength.

- Ask a member of your Fearbuster Team to listen to one Acknowledgment a day without judgment, and then to congratulate you as if you had just won the Nobel Peace Prize. After all, for most of us, doing something positive for ourselves in a consistent and persistent manner is just about that important! For years, I was unwilling to believe in myself for longer than a millisecond because of all of my past failures. I had reached a certain level of success, yet I thought I was still a loser who was going to be laughed at one day soon. Hearing my team member congratulate me time after time helped to change that so I could believe in myself and attain the success I had thought was out of reach.

- After you are comfortable writing your Acknowledgments, begin the process of absorbing them at a deeper level by reading over each Acknowledgment five times slowly to yourself. This process can be painful at first because of all our past conditioning, yet it is vital because it reinforces the message of your Acknowledgments.

- Look at yourself in the mirror and acknowledge yourself out loud. Try to look into your own eyes as you speak. This is a powerful exercise of self-love.

- When you have grown accustomed to acknowledging yourself, start expanding this skill by acknowledging others. You'll find that giving genuine compliments is now easy. And remember, people are dying for attention. The greatest gift you can give another person is an acknowledgment of who the person is as a human being. No matter how confident people appear on the outside, they still have fears and anxieties that they don't measure up in some area or another. Don't wait until something major happens. Compliment people on little things, just as you have learned to acknowledge yourself for little things. You might say, "I love the fact that you are always on time. I really appreciate the way you respect my schedule." Or "Thanks for seconding my motion at the meeting. I value your opinion." Or "You look great in that color! You've got such a terrific fashion sense."

Here is the list of Acknowledgments I wrote today:

1) Today, I acknowledge myself for reaching out for help regarding a difficult task.
2) Today, I acknowledge myself for speaking up even when the fear of being thought of as a loser came up.
3) Today, I acknowledge myself for saying yes to an opportunity to do something with which I have had no previous experience.
4) Today, I acknowledge myself for calling my venting partner instead of complaining.

5) Today, I acknowledge myself for scheduling a vacation even though my fear of feeling worthless wants me to believe it is an indulgence.

When you begin acknowledging yourself every single day, complimenting others as often as possible, accepting compliments with ease, and giving up impossible standards of perfection, you will turn that primal fear of not being good enough into a force that sets you free to fulfill your essential nature and express your innate wholeness, thereby becoming who you were meant to be. What was once anxiety will become excitement. What was once apprehension will become exhilaration. What was once stress will become stimulation. What was once uncertainty will become a quest. What was once impatience will become eagerness. What was once fear will become awe and wonder at the magnitude of life's possibilities. You will leave behind the old restrictions of your expectations in order to embrace the unlimited potential of your Fearless Path.

The Fearless Path

When James B. Conant was president of Harvard, he kept on his desk a statuette of a turtle. The base was inscribed with this message: "Consider the turtle. He makes progress only when he sticks his neck out."

Fearless Living is about sticking your neck out. It's about finding the courage to take risks, to change, and to keep going even if you falter. It's about mastering the fear that comes from past regrets and using it to summon the strength to take another chance. It's about taking each new risk without regret.

The work you've been doing so far has given you concrete ways to master your fear and to move toward the freedom that is your true self. Now you are ready to learn another secret that I, along with thousands of others, have learned about Fearless Living: The very act of setting yourself free from fear protects you from the pain you've been trying to avoid all along. The paradox of Fearless Living is that you are safer when you're free than you are when you're attempting to stay safe by avoiding risks.

An incident in my friend Marta's life is a classic example of this. She had wanted to be a singer, but after a brief, early attempt at making her dream come true, she had abandoned the idea. Years later at midlife she started thinking again about singing professionally. I knew her by then, and she talked to me about her plans. She said she envisioned giving a solo show. She'd hire an accompanist. She'd rent a theater. She'd hire a tech crew. She'd do a lot of publicity. I heard about this for months and months. After a while, although I had acknowledged Marta for coming up with the ideas—which after all is the first step in taking a risk—I started to wonder whether she was ever going to do anything but talk about her dream. She hadn't even picked out the music yet. She said the music had to be perfect, since this would be her second debut. But she said someday soon, she'd find the perfect music and get on with it. At that point I recognized that her fear of being a fake was stopping the show. It was keeping her in perfection mode. So as her Powerful Partner I knew I had to say something.

Finally, the opening I needed presented itself. I looked her straight in the eye and told her gently but firmly that she was kidding herself. Her eyes widened with disbelief. "What?" she said.

I repeated very clearly, "You are kidding yourself." I went on to tell her that she had been talking about this show for over a year and no real progress had been made. I told her that the talking was making her feel as though she were doing something. I told her that although I love her very much and would support her always, I had come to doubt that she would ever actually do anything about this show. Her Wheel of Fear was in complete control.

Marta was furious. She stormed out of the restaurant. We didn't talk for days. Then she called me. She told me how much she had hated me when I had confronted her with the fact that she had been stalling when it came to making the show happen. She said she had gone home and vented to her husband about what I had said to her. He had listened while she got everything out. Then she had looked to him for validation, saying, "You don't believe that, do you?" And he had the courage to say he agreed with me. He didn't believe she would ever do the show either. She didn't have music. She didn't have an accompanist. She didn't have a location. Because nothing was right or good enough. Everything had to be perfect. Her fear of being a fake was calling the shots, telling her to have everything "just right." Otherwise she would surely be found out. And that impossible goal was keeping her from taking the risk she wanted so dearly to take.

At that moment, Marta surrendered. Her husband and her best friend had been willing to tell her a painful truth. She heard us. In turn, she became willing to learn how to risk. She asked me to coach her. I shared with her the formula I have used successfully with scores of clients when they have reached the stage Marta had just reached. The formula is a capsule version of everything you've been learning and putting into practice as you have worked your way through the Fearless Living program, chapter by chapter and day by day. Marta had been working through the program as well, yet until I gave her the formula, the various aspects of the program had not crystallized for her into a cohesive, easily accessible way to move from fear to freedom. Yet as I have learned over the years, the formula is most effective after they have experienced the work. At just the right time, the formula has the power to change lives.

Now, at last, is the right time for you to receive the formula. It is my gift to you because you have done the work thus far and made a commitment to continue doing it. You have internalized the tenets and exercises of Fearless Living. You are ready to use the formula anytime from this point on as a surefire way to get on your Wheel of Freedom as fast as possible when something happens that triggers your Wheel of Fear.

R*I*S*K

Release your attachment to the outcome.
Invest fully in your intention.
Stand for the truth.
Keep kindness a priority.

Release your attachment to the outcome.
In Chapter 6, you learned to let go of unrealistic and unspoken expectations. This is the fundamental first step in putting the Fearless Living program to work for you. If you skip this step, the power of the rest of the steps will be diminished.

The "R" will help you access the skill of releasing expectations immediately. Taking a risk—the essential element integral with all aspects of Fearless Living, after all—is not about winning or losing, rather it is about having the courage to try something new. However, that doesn't mean being foolhardy. Fearless people have the wisdom to consider all the possible outcomes of taking any given risk, especially a big one such as starting a new business. They learn all they can about the venture. They know there's a difference between hesitating out of fear of failure and taking the time to do research and get advice. Ultimately, they let go of the goal. They focus on the process. If they don't reach the goal, they are not devastated. They have the emotional stamina to pick themselves up and take a new risk. That gives them the fortitude to stretch themselves even further because they know intuitively that with each risk they are being more true to themselves.

Each time you take a risk, be honest about whether you have expectations regarding the outcome. Let's say you've begun dating someone new. Are you thinking constantly about whether he or she is spouse material? Are you calculating every move and every sentence with the hope of making this relationship "the one"? Or are you reveling in the pleasure of a newfound friend, allowing each of you to learn and laugh and, yes, love without your eye on a goal? If you can do the latter, then the outcome will take care of itself. If this is the right relationship, you'll stay together. If it's not, you will go your separate ways. In either case, you'll have no regrets.

The same is true for any area of your life. Are you working on your novel so you'll be rich and famous? Or are you writing because you have something to say and you take pleasure in the process? Are you starting a new business so you can prove to your parents that you're smart and capable of making more money than your brother? Or are you itching to be your own man and do something you believe in? Are you having a baby to keep up with your sister and your best friend? Or are you aching to hold a new life in your arms and heart and guide the child toward a time you will never see? Beyond all of that, are you prepared to accept that your novel might get bad reviews? That your business might not get off the ground? That your child may be born with special needs? The only true way to live fearlessly is to take risks without expectations and then to do all you can to make the risk worthwhile even as you prepare to accept the outcome without regret.

Invest Fully in Your Intention

The "I" in the Fearless Living formula will remind you that intentions, as you learned in Chapter 6, are the antidote to expectations. The "I" will also encourage you to continue the Life Log you started in Chapter 7 as a method of eliminating the excuses that are taking up your precious time. Once you have identified your intention in any given situation—for example, writing your novel because you have something to say rather than because you expect to become famous—go for it with all you've got. Keep your Life Log faithfully so you won't be able to tell yourself you don't have time. Find the time. Scrape up the money. Learn everything you can. Ignore your detractors. Enlist your Fearbuster Team. And on the days when some bureaucrat sits on the paperwork or an ice storm makes you miss a crucial meeting or illness saps your energy or a loved one needs your full attention, don't give up. Postpone maybe, but don't give up. You are not at the mercy of fate. Accomplishments happen when you invest fully and purposefully in yourself. And the Life Log becomes proof that you are doing just that.

Stand for Truth

As you learned in Chapter 8, complaining is nothing but a way of avoiding the truth of who you are. Gratitudes, on the other hand, teach you to speak and act true to who you are. They show you how to transform negative experiences into meaningful and positive lessons. Many times we get off track because we get caught in our fear-based feelings and stories, forgetting what we are committed to. At those times, we are refusing to surrender to the life before us and cherish the gift that it is. When someone does something that affects us adversely, we tend to lose sight of our essential nature. Remember, the only person left to face at the end of the day is you. And your life is a reflection of how you perceive the world. Gratitudes shift your focus, giving you the clarity to reclaim your commitments. Without clear commitments, you can easily be blown off course and rendered powerless. Instead, decide a course of action based on what you value and the type of person you would be proud to be. The "S" in the Fearless Living formula will help you stand for your essential nature and focus on Gratitudes instead of complaints. When that happens, your wholeness will naturally expand.

Keep Kindness a Priority

Remember Chapter 9? No beating yourself up! Acknowledgments override your negative self-talk and nourish your soul. They are the key to treating yourself—and for that matter, everyone else—with the kindness that allows fearlessness to flower. Being kind to yourself keeps you on the path toward joy and peace of mind, and eases the pressure to be better or more perfect than you are. Kindness to others puts compassion to work and overrides your need to be "right." Being kind gives you the space to breathe while integrating the changes you would like to make, and allows you time to process these new ways of being. Learning to love yourself through any situation rather than just the ones you or others approve of is absolutely necessary. This is a vital component of the internal permission you need in order to follow your own fearless path.

The **R*I*S*K** formula can change your life, just as it changed Marta's life. The minute she let go of her fear that all would be lost if everything were not perfect, she was able to take a risk. She began to focus on the process instead of the goal. She began to enjoy every minute of the process. Within a few months, she had put on her solo show.

Since that time, she has found the courage to take one risk after another. She formed a female a capella group. She began booking the group into supper clubs and theaters all over town. She hired a publicist. She invited the press. To her delight, the group almost always performs to rave reviews.

Yet when things are not perfect—when a review is mixed or the theater isn't sold out or she has given a performance that was less than her best—Marta doesn't let her Wheel of Fear intervene. Freedom from her fear and of the emotional pain that would be its consequence has inoculated her against that pain. Of course, like all of us, she is more pleased when things are going well than when they aren't, and she works hard to do a responsible and professional job of her singing. But she no longer lets her Wheel of Fear hold her back. The pleasure of the process has overridden that fear.

Yet if the process is an end in itself, then what it produces benefits not only a risk taker like Marta, but others as well. Marta gives pleasure to her audiences by using the gift of her voice. In a sense, this accomplishment is but a by-product of the pleasure of the process. Also Marta has ended up making a genuine contribution to other people's happiness. And that is the true measure of success.

Think of your definition of "risk." Is it going back to school, falling in love, or shooting for that promotion? It could be saying you're sorry or admitting you need help or sharing your feelings with someone you love. Risk is different for different people. That is one reason our Wheels are individualized. We are all afraid of different things and in turn, what we perceive as a risk is different. This is another reason to practice compassion for yourself and others. And our Wheels of Fear also remind us, whenever we experience feelings of fear, that we are in fact risking much more than we give ourselves credit for. Acknowledge yourself. In their unique way, our Wheels of Fear guide us through our fear, giving us the courage to risk expressing who we truly are.

Meredith took a risk when she began the Fearless Living program. Doug was risking when he shared what he was thinking about when the cute girl walked up to him. Connie risked when she asked her mother-in-law to watch the baby. Kara risked when she was willing to reevaluate her happiness quotient even though to the outside world everything was peachy. Marta took a risk when she gave up her idea of perfection and just started singing, anywhere and everywhere. My sister Linda took a risk when she was willing to admit she was afraid of being ordinary. I risked by forgiving myself.

Each of us takes risks that go unnoticed. Sometimes we don't think they are big enough, difficult enough, or good enough to be called a risk. Yet, every time we acknowledge the risks we take, no matter how small, we are creating a foundation that will sustain us through our fear. We will know we can count on ourselves to follow through and we will believe that no matter what we are doing, we are contributing to the world just by being willing to be ourselves. That is the biggest risk of all. To risk is to fight for you, the you that dares to dream. You have the formula RELEASE (no expectations) . . . INVEST (no excuses) . . . STAND (no complaining) . . . KIND (no beating yourself up) . . . R*I*S*K.

FEARBUSTER EXERCISE:

To get yourself ready to take risks, list all the situations in your life that you would like to change.

- Name the top three risk-producing situations in your life.

- What makes them risky?

- What part of those situations do you have control of?

- What do you have no control of?

- Brainstorm—that means no judging what you come up with—a minimum of ten things you could do to change a situation that you have some area of control over. This is a good time to ask a Fearbuster Team member for brainstorming support.

- Brainstorm a minimum of ten ideas you could do to change a situation that you think you have no control over.

- What factors contribute to the difference between the areas you can control and what you can't control? Money? Authority? Rules? Relationship? Family?

- Accept the areas that you have no control over and find ways to empower yourself. Reread the sections on intentions and letting go. Write a minimum of three Acknowledgments regarding this area to put some power behind you. Remember, when we focus on why we don't have control, we are squandering our precious resources called our energy, creativity, and time.

- Pick one of the ten actions in the area where you have some control and *do that action within the next three days*. If you have always wanted to play the flute, call the music store and find out how much it costs to rent a flute. If you are lonely and between relationships, join any group of people with like-minded interests—volunteers who clean up the city's parks, weekend backpackers, the community theater, a chapter of Parents Without Partners. If you are stuck in the wrong career, open a savings account ear-marked for giving you the cushion you'll need to make a change. Risks are often taken one step at a time. The result is just as good as if they are taken at the edge of a chasm in a giant leap, as sometimes happens in an emergency.

- Pick one of the ten actions in the area you have no control over and *perform that action within the next twenty-four hours.* Don't think about it, evaluate it, or debate it. Just do it. If property taxes have recently gone up and you've been downsized, call a realtor and get an estimate on how much the house is worth. If diabetes runs in the family and you've just found out you have it, call the American Dia-betes Association and ask for a referral to a diabetes educa-tor and a support group. If you're worried about what the weather will be like the day of your garden wedding, rent a rain location as a backup.

When we take some movement in an area where we feel pow-erless, we come to find that we are more powerful than we had previously realized.

The Uncomfortable Zone

The actions you take when you're working through the Fear-buster Exercise just described will definitely go a long way toward helping you master your fear and encouraging you to risk. As the poet Ralph Waldo Emerson said, "Do the thing you fear, and the death of fear is certain." He was right, of course, in that when you do the thing you fear, the unknown becomes known. However, the process is far from instantaneous. The transition period between what you were and what you are be-coming is fear-producing in and of itself. I call it the Uncom-fortable Zone. For many of us it feels as though we don't even recognize ourselves. It's almost like we don't know who we are anymore. We want to shout, "Will the real me please stand up?" That is normal. What is actually happening during this transition is that you are redefining who you are and refining your actions, behaviors, and thoughts. Surrendering who we thought we were for who we are meant to be can get a little scary. The Wheel of Fear will almost certainly be triggered. Don't let it stop you. It stopped me far too many times. To help you stay master of your fear, I'm going to share with you what I have found to be the three stages risk takers typically go through:

Stage 1) Believing the Messages of the Past

When you risk, past fears will come up. "You're a loser, remember?" you might say to yourself. "Why open yourself up for getting hurt? You're better off not taking any chances. You don't want to make a fool of yourself, do you? Trying to make your mark just isn't worth it. You'll end up licking your wounds. Don't you remember the last time you went out on a date and he never asked you out after that? And what about when you started that side business? It was a disaster. Anyway, really, is life so bad right now? Why rock the boat?"

Marta's message from the past was crystal clear. "Remember the time when you were twenty and that famous agent said your singing voice was nothing special? Well, it isn't." That stopped her career from moving forward then. It would have brought her new venture to a halt as well, yet through our coaching she knew that the message from the past was just the Wheel of Fear warning her of potential danger. This time, she chose risk instead of safety.

Do not believe messages from the past. When you do, you are courting fear. You may be able to manage your fear but you'll never master it. As we learned in Chapter 2, there's a big difference. Managing your fear is a temporary solution to a permanent problem, like putting a lid on a pressure cooker that's sure to blow sooner or later. Mastering your fear means accepting it, owning it, and making it work *for* you instead of *against* you. The irony is that when you're on your way to freedom, your fear will be more potent than it's ever been. That should be no surprise. Your fear is trying to stop you from whatever you are doing that is risky. That is no reason to turn back. Because don't forget fear is an affirmation of your growth. If you keep going, your fear will eventually lose its power to hinder you and become a force that propels you forward. I promise you that.

Stage 2) Feeling Like a Phony

When you attempt something new, you may get a sense that you're not the "real thing." You want to be a novelist, but when you start spending evenings sketching out your plot and characters, you chide yourself for even trying. Joyce Carol Oates is a novelist. John Grisham is a novelist. Toni Morrison is a novelist. They are the genuine articles. You are a phony. This, needless to say, does nothing for your creativity or self-esteem or productivity.

Ginger, a client of mine, is a case in point. She came to me because although she was doing fairly well at selling Mary Kay cosmetics, she was unable to push herself to the next level and begin to recruit salespeople who would help her expand her business. "My neighbor hosted a skin-care class to kick off my sales when I started out about nine months ago," Ginger said. "It was a big success and I got some steady customers. After that, I was really encouraged. I had some flyers made up right away. I got a lot more customers as a result, and word of mouth has done the rest. I have surpassed my personal sales goal. But I just can't bring myself to call other people and pose as this big sales trainer. I feel like I'd be putting one over on them. Everything I know I learned on the job, and I've only been doing this for a matter of months. Who am I to pass myself off as an expert?"

I worked with Ginger for several weeks. I pointed out to her that she had been working with the end in mind and judging her experience based on quantity of time rather than quality of performance. We discussed expectations and identified her

Wheel of Fear. She was still hesitant and still not thoroughly convinced that the Fearless Living program was going to work for her. As I always do when that happens—and it happens more often than not—I instructed Ginger to ignore her feelings and simply take a risk based on her commitments. We picked a very simple, concrete first move: she was going to call someone nonthreatening and talk about the joy and success she has experienced since becoming a Mary Kay consultant. This was in alignment with her Wheel of Freedom's proactive behaviors. Ginger chose the neighbor who had thrown the Mary Kay class.

She came back the next week and said, "Well, I did what you said, and to my surprise, my neighbor was so thrilled for me she ended up asking how I had gotten involved. I told her I wanted to do something where I could grow and expand as a person as well as help other women. She shared that that was her dream as well. Based on what you and I had talked about, I knew this was an opportunity to take a risk. I explained I was presently looking for additional consultants. She was so excited. We scheduled an appointment to talk more this weekend. But to be honest, I still felt a little like an impostor. Even while I was on the phone and she was so excited, I was thinking, 'You can't teach her anything.' "

I told Ginger that she was in good company. Most people feel the same way at that juncture in their journey to freedom. I congratulated her for her small act of courage and encouraged her to go on from there *no matter how she felt or what she thought.*

When the sense of being a fake comes up for you, I want you to do the same. When you are feeling like a phony, fear is trying to keep you where you are, safe and sound. Without the understanding that your Wheel of Fear is spinning, you may believe that your intuition is warning you not to take this chance. Remember, though, intuition never disempowers you. Feeling like a phony—or worse, a liar—definitely disempowers you. You may want to give up this new you and go back to what is familiar. You'll find yourself thinking, "Who do you think you are? . . . This isn't you. . . . You can't do this. . . . The timing is off!" But when will the timing be right? Remember Marta? She stalled because everything wasn't perfect. She believed that if she could just get everything right, then nobody could call her a fake. Yet, trying to control all the events won't make you feel less of a fake. The fear of being found out is your accumulated conditioned beliefs and thought patterns telling you that you are a phony.

And there is no right time to begin expressing more of your essential nature. Still, fear can trick you into thinking there is one. Just wait a little while longer and then you can begin to date, go to college, or change jobs. Yet you and I both know that never happens. After that first phone call to her neighbor, Ginger pushed herself past her fear by focusing on R*I*S*K and her proactive Wheel of Freedom action list. Pretty soon, with four very productive members of her sales team looking to her for support and guidance, she got over her initial sense that she was phony. "I'm very good at what I do. I see that now," she told me. "Nothing can stop me! I'm going for that Mary Kay pink Cadillac. And you know, even if I don't get one, I'll still feel great. I'm growing as a person, love this line of work, and I'm proud of my team. That's what really counts!"

Stage 3) Feeling Lost

Confusion. A sense of being disoriented. The inability to make a decision. All of the above may happen to you when you're taking a risk. There is a kind of dizziness, an emotional vertigo, that goes along with being en route to a reality that is foreign to you. You aren't sure if you are upside down or right side up. Hang in there. It's just another way the Wheel of Fear uses to alert you that you are approaching the edge of your comfort zone. In fact, it is precisely when you've lost the certainty of who you are that you can actively choose who to be. Soon enough, you'll get your bearings again. Listen to Brent, a client of mine who had been groomed from childhood for the day he would take over the family business.

"My father is a brilliant guy, a real powerhouse," Brent told me. "Dad started his import-export company when he was still in his twenties and he's made a fortune. I'm the firstborn son, and I was expected to follow in his footsteps. He used to take me to the office when I was little kid and give that someday-this-will-all-be-yours speech. Being the heir apparent seemed like a piece of cake, but within my first week of working for him after college, I realized his dream was not my dream. Yet how could I tell him?

"I mean, I didn't know anything else. I didn't know what I would do if I didn't do that. I began to think back about what I loved to do when I was a kid. That's when I remembered something I saw on the Discovery Channel when I was about eight. It was about mountains and rivers and I was all excited. And I realized that all my best memories were about kicking around in the dirt and dreaming of going on expeditions, climbing mountains and fording rivers. That was when I figured out I wanted to make a difference and maybe help save the environment. That was the real me, but what could I do? I had to keep it to myself. My parents would have been devastated if I left. And my father worked hard. I couldn't throw it all away. He was depending on me."

As Brent and I began to work together, I suggested a small shift in his downtime. He could use his weekends as an opportunity to volunteer for organizations that did just what he dreamt about doing. As he came back week after week, he said he was beginning to realize he had to quit his job at his dad's office. Then Brent was offered a job at one of the volunteer organizations, so that seemed to be an easy transition. I coached him on the conversation that he would be having with his father to break the news. He was ready—or so he thought.

When his father gave him the look of disappointment, Brent hesitated. He became confused about what was fear and what was freedom. His father's expectation had been Brent's reality for so long that he was lost without it. Brent says that rather than press on, he almost told his father he wanted to stay. Fortunately, he didn't do that. Before long, he began to find his own way.

And that happens. You lose sight of what feels like freedom and what feels like fear. They get intermingled and mixed up. When you aren't sure which way is up, stop. Breathe. Look over the qualities of your Wheel of Fear and Wheel of Freedom. Compare the feelings you are having about the situation with your Wheels. If you feel rushed, frantic, or afraid you might miss something if you don't jump, that is a sure indication that the Wheel of Fear is in control. If you feel a sense of calm excitement, the Wheel of Freedom is in charge. It will become easier and easier to know the difference. Again, remember that this is a process, yet one that you are integrating permanently into your daily life.

When I last heard from Brent, he was the head of an inventory crew in the forests of the Pacific Northwest. To Brent's surprise, his dad is not holding any grudges and is proud of his trailblazing son.

FEARBUSTER EXERCISE

To help you get through the three stages of the Uncomfortable Zone—believing the messages of the past, feeling like a phony, and confusion—complete the following exercises:

- If I acknowledged myself daily, how would I feel about myself?

- If I noticed five things a day to be grateful for, how would my life change?

- If I took control of my time rather than allowing it to control me, what could I achieve?

- If I did the exercises as best as I could, how would my life be different one month from now? Six months? A year?

- What is one exercise I will complete today?

- For five minutes today I will:

- I will tell one Fearbuster Team member my daily and weekly commitments. If I am unable to fulfill them, I will take responsibility and renegotiate.

- One year from now I want to say I am:

- In order to do that, I must:

- Look in the mirror and repeat daily, "I am willing to live fearlessly."

- The key to living fearlessly for me is:

My Fearless Journey Home

I hope you'll do the exercise above, and all the Fearbuster Exercises, not just once but over and over whenever your Wheel of Fear is activated. I do exactly that, and I know it works. I have become my own best pupil. I have worked through every exercise of my Fearless Living program, and I continue faithfully to read my Intention Statement as well as write my five Gratitudes and five Acknowledgments a day. I keep my Life Log. My laminated card is well worn. I use the R*I*S*K formula as shorthand when fear threatens to destroy the moment and prevent me from moving forward. As a result, I am true to my essential nature and I feel whole. Joy fills my soul and bubbles up at the most unexpected times. It happens without warning. This sudden urge to smile and be thankful for all that I have and all that I've been willing to embrace is something that I didn't think I could ever attain. When my parents died, I thought any capacity I had for joy had been cut off. Yet, I kept being willing to be wrong. I kept looking for something that would tell me there was more. I found it in the Fearless Living program.

The day I knew for certain that my life had been completely changed was my twentieth high school reunion. I was going back to my little hometown in northern Michigan. By then I had been a successful coach and speaker for several years. My

tapes, videos, and workbooks were selling briskly. In Los Angeles, where I had made my home since young adulthood and on
the road giving seminars and keynotes all over the country, I was
a genuine model of Fearless Living in action. Not that I never
felt fear. We all feel fear all our lives. Yet I was masterful at knowing my fear and turning it into a force for freedom.

But nothing had prepared me for the experience of facing
my fear in the very environment where it had first been bred.
When I sent in my check to the reunion committee, all I
thought about was how exciting it would be to see everyone and
let them know I had turned out all right after all. In fact, I had
decided that I would give one of my Fearless Living seminars in
a local motel. I had rented a room and sent press kits to the area
radio stations, the lone TV station, and *The Daily Mining Gazette.*
I was eagerly looking forward to sharing my revolutionary program with the people who had known me when I was a fearful
young girl unable to cope in the aftermath of tragedy.

But as I drove the rental car from the airport and saw on either side of the road the familiar stately pines of the place
where I had spent my girlhood, my fear completely overcame
me. I was a loser. I was worthless. Nothing I had to say in the
seminar would make any sense. They would laugh me out of
town. I was in a cold sweat. By the time I pulled into the parking
lot of the motel, I thought that my fear had gotten the better of
me once and for all. Then I sat there calmly for a moment.
"R*I*S*K, Rhonda, R*I*S*K," I said to myself. "R"—release attachment to outcome, no expectations. So what if no one came
to the seminar except my uncle David and my uncle Evald, who
had agreed to help me set up chairs? Maybe the two of them
would get something out of my message. So what if people did
come, and they were just a bunch of my parents' friends who
wanted to see what the crazy little suicidal orphan was like now
that she was living out in Los Angeles and purporting to know
what she was talking about? Maybe one or two of them would
buy videos and change their lives. I took out my Intention Statement and read it aloud. Then I went on to "I"—invest fully in

your intention. I wasn't giving the seminar to show off. I wasn't trying to prove I was better than my classmates. I wasn't attempting to impress the town with my accomplishments. I was giving the seminar because I believed in my message with all my heart and wanted to share it in my hometown just as I share it elsewhere. As for "S"—stand for the truth—I listed five Gratitudes that centered me in my essential nature, chief among them "I am grateful today for the opportunity to share my Fearless Living program with others." Finally, "K"—keep kindness a priority. I consciously stopped beating myself up. When my brain began to form a thought such as "You were an idiot to expose yourself to this situation in the first place," I reframed it into "I acknowledge myself for taking the risk of ridicule because I believe in the value of what I have to share."

Uncle Evald set up the chairs. Uncle David arranged the tapes and videos and workbooks on a table. The two of them were silent. But then, neither one of them had much to say to me except to make jokes about me that amounted to thinly veiled put-downs. So the silence was better than criticism. The clock ticked away. Finally, it was time to unlock the door. We had forty seats ready. I figured maybe ten people would show up.

As the door swung open, I have never been so stunned in my entire life. There was a line down the hall and clear around the motel swimming pool. I recognized a few faces, but there were also plenty of strangers who turned out to be tourists from Detroit and Chicago in town on their way to a lake resort. The forty seats filled up fast. The motel staff frantically began setting up the maximum amount of chairs, bringing the total to sixty-five. Another ten people were happy to stand in the back of the room just to have a chance to hear me. Buoyed by the enthusiasm I felt from my audience and emboldened by a quick inner checklist of R*I*S*K, I gave one of the best presentations of my life. When it was over, people bought all of the books and tapes I had brought with me, placed orders for more, and came up to me to thank me and get my autograph.

Tammy, the high school friend who had sung "I Honestly

Love You" with me at my mother's funeral when we were fourteen years old, was one of the last to approach me. We hugged
and cried happy tears.

"I'm the manager of a temp agency in Atlanta, Georgia," she
said. "We have annual national conferences. You absolutely
have to come and speak this year. The people in my business all
need Fearless Living. In fact, everyone does. You are proof of
what this program can do."

And then my uncle Evald, who had busied himself folding
the chairs while the room emptied out, came over to me. He
cleared his throat. Then he broke into a rare grin and gave me
one the greatest compliments and strongest acknowledgments
I've ever received in my life: "You did good, kid." Uncle David
nodded in agreement. I was, for once, speechless. But the tears
of gratitude that welled up in my eyes said it all.

That night, I danced at my high school reunion. The old,
fearful Rhonda was gone. Fearless Rhonda swayed and swirled
and laughed and loved and felt loved in a celebration of a life
transformed.

Fearless Vision

Imagine that it is one year from today. You have been faithfully giving yourself credit through Acknowledgments. Gratitudes have become so effortless that they form in your mind all
day long, not just when you're sitting there with a paper and pen
trying to think them up. You have embodied your Intention
Statement and it has become a way of life. The Life Log has
given you more time for the things you desire to accomplish and
the power to see that your life is truly up to you. As you look over
the past year, those Fearbuster Exercises have become an archive
that allows you to see your shifts and changes in black and white.
Claiming them has become easier and so has owning your essential nature. Wholeness is your primary state of being now.

You have given up being codependent, blaming others, getting caught in gossip, taking things personally, giving your power away, minimizing yourself, turning down compliments, letting opportunities slip by, wasting time, being resentful, bitter, or angry. You have let go of trying to be perfect and controlling everything around you. You have concrete evidence of these changes through your daily homework. Congratulations!

Your Wheel of Fear has become nothing more than a way to let you know you are becoming more of who you are meant to be. The proactive behaviors on your Wheel of Freedom are easy and natural, while the self-affirming behaviors have become second nature. You are no longer caught up in the world of what "should be," but rather the power of choice is in your hands. You have embraced compassionate accountability by learning how to give yourself (and others) a break yet, never let yourself (or others) off the hook. You understand what it means to invest fully in everything yet attach to nothing. It's exciting to realize how differently you feel about yourself in just a year. When you look in the mirror, you see someone that you are glad to know. You are home.

This is the truth. This is what happens when Fearless Living isn't just a theory but a way of life. As you begin to invest in your life, your purpose becomes clearer and passion is present whether you are reading a book or cooking dinner or making love. I want you to take a moment and think about what a year from now could look like in regard to work, play, relationships, family—every aspect of your life. How would your life be different from the way it is today if you lived fearlessly? The difference may not be accomplishments. It may be something as revolutionary as daily peace of mind or an ability to be compassionate with yourself or to forgive the unforgivable.

I believe with my whole heart that if I can be where I am today compared to where I have been, you can fulfill your potential by living in your essential nature. All I used to think about was how I either didn't want to live or didn't deserve to live. Now, those thoughts are the farthest things from my mind.

I am alive and I want to live a long time. Fearless Living has made all the difference.

Fearless Beginnings

The Fearless Living program is more than just happy endings. It's also about fearless beginnings. It's about savoring the thrill of a challenge instead of shrinking from it. It's about curiosity and creativity without fear of ridicule or reprisals. It's about having the courage to explore, to change, to grow. It's about turning life's inevitable losses into gains. It's about living every moment instead of wasting time getting ready to live. It's about the joy of the journey instead of about striving to reach a goal.

When you become fearless, fear turns into your guidance system. It shows you when you are risking or when you are playing it safe. That is the real purpose of fear. Fear is an affirmation of your growth because it proves that you are risking. You have learned to use fear instead of allowing it to use you. Now, though, instead of cowering and changing your mind about the risk, you experience fear as power, passion, and purpose. Fear propels you forward again and again as you take the risks that keep you free.

Think of Meredith, Kara, and Doug. What about Connie, Ginger, Frank? And don't forget Jennifer, Wayne, and Marta. There are thousands more. If they can do it, one exercise at a time, you can too.

May you tap into the truth of who you are. And may you be awake to the wonder of living fearlessly, without excuses and without regrets, all the days of your life.

This is your life. Do the work. You can do this.

GRATITUDES

Today, I am grateful for:

Sondra Forsyth, for being undaunted under extremely challenging deadlines. As my collaborator, she stayed true to the simplicity of Fearless Living. Using her writing expertise to make my words sing, Sondra captured the vision and nurtured it until it glowed. Her belief, support and caring are gifts beyond measure.

Linda Sivertsen, whose enthusiasm for Fearless Living gave life to my proposal, making this book a reality.

Elly Sidel, agent extraordinaire. Elly has walked beside me through every step of this process. As my number-one career Powerful Partner, she takes care of the details, which allows me to stay focused on the big picture. Elly is indispensable as an agent and friend.

Brian Tart, editor in chief of Dutton Books. Brian instantly understood my passion for this work and embraced the vision, brilliantly keeping the book on course through rewrite after rewrite. Brian has been there for me above and beyond the call of duty, as a gentleman, mentor, and friend.

Jennifer Repo, editor of Perigee Books. Her determination to bring the Fearless Living program into book form was instrumental in moving it from dream to reality.

Lisa Johnson, Kathleen Schmidt, Erin Sinesky, Robert Kempe, and the rest of the PR and marketing team at Dutton, for taking *Fearless Living* into their hearts and committing time and resources to getting the word out.

Kara Howland for handling innumerable details each day with grace and ease.

To the entire staff at Dutton for your caring support. You have made this process effortless.

And of course, Carole Baron, president of Dutton, for her stamp of approval. I am grateful for your trust and blessed to be part of your publishing family.

To my foreign editors: Thank you for diving in. Your faith in this project makes me speechless. Rowena Webb, editor of Hodder Headline UK, for her enthusiastic support. Lisa Highton, publishing director of Hodder Headline Australia, for taking the Fearless Living message Down Under.

To Aline Akelis, my foreign rights agent, whose authentic commitment to bring the book *Fearless Living* to the world makes every foreign reader possible.

To My Wise Council. I can't thank you enough for your wisdom and enduring contributions: Dr. Rev. Michael Beckwith, Breck Costin, Barbara Duetsch, Richard Golden, Warren Hogan, Paul Roth, Rev. Joan Steadman, Rev. Coco Stewart, Marianne Williamson, and Lou Paget, author of *How to Be a Great Lover*, for earnestly sharing her invaluable publishing expertise with this novice writer.

To My Voices of Experience. For their loving guidance, creativity, and expertise in support: Jenna DeAngeles, Michele Cohn, Debbie Leaper, Dave Morton, Sarah Reeves-Victory, Dr. Mark Stein, Vicki Sullivan, and Gary Tharler.

To My Support Team. Whether they read various versions of *Fearless Living* or patiently loved me during this process or actively pushed me to higher heights, this support team deserves an A+:

Anni and Bert Atkinson, Suze Baez, Bonnie Barnard, Debbie Bermont, Greg Cortopassi, Stephanie Davis, Kathryn Fadness, Kandace Forseca, Sam Khoury, Doug Knoll, Terry Oxford, David Powell, Mark Sansoucy, Sandra Silvey, Steve Sisneros, Ras and Tina Smith, Kaiopa Stage, Kim Terranova, and Jodi Walker.

To My Wild Women's Writing Support Group, who have truly held me up through the creation of this book. I am filled with gratitude for their cheerleading, writing expertise, commitment and love. Carol Allen, author of *Adventures of a Hollywood Dog Walker*, Chellie Campbell, author of *Financial Stress Reduction*, Linda Sivertsen, author of *Lives Charmed*, and Victoria Loveland-Coen, author of *Itty-Bitty Baby Bonding Book* and *Manifesting Your Desires*.

Deep abiding gratitude to Minda Burr, Stephanie Hagen, and Nancy Hardin who put many things into motion.

A special thank you goes to Alexandra Reichler and her two fab roommates, Amy and Laura, for the generous hospitality of opening up their New York home to me. And Bill and Wendy Ostlund for the same in St. Paul, plus double thank you to Wendy for her meticulous detail while reading early versions of *Fearless Living*.

To My Powerful Partners: Thank you for your continued support, passion, and focus. Greg Cortopassi, president of Team-Works; Grant Doyle, president of GetSpeakers.com; Gary Good and Cathy Story of Gary Good Speakers Bureau; Lori Otelsberg, president of Signature Entertainment; Craig Robinson and David Naishtut, principals of Discovery Concepts; Laura Rubinstein of LBR and Associates and my dedicated marketing director, Susan Guzzetta.

Heartfelt gratitude for Ann Ben-Porat and Joe Decker for being the first coaches trained through the Fearless Living Institute. Their endless dedication and caring for the people and the program are priceless.

Unending gratitude for my assistant, Jennifer Brynes, for keeping me in stitches, taking care of my stuff and truly loving this work.

In my lost years, I received signposts and moments of synchronicity on my path. At the time, I had no idea of the impact they would have on the rest of my life. Yet, as I look back in gratitude, the following people were there just at the right time to give a loving push, a caring hand, or wise advice that would eventually help me find my purpose. I am extremely grateful to finally have the honor of publicly thanking you:

Sharon Eckholm Hill, for being present whenever my sisters and I needed an adult to guide us through a challenge or celebrate a success. Joe Berini, my high school counselor, for seeing past my Badge of Fear and encouraging me to shine. Bob Caton for opening my eyes to my creativity. Bob Cooper for loaning me *Living in the Light*, by Shakti Gawain. Bill Gamble for suggesting sobriety. Maria Gobetti for waking me up when she asked, "Why do you work so hard to push people away from you?" Samantha, my DUI counselor whose last name is long lost, for her guidance, wisdom, and handing me the book *Father Loss*. Coworkers at Tony Roma's for repeatedly telling me I was funny. Laura Clear for inviting me to hear Marianne Williamson. Mark Chaet for introducing me to coaching. Gil Christner for giving me my first paid writing job.

Lisa Ferguson Lessa. As my first client, she stepped up to the plate when I needed someone to take a chance on me. She was tireless in her thirst for change and willing to do the work necessary. Lisa brought Fearless Living out of the one-on-one coaching arena. Her enthusiasm and love for the work was the impetus for me to do my first public workshop. Thank you, Lisa, for continually telling me that Fearless Living has changed your life. You have changed mine.

To Marta and my sisters, Cindy and Linda.

There are no words to truly describe my gratitude for my best friend, Marta Weiskopf. She has nurtured my transformation as if she were a guardian angel assigned to guide me back to myself. She has shared my pains, helped heal my wounds and awakened me to my truth. I am thankful for her willingness to walk this path with me. Thank you for being my best friend. In fact, major gratitude goes to her husband, Kreigh, for enduring my late-night phone calls and frequent lunch dates with his wife that turned into marathon coaching sessions. He is a man among men and his relationship with Marta inspires me. Thank you for being in my life!

My older sister, Cindy, has been willing to tell the truth, face her own fears and share her secrets with me. Our intimate connection and our laugh-filled shopping trips are memories I cherish. For her greeting cards that always appear at the perfect moment, her wonderful cheerleading chants and her open-door policy. I know I always have a home with her family, Dean, Jason, Deena, and Adam. Thank you for seeing past my mistakes and allowing me to change before your eyes. You are a true Powerful Partner.

My younger sister, Linda, was given more love than the rest of us growing up and she has generously showered me with that abundance during my life. Her genuine enthusiasm for Fearless Living and her endless support have been invaluable. She takes my bookmarks to her craft shows, tells her fellow teachers about the book, and is clearly proud of her older sister. And her family, Joel, Rachel, and Zachary, always make room for me at holiday dinners giving me another home away from home. Thank you, Linda, for accepting me exactly as I am and supporting my dreams.

To my parents: Thank you for the opportunity to be your daughter. Our destinies merged on June 15, 1975, and Fearless Living was born that day. It just took me a while to understand my part. Because of you, I have learned how to forgive, love, and accept who I am. Thank you for all you gave me while you were alive and for watching over me since your passing. I can truly say I love you without doubt, hesitation, or restriction. Thank you for loving me the best way you knew how. I miss you.

And lastly, I want to thank anyone who has ever heard me speak, listened to my tapes, read one of my books, e-mailed a thought or question, attended a workshop, or come to me for private coaching. This book is for you. It was your genuine interest and desire to know more about living fearlessly that drove me to write this book. Without you, there would be no Fearless Living. Thank you for your willingness to do the work and for trusting me with your heart. I have no words to express the joy I feel when I see you shine from the inside out. Your courage touches my soul daily. Your light inspires me. Thank you.

We Want to Hear From You . . .

How has Fearless Living changed, helped, or altered you? What qualities or behaviors have you incorporated into your daily living? How has Fearless Living affected your work or home life? What have you accomplished that had previously been out of reach? Tell us about you!

We want to hear how Fearless Living has affected you and your life. How are you choosing to live more fearlessly each and every day? Please send your success story (typed or neatly hand-written) along with your name, phone number, e-mail (if available), address, city, state, and zip.

Thank you for sharing your success stories with us.

Please send your story to:

Fearless Living Success Story
P.O. Box 261775, Encino, CA 91426

Fearless Living Institute

Private Coach? Fearless Living Workshops? Corporate Training? Become a Coach?

If you would like to work with your own private coach or attend a Fearless Living Workshop, the Fearless Living Institute can help. We can tell you about the latest classes available as well as connect you with our list of pre-approved coaches.

If you are looking for new career opportunities for yourself as a coach or trainer, the Fearless Living Institute has programs that will suit your needs. Attend our extensive and in-depth coaching program and you will become a certified Fearless Living Coach. If you prefer to work in a group setting or in the corporate environment, becoming a Fearless Living Corporate Trainer may be the perfect fit. For the latest information:

Visit our Web site at http://www.FearlessLiving.org
and click on Institute

Or request information:
Fearless Living Institute, P.O. Box 261775 Encino, CA 91426

Rhonda Britten

If you would like Rhonda to speak at your next corporate meeting, association conference, or public event, please visit Rhonda's Web site at **http://www.RhondaBritten.com**

Or contact the Fearless Living office at: 818-907-8959

Be sure to check out the list of topics available including: Fearless Leadership, Fearless Selling, The Language of Fearless Living, and Creating Accountability: The Fearless Approach to Empowering Your Employees.

Thank you for your support and enthusiasm.
Be Fearless!